MANAGEMENT AND ORGANIZATION:
RELATIONAL ALTERNATIVES TO INDIVIDUALISM

Management and Organization: Relational Alternatives to Individualism

Edited by
DIAN-MARIE HOSKING
H. PETER DACHLER
KENNETH J. GERGEN

Avebury
Aldershot • Brookfield USA • Hong Kong • Singapore • Sydney

© D. M. Hosking, H. P. Dachler and K. J. Gergen 1995

All rights reserved. No part of this publication may be reproduced, stored in a retrieval system, or transmitted in any form or by any means, electronic, mechanical, photocopying, recording or otherwise without the prior permission of the publisher.

Published by
Avebury
Ashgate Publishing Limited
Gower House
Croft Road
Aldershot
Hants GU11 3HR
England

Ashgate Publishing Company
Old Post Road
Brookfield
Vermont 05036
USA

British Library Cataloguing in Publication Data

Management and Organization: Relational
Alternatives to Individualism
I. Hosking, Dian-Marie
302.35

ISBN 1 85972 167 2

Library of Congress Catalog Card Number: 95-79846

Printed and bound by Athenaeum Press, Ltd.,
Gateshead, Tyne & Wear.

Contents

Figures and tables · vii

Acknowledgements · viii

List of contributors · ix

Preface · x

1 The primacy of relations in socially constructing organizational realities · 1
   H. Peter Dachler and Dian-Marie Hosking

2 Relational theory and the discourses of power · 29
   Kenneth J. Gergen

3 Constructing power: entitative and relational approaches · 51
   Dian-Marie Hosking

4 The social construction of grievances: organizational conflict as multiple perspectives · 71
   Paul Salipante and Rene Bouwen

5 The social construction of grievances: constructive and constructionist approaches to a relational theory · 98
   Mary Gergen

6	The case of group sado-masochism: a dialogue on relational theory *Kenwyn K. Smith and Mary Gergen*	104
7	The manager as a practical author: a rhetorical-responsive, social constructionist approach to social-organizational problems *John Shotter*	125
8	Social constructionism and the postmodern turn of management theory *Emil Walter-Busch*	148
9	Social construction and appreciative inquiry: a journey in organizational theory *David Cooperrider, Frank Barrett and Suresh Srivastva*	157
10	Relational knowledge in organizational theory: an exploration into some of its implications *Thomas S. Eberle*	201
11	Reality is the basis of social construction which in turn creates reality *Mario von Cranach*	220

Figures and tables

Figure	4.1	A kaleidoscope model of grievance perspectives	88
Table	4.1	Perspective formulation and interaction outcomes	91
Figure	7.1	Processes of making and finding	142
Table	9.1	Means, standard deviations and T-values for administrative division practices across time	190
Figure	9.1	The ripple effect of the power of theoretical language	196
Table	9.2	Means, standard deviations and T-values for the medical department's practices across time	192
Table	9.3	Positive changes attributed to appreciative intervention ('E.T.') by members of the administrative division	194
Figure	11.1	Model of information elaboration and action organization, information processes within a loop	226
Table	11.1	Frequencies of attribution by client-centered therapists and by vertical behaviour analysis therapists	229

Acknowledgements

A book such as this could not have been produced without the help and support of many persons and institutions. We gratefully acknowledge the generous financial support of the University of St. Gallen for Business Administration, Economics, Law and Social Sciences who funded and hosted a conference which enabled this project. Yvonne Hungerbuhler, secretary to the department of organizational psychology at the University of St. Gallen, was a central figure both in organizing the conference, and in coordinating and conducting the many subsequent communications between editors and authors. We very much appreciate her dedication to the book and her organizational skills. The final formatting, proof reading and computer work would have been nearly impossible for the editors but for the dedicated help of a number of persons at St. Gallen and at the University of Aston Business School. In Switzerland, our team included Nicola Pless and Sabine Raeder; we thank them for the valuable time they took away from their dissertations. In the UK, Viv Golder and her collegues in computing services took time out to solve problems and provided cheer and support when it was much needed. Finally, we must thank our authors for responding so constructively to our editorial suggestions, requests and deadlines.

List of contributors

Frank Barrett, Case Western Reserve University, U.S.A.

Rene Bouwen, Catholic University of Leuven, Belgium.

David Cooperrider, Case Western Reserve University, U.S.A.

Mario von Cranach, University of Berne, Switzerland.

H.Peter Dachler, University of St Gallen, Switzerland.

Thomas S. Eberle, University of St.Gallen, Switzerland.

Mary Gergen, Pennsylvania State University, U.S.A.

Kenneth J. Gergen, Swarthmore College, U.S.A.

Dian-Marie Hosking, Aston University, UK.

Paul Salipante, Case Western Reserve University, U.S.A.

John Shotter, University of New Hampshire, U.S.A.

Kenwyn K. Smith, University of Pennsylvania, U.S.A.

Suresh Srivastva, Case Western Reserve University, U.S.A.

Emil Walter-Busch, University of St.Gallen, Switzerland.

Preface

Over the course of the century management and organization theory have been dominated by two major forms of explanatory discourse. The first, and perhaps the most broadly circulated in the working world, is lodged in the presumption of individual agency. Organizational life is viewed as the result of individual action. It is the individual, thought of as an entity with clear boundaries between his/her internal and external environment, who is understood to possess the capacity to reason, to learn, to invent, to produce, and to manage. Given these presumptions, the 'reality' of management is understood as individual creation and control of order, for example, on the basis of rules, regulations, operating procedures, strategic plans and visions. With reference to these same assumptions, organization is viewed as an object formed and directed by 'powerful coalitions', according to their priorities, and by other 'entities' in and outside the organization. On the one hand, it is taken for granted that organizations are created through the co-operative efforts of individuals. On the other hand, it also is assumed that management acts as subject directing, energizing and controlling objects; the contradiction goes unrecognised. The actual process of co-ordination, creating what is understood to be 'real' in the organizational world, is understood in terms of the presumed properties of entities (e.g., power, rationality) and can only be understood in this way. As a result, crucial questions and their answers are taken for granted, as they form the implicit context within which specific questions for research and practice take on their 'natural' meaning.

The second orientation to understanding organizational life is based on the presumption of macro-social structures and causal influence relations including, for example, structural-functional interdependencies, information systems, and structures of power. These understandings go 'hand in glove' with the individualistic perspective described above: both assume entities and the meaningful separation of 'micro' and 'macro'. However, in the discourse of macro-social structures, individuals are typically viewed as a by-product, i.e., as entities whose attributes are created by macrosocial configurations, and who therefore have explanatory value for issues of aggregated behaviour.

In this book the authors, who come from different disciplinary traditions and cultures, offer other arguments which share a common doubt in the prevailing entitative assumptions. The authors focus on different aspects and implications, draw from a variety of theoretical traditions and deal with a range of practical concerns. However, they all centre their attention on the social-relations implied by organizing processes and, in one way or another, take seriously the fundamental relatedness of human life. In other words, that which is taken-for-granted, if not muted to theoretical insignificance in the prevailing entitative perspective, is, in this book, given central voice.

Also expressed in this book is the increasingly felt inadequacy of prevailing understandings to deal with the growing complexity and ambiguity, with the rapid changes and the increasingly multicultural organizational world. These challenges all have their roots in relational issues, i.e., issues that concern social interdependencies, the social processes by which mutual understandings as well as misunderstandings are created and continuously redeveloped. Various kinds of relational approaches are offered in an attempt to provide a more meaningful basis for approaching collective problematics, such as intercultural communication, the social processes of knowledge generation, organizational culture and learning. The topics addressed include leadership and management, the evolution of privileged knowledge, grievances and organizational conflict, and power and politics in organizations.

The contributions variously make reference to different literatures which critique the individualistic orientation and attempt to reorient the discourse toward a relational perspective of knowledge. In part, the discontent with individualist constructions of the social world grows from a range of philosophic, literary, and ideological critiques of knowledge as an individual possession. For many philosophers, the long standing empiricist assumption of individual minds reflecting the character of an independent world, no longer seems credible (e.g., Rorty, 1979). Without the pivotal assumption of a 'knowing mind' the remainder of the individualistic vocabulary of explanation (e.g., motivation, emotion, intention) loses its justification and ontological base. Literary theory has added further weight to such arguments in its multi-faceted attack on the presumption of individual authorship. For example, it is argued that reading is not a matter of accessing author's intentions but reflects the conventions of interpretative communities (Fish, 1980). Similarly, literary deconstruction theory (Derrida, 1976) demonstrates the way in which texts gain their meaning through their referential relationships to other texts. These conceptual critiques go together with a broad range of ideological assaults on individualistic presumptions. So, for example, individualistic explanations have been excoriated for their promotion of cultural narcissism, detrimental effects on personal and communal commitment (Bellah, 1985), incapacity to generate moral foundations, and their reflection of an androcentric world view (Haraway, 1988).

The above critiques have been inter-textual with what now is broadly conceived as a social constructionist view of knowledge. Reflecting widespread intellectual developments for example, in the sociology and history of science, semiotic and rhetorical theory, critical and feminist theory, and ordinary language philosophy, accounts of reality are traced to relationships among persons (cf. Gergen, 1994). Propositions about the world are, in this view, dictated by active processes of relations - negotiating, colluding, collaborating, and so on. If we view such processes as the matrix from which the conception of both individual selves and social structures spring, then we are drawn as well to the possibility that a relational focus may give us substantial leverage in accounting for organizational life. That is, constructionist views of knowledge production may be fruitfully extended to give an account of organizing processes. To be sure, we may not pursue such inquiry because it will result in an accurate picture of organizations as they are. Rather we see the dialogues of relationship as giving birth to a new array of texts. It is from these texts, in turn, that a new array of organizational textures may be given life.

It is within this conversational context that the present volume was brought into being. Variously informed by the issues summarised, the authors have explored the potentials for theory lodged neither within the individual nor the social-structural orientations to understanding organizational life. Themes of social construction are woven into these accounts, but remnants of both the individualist and social-structuralist views also are present. The attempt here is not so much to silence these long-standing traditions as to soften their seeming certainties, and thus enable new forms of discourse. Because discourse and relationship each implicate the other new forms of discourse will implicate new forms of relationship. It is our hope that this volume may enable a richer variety of textures of organising and being in relationship.

References

Bellah, R.N. (1985), *Habits of the the Heart*, University of California Press, Austin.

Derrida, J. (1976), *Of Grammatology*. Trans. Gayatri Spivak, Johns Hopkins University Press, Baltimore.

Fish, S. (1980), *Is there a Text in this Class? The Authority of Interpretive Communities*, Harvard Universtiy Press, Cambridge.

Gergen, K.J. (1994), *Realities and Relationships*, Harvard University Press, Cambridge.

Harraway, D. (1998), 'Situated knowledges: The science question in feminism and the priviledge of partial perspective', *Feminist Studies*, 14:3.

Rorty, R. (1979), *Philosophy and the Mirror of Nature*, Princeton University Press, Princeton.

1 The primacy of relations in socially constructing organizational realities

H. Peter Dachler and Dian-Marie Hosking

A long history is attached to the view that realities are socially constructed and that knowledge is in some sense relational[1]. This position has been discussed, and in varying degrees adopted, in areas of philosophy, sociology and psychology, and is most obviously at the forefront of theoretical traditions such as symbolic interactionism, cognitive sociology, phenomenological sociology, and system theory (e.g., McCall & Simmons, 1978; Cicourel, 1974; Schutz, 1962; Mead, 1934; Berger & Luckmann, 1966; Garfinkel, 1967; von Glasersfeld 1985; Watzlawick, Weakland & Fish, 1974).

A relational view has gone largely unconsidered in the literatures of management and organization. These literatures are dominated by a perspective that variously has been characterized as 'entitative' (e.g., Hosking & Morley, 1991), as 'possessive individualism' (Sampson, 1988) or as 'realist ontology' (e.g., Dachler, 1988). The term 'relational' means many different things to writers working from different theoretical traditions and practical concerns. In this chapter we work towards an explicit and systematic statement of the central features that need to be addressed in a relational position.

In our view the key issue in any relational approach lies not in matters of content, e.g., competitive vs. collaborative relationships, and not in justifying the truth value of propositional statements; the central issue is epistemological. By epistemological we mean to address the following assumptions: the processes by which we come to ask particular questions in the first place (and not others); the processes by which we come to know, and; the processes by which we justify claims to reality. What is experienced as real or true depends on (usually implicitly) held assumptions about processes of knowing. In debates about the reality of different knowledge contents many misunderstandings are a result of unreflected taken-for-granteds with respect to the underlying epistemology.

It is on the basis of epistemological processes that individual and social phenomena obtain ontology, that is, are interpreted as real or as having a particular meaning. Epistemological principles are discussed to varying degrees in different literatures. For this reason we will make a beginning by summarizing and integrating them. We do so in order to suggest what it may mean to talk about relational processes in the social construction of managerial and organizational realities. In the first part of this chapter we will discuss the epistemological assumptions of the prevailing entitative perspective and those of the alternate relational perspective. This shows the very different understandings of managerial and organizational realities that follow from incommensurate epistemological assumptions. In the second part we illustrate our arguments by showing how diverse epistemological assumptions result in very different understandings of leadership, networking and negotiation.

A relational perspective

The underlying epistemology of the relational perspective is best understood in contrasting relation with the epistemological assumptions and related concerns of 'entitative' or 'possessive individualism'[2]. Therefore, we give a brief and critical overview of the epistemological assumptions inherent in the entitative perspective; we then lay out the equivalents in a relational perspective.

The epistemological assumptions of the entitative perspective

Possessive individualism has two central epistemological themes[3]. The first is the assumption of a knowing individual, in principle understood as an entity. This is the constituting idea of Cartesian philosophy. The individual is understood to be endowed with a knowing mind whose ontology is differentiated from internal and external nature; 'the mind' is the locus of knowing about nature. Individuals are assumed to have access to the contents of their mind; mind contents and knowledge are viewed as properties of entities, as individual possessions. On the basis of such properties one entity can be distinguished from other entities, such as other people or their environment. It is but a short step from this position to view all aspects of a person as personal properties, possessed in differing amounts. Individuals are treated as if possessing properties such as expert knowledge, mind maps and personality characteristics, as well as physical properties such as height and weight. This kind of individualism also can be seen in the treatment of groups and organizations as some form of aggregation of individual possessions and performances (e.g., Belbin, 1981; see Dachler & Enderle, 1989; Hosking, 1988).

The second assumption follows directly from the first. Namely, individual possessions, including certain interests and goals, are the ultimate origins of the design and control of internal nature and of external nature, including other people or groups. On the bases of his or her personal properties the knowing individual is understood as the architect and controller of an internal and external order which makes sense with respect to the array of the personal possessions. Consequently, if one starts from the common, historically grown definition of individual rationality, the idea of orderly relations among 'known' components of the internal and external world becomes a central principle of understanding self and the surrounding world. As a result, the guiding project becomes the creation and control of order, including social order. It is this assumption that leads some commentators to speak of 'self-contained individualism' and the 'egocentric' metaphor of personhood (Sampson, 1985).

It must be stressed that possessive individualism makes sense with reference to the prevailing epistemology of an objective truth. The Cartesian dogma of a clear separation between mind and nature leads to the need to know internal and external reality as entities separate from the knowing person. The implicit assumptions about person described above make meaningful the epistemological assumption of a required correspondence (so to speak as a mirror) between the 'contents' of mind and the contours of the surrounding internal and external world (Gergen, 1993; von Glasersfeld, 1985). Knowledge is objective as far as the contents of mind match the properties (possessions) of the entity to be known. Thus, criteria of truth are 'physicalist' (Allport, 1955) and knowledge claims are assessed as true or false, right or wrong.

Given our present interests what is crucial is that these epistemological assumptions only allow what we call a subject-object understanding of relationships. When person is understood as a knowing individual s/he is being viewed as a subject, distinguishable from the objects of nature. The latter implicitly are viewed as passive, as knowable and malleable only by the subject. In other words person as subject is active in object relations, with external nature for example by motivating employees, or with internal nature for example through the mind influencing internal states. Since other people are an important part of external nature, it follows that social relations are understood as subject-object relations and can only be understood in this way. Social relations are enacted by subjects to achieve knowledge about, and influence over other people and groups. Relations are considered only from the point of view of the entity considered as the subject in that relationship. Relations, and therefore knowledge and influence, are understood as more or less instrumental for the subject's understanding of order.

Within the epistemological premises of the entitative perspective relationships are explained and understood on the basis of the properties and behaviours of interacting individuals or organizations. As a result, relational processes are left largely untheorized. Relations are given little explanatory power beyond an unexplicated view that influence results from relationships between certain properties possessed by the interacting entities.

The above assumptions are rarely made explicit. Nevertheless the traditional literatures of management and organization make sense precisely because they implicitly reference them. In the second part of this chapter we will illustrate these epistemological processes with respect to leadership, networking and negotiation.

Relational epistemological assumptions

It is important to recognize at the outset that within a relational perspective the borderline between epistemological and other kinds of arguments (often thought of as content issues) becomes very blurred. This is because talk about social relations and social processes is also talk about knowledge, shared understandings, and truth. To simplify discussion, however, we will make an analytical distinction between epistemological premises and social processes and discuss each in turn.

The relational perspective views knowledge as socially constructed and socially distributed: not as 'mind stuff' constructed or accumulated and stored by individuals. As will be shown, that which is understood as real is differently constructed in different relational and historical/cultural settings. From a relational perspective the truth value of knowledge becomes a matter of assessing meaning with respect to interwoven narratives recounted within a cultural community. The issue of ultimate truth is shifted from its previously central position and questions of cultural meaning and significance take its place. When knowledge and truth are viewed as a social endeavour then constructions of what we variously shall call understandings, descriptions, or meanings (i.e. knowledge), are always a part of 'what is going on' in any social relational process. Whether the social process is leadership, management, networking, or negotiation, knowing is an ongoing process of relating.

Knowing is always a process of relating In a relational perspective knowing is viewed as an ongoing process of meaning making. A claim to know is a claim to be able to construct the meaning of a running text. In the philosophical tradition of hermeneutics, and in studies of the meaning of literatures whose authors and social context are no longer available for conversation, 'text' usually refers to written or spoken documents. In contrast, we think of text as a narrative about the way something could be understood (known). What we call facts, events, utterances, documents, physical objects or any kind of individual or collective behaviour are texts, in and of themselves meaningless; their meaning is equivocal. In this sense texts acquire meaning only to the extent that they can be related, through narration and conversations, with ongoing stories in the social/cultural context.

To elaborate, to the extent that there are other actors, physically present or symbolized in ongoing narratives, the behaviour of an actor acquires meaning when other actors coordinate themselves to the behaviour through some form of reaction. For example, wildly waving an outstretched hand is knowable only relative to (some of) the multitude of stories in our culture about being separated from a valued person and in a context such as a train slowly moving out of the station. Otherwise the action of 'wildly waving' remains as a potential for absurdity. In other words, meaning or understanding is not a picture, is not something static, something already attached to 'some(thing)'; it is a narrative process in which meaning is constantly in the making. That is why we speak with others (Gergen, 1993; Hodge & Kress, 1988) of a running text. In narration an ongoing text talks about something and makes it real. As we shall see, narration is language and therefore knowledge becomes a 'language game' (Wittgenstein, 1963).

The next crucial point to appreciate is that text is always in mutual relationship with a context. While it is helpful to distinguish between text and context they are mutually interrelated: text implies reference to context and context already contains text (Culler, 1988; Vaassen, 1994). The meaning of a text does not start from a tabula rasa, but always brings to bear a preconception, an already recounted narrative to which a text makes reference. For example, the act of a person signing a document is by itself equivocal. Only by reference to a very complex interrelated network of ongoing narratives regarding the act of writing, the signing of documents, hierarchies of authorities, legalities of contracts, dominance of men over women, etc. can we construct the text of a manager (male) who, through his signature and formal authority, accepts a contract that a secretary (female) has typed and put on his desk for his act of accepting certain obligations and responsibilities. Obviously by reference to a large but limited set of other potential interrelated narratives very different texts about signing could be reconstructed, for instance signing a parking ticket, or a divorce agreement. Thus, the same text will mean different things depending on the particular contexts to which it is referred and in relation to which the text is narrated (e.g., Garfinkel, 1967; Cicourel, 1974). One important way of putting in relation is the referencing of a text to the context of what it is not. Just as light, as a text, derives its meaning in contrast to the context of dark, the text of leader as subject derives its reality with reference to its differentiation from the context of follower as object.

Relating is a constructive, ongoing process of meaning making, through language, in multilogue Given that meanings are made through relating, or referencing, it is these processes that become the unit of analysis so to speak.

We use the term multiloguing to refer to these processes in which meanings are made in mutual relating, or referencing of texts to contexts. It is in the processes of multiloguing that realities are constructed. Multiloguing is founded in some minimum necessary degree of commonality and collaborative work based on language. As Shotter (1980) and others have shown (Grace, 1987; Vaassen, 1994), language is the coordination of action. From language follows the multitude of ontological assertions, such as 'individuals have minds' or 'relations between people depend on the possessions and behaviours of participants'.

Coordination of action involves several interrelated issues. Conversation is impossible if participants refuse to allow each other (that is, refuse to agree) to reference certain contexts. It can continue only if speakers act as though both share the same basic view about what is the topic of conversation (Garfinkel, 1967; Gergen, 1993). In this sense, and based on a language already in place, participants in multiloguing are engaged in ongoing processes in which they take for granted some shared agreement. Of course such a belief is, in itself, a social construction of the participants. Talk about shared understandings or shared meanings is talk about a community of language users in the sense that participants reference at least some interrelated narratives as common contexts for meaning making. This is a crucial point. References to 'shared understandings' do not concern overlapping substantive content, as they would in an entitative perspective. Instead, they refer to usually implicit agreements about a set of interrelated narratives that serve as an interpretative context[4]. In sum, reference to shared understandings or shared agreements is reference to a more or less widely shared sense of a local reality. Local reality or social order contributes to, and emerges from, ongoing processes of multiloguing. This makes clear that the individual cannot be the sovereign author of meaning. Therefore, what is traditionally described as subjective knowledge no longer makes sense in a relational perspective.

This view of multiloguing answers the question of how it is possible for participants constantly to reference texts implicitly and explicitly to different contexts and yet, out of difference, can achieve what are experienced as agreed, shared understandings. In the context of possessive individualism the question does not arise, because (a) truth is defined by the correspondence between knowledge claims and object properties, and (b) collective action and achievements are simply an aggregation of individual contributions.

Many terms are used in the literatures to discuss meaning making processes. They vary in the degree to which they emphasize the social-relational aspects:

in live, face-to-face processes for example, by speaking of enactment, discourse, conversations, dialogues, or accounts (e.g., Potter & Wetherell, 1987; Harré, 1979; Winograd & Flores, 1986; Garfinkel, 1967; Weick, 1979); in the socially distributed knowledge/cultural history of a society, tribe, or subculture, for example, using terms such as stories, narratives, and saga (e.g., Bennett & Feldman, 1981; Clark, 1972; Orr, 1990); or in terms that may be equally useful for discussing present social processes in relation to the past and possible futures - the term communications (e.g., Watzlawick et al, 1974) is more of this kind. We use the terms multiloguing and narrative to talk about knowledge as a process of relating. Next, we turn to explicate their meaning since we use them in rather special ways.

With the term multiloguing we want to emphasize the speaking of many, with reference to many contexts, through language. The term has the advantage of a strongly active, ongoing, processual connotation. Multiloguing need not only refer to explicit live, face-to-face social processes as the term conversation usually connotes. It takes place implicitly, in the sense that by working on a text (as is happening in writing this text) we are speaking with reference to a complex set of contexts made up of many interrelated texts told within psychology, sociology, philosophy, in our society, or in other communities. If we were asked to tell a story about the contexts to which we are relating in writing the sentences just completed, we could specify some of the (to us) more obvious ones. At the same time, we would get into more and more difficulties, becoming entangled in an increasingly complex network of contexts to which reference could be made. Thus while the meaning of a text is context-bound, the contexts are, in principle, unlimited. With every additional reference of a text to another narrative within the context, the meaning of the text changes. And in trying to reflect on the meaning of the context, it becomes a text whose meaning we understand from another (meta)context. Theoretically this process of meaning making is endless (see Gergen, 1993).

The term narrative is used to mean many widely different things in the literatures. First, it forms part of a vocabulary for talking about cognition, the most common tendency being to treat narratives as just one of many categories. In contrast, a few use the term very broadly to embrace all kinds of cognitive processes or thinking including, for example, scientific theories and mathematical thought (Howard, 1991). Second, there are those who restrict the concept to refer to one kind of knowledge, that is, knowledge as a subjectively imagined fiction or story, as contrasted with other kinds such as factual knowledge. Third, many locate the term firmly in the context of discourse but then distinguish between different kinds of discourse of which narrative is only one. Last, there is the common practice of viewing story telling as one kind of data, different from other kinds of data such as physical objects; the investigator can collect stories of heroes and villains and, in this way, learn something more about a particular organization or culture (e.g., Martin, 1982).

However, when relational epistemological principles are assumed, it is only through processes of narrating that knowledge, or rather knowing, is possible. We use the term narrative to speak of what we earlier defined as text. But with the concept of text as narrative we want to underline our position on a key issue: the impossibility of static, picture-like, entitative knowledge, which has its ontology in the so-being of some fact. In a relational perspective as we have outlined it, factual knowledge is in that sense meaningless - a fact cannot be knowable in its so-being. The literatures convincingly demonstrate that the epistemological assumption of objective knowledge raises many questions for which there are no adequate answers (cf. Gergen, 1993, Vaassen, 1994). Given that knowledge (understanding) presupposes language and language is a process of speaking, knowing is always a process of narrating.

In summary, we view knowing as a process of narrating. This means that (a) narratives are not stored documents (as in an entitative perspective), but are always in the process of being retold; (b) narrating is being in relation, speaking with others, actively engaging in what we earlier called multiloguing and coordinating with others in the neverending construction of a local ontology, that is, a common understanding of local reality; (c) speaking or narrating includes all forms of acting. Notice that this also means it is impossible not to act, since any action (including what appears as not acting at all) is text, ambiguous until others coordinate themselves to it and make reference to other ongoing narratives (cf. Gergen's chapter in this book).

Meanings are open, have no ultimate origin or ultimate truth The relational epistemology, by recognizing knowledge as socially distributed and truth as socially certified, does not privilege any particular knowledge claim as more true, in the sense of the entitative epistemology, than others. The argument that meaning emerges though the cross-referencing of texts with possible contexts implies that for any particular text, the meaning created does not have to be that way - references could be made to other possible narratives (e.g., Potter & Wetherell, 1987). Multiple realities, in the sense of multiple meanings, descriptions or knowledge claims are a part of the local ontology in the process of being narrated (e.g., Cicourel, 1974; Garfinkel, 1967). The significance of this epistemological position is considerable. Reality no longer is viewed as a singular fact of nature but as multiple and socially constructed. We see why 'truth' loses the significance it had in the entitative perspective.

Meanings are bounded by socio-cultural limits A relational epistemology greatly broadens the possibilities for meaning and disallows one true meaning. However, there are socio-cultural limits to what will be allowed as real or true, right or wrong, desirable or undesirable; not anything goes. Limits are constructed and reproduced in multiloguing. In narrating a particular text reference is made, usually implicitly, to a cultural context whose meaning is taken for granted. As a result its appropriateness for the reality constructed in the current text cannot be questioned. It is the unavailability for questioning the taken-for-granted context that preserves the status quo (Argyris, 1982; Schattschneider, 1960) and often leads to seeming changes that in fact are simply more-of-the-same (Watzlawick et al., 1974).

This muting of other possible meanings could be seen as an avoided sense-making process. Moreover texts, whose meanings emerge from a particular taken-for-granted cultural context, when viewed from a different cultural context, are usually not recognized or are misunderstood. As a result they are ignored, or devalued as wrong, weak, ineffective or worse (Dachler, 1992). The ubiquitous devaluation and neglect of the feminine voice in science, organizational, and world affairs, offers a good example of how feminine texts simply make little sense when implicitly referenced to a taken-for-granted masculine culture (see, for example Dachler, 1992; Gilligan, 1982; Harding & Hintikka, 1983; Sampson, 1988). Possessive individualism and its implied narrative of relationships can be argued to be a context so pervasive and taken for granted in recent western cultures that other relational models are (mis)understood as unrealistic and therefore are almost impossible to reference for meaning making. However, if implicit referencing processes are made explicit, they can be addressed and questioned as text in relation to some shared project (e.g., Schutz, 1962). In this way the limits that previously maintained the status quo can be (re)constructed.

Socially constructing and referencing narrative themes of self, other and relationships A crucial boundary to the meanings of relational processes is the way in which self, other and relationship are understood. We have earlier attempted to relate the story of possessive individualism as a narrative about subject (self or other), object (self or other) and relationship (instrumental; subject-object). In contrast, relational epistemology invites questions about the many possible narratives about self, other and relationship. They emerge in the historical/cultural context of multiple ongoing narratives about personhood and being mutually related. Our point is that the interdependent running texts of self, of other, and of relationship, are fundamental to the social reality in the context of which our behaviour becomes meaningful. In other words, in a relational perspective, multilogues are processes of meaning-making in which narratives of self, other, and relationships are referenced and are themselves in the making. We shall return to develop a more extended discussion of self, other and relationships as narratives and their role in meaning-making processes.

We now can summarize the key premises of relational epistemology as follows:

a   The claim to know is a claim to be able to construct the meanings of a running text.
b   Meaning making is a process of narrating and a reflection of the oppositional unity of text and context.
c   Text and context cannot be separated as if they were entities, since both entail each other and derive meaning only from their opposition or difference.
d   Meaning is produced through multiloguing: an actively relational process of creating (common) understandings on the basis of language.
e   Meaning can never be finalized, nor has it any ultimate origin; it is always in the process of making.
f   Meanings are limited by socio-cultural contexts.

Towards a relational perspective in organizational theorizing: some illustrations

In the second part of this chapter we would like to illustrate the epistemological arguments of a relational perspective by looking at three commonly used explanatory concepts namely leadership, networking and negotiation. We will use the relational epistemology to deconstruct the entitative taken-for-granteds which underlie current understandings of social relations. In particular, we will analyse the central concepts of self, other and relationship, as they are referenced in common conceptions of leadership, networking and negotiation. We then can show that a relational perspective makes alternate constructions of social relations possible.

Narratives of leadership

Possessive individualism and the narrative of leadership   Consistent with the meta-narrative of possessive individualism, theories of leadership typically emphasize individuals as entities and locate explanatory force in their assumed properties. Moreover leadership is understood by crosscutting reference to the prevailing narratives of management as the originator of rules and order, guidance and orientation. The meaning of management is embedded in the corresponding understandings of organization as hierarchically structured entities in which the flow of activities follows an ordered preference based on the logic of the division of labour. By implicit reference to such a context leaders are understood to possess certain characteristics on the basis of which, and in interaction with measurable characteristics of their context, they carry out their leadership functions. Leaders are understood as subjects set apart from the objects which make up their context including their subordinates, the subordinates' tasks and the organization. People are leaders based on their superior (compared with subordinates) knowledge and certain other possessions for example, charisma. Given the assumption of these attributes, leaders are understood as active in two respects. First, as subject, it is the leader's goals and interests that are privileged relative to those of the objects of leadership. Second, and on the basis of the above, leaders are the architects of order and control. It is they who are understood to act through leadership styles and behaviours, who influence the values of others, who influence others to make sense of their contexts in certain ways (Dachler, 1988; 1992; Dachler, Pless & Raeder, 1994; Hosking, 1988).

By implication, and in contrast, subordinates are treated as the objects of leadership: as less active, less knowledgeable and as having less access to the (privileged) goals and interests possessed by the leader. It is vital to note that within this narrative of leadership subordinates cannot, in principle, be understood to be as self developed and self responsible as is the leader. Rather, the central concern is implicitly always that of how the leader/subject gets follower/object to think, talk, or act in ways that reflect the leader's perspective. In the context of the entitative epistemological assumptions leaders become the energizers of their leadership context. They are understood as the prime originators of what happens within their area. They are responsible for their employees' policy compliance, their motivation, and how successfully their group performs, and so on. It is because leaders are seen as the originators of activity that they must carry the consequences when performance is deemed inadequate. A closely related taken for granted is that in leader-member relations it is one voice, that of the leader, which ultimately must prevail. Even if leaders invite participation it cannot be to have open critical discussion in which all points of view have equal legitimacy. Rather, it is the leader's perspective that is taken for granted as setting the limits to what is thought of as right or wrong. Leaders would have difficulties in understanding themselves as in charge if the possibility were accepted that other perspectives are, in principle, equally legitimate.

The meaning of leadership is constructed not just with reference to certain kinds of narratives regarding management and organization. Leadership also takes its meaning with reference to a pervasive socio-historical narrative that some call a masculine culture (Dachler, 1992; Dachler & Hosking, 1993). The observation that a review ' ... of true leadership traits ... is a description, nearly a caricature, of the dominating, competitive, aggressive, manipulating, and achievement-driven male' (Dachler, 1988 p.264) illustrates a masculine standpoint in the leadership literatures (Calas & Smircich, 1988[5]). Eisler (1990) and others draw attention to important cultural differences that arise from the division of labour in gender relations. Over the centuries women have mostly been involved in 'care' work (Gilligan, 1982) and males in 'world structuring' work (Dinnerstein, 1976). Out of these contrasting life experiences important cultural differences have evolved as reflected in different understandings of self, of other, and of being in relationship.

Eisler (1990) has used the term 'dominance model' to refer to the understanding of relationships whose meaning is constructed by reference to narratives of the masculine culture. In its different descriptions (e.g., Dinnerstein, 1976; Eisler, 1990; Gilligan, 1982; Marshall, 1993) it includes: a self-concept that depends on differentiation and social-emotional separation from others; self determination based on criteria of personal achievement and success; mastery or world structuring and; emphasizing rules, rationality, and general, value-free principles. Within such a cultural context it is taken for granted that leader relationships are: artificial not natural; instrumental not self-developing; short-lived, not long-term and involving. Exchange and path-goal theories of leadership (e.g., House & Mitchell, 1974) are good examples of the dominance model. The dominance model is an implicit narrative in all our leadership theories. This is only to be expected since the entitative epistemological assumptions and the masculine culture derive their reality in their text-context relationships: the masculine culture is context for the entitative perspective and vice versa.

While some leadership theories may appear to espouse a less individualistic, perspective, the implicit assumptions briefly sketched above remain (Dachler, Pless & Raeder, 1994; Hosking & Morley, 1991). For example, some have observed that within the context of understanding organizations as systems of shared understandings and common goals, leadership becomes a process of interpreting and socially constructing organizational reality to provide meaningful definitions for employees (e.g., Neuberger, 1990; Pfeffer, 1981; Smircich & Morgan, 1982). Leadership thus takes on an additional function, that is, to provide meaning within an 'interpretation community' (Neuberger, 1990) and to help in making events and expected behaviours more understandable. Others also have suggested that organizational culture can be manipulated by skilful leadership (Schein, 1985; Smircich, 1983). From a relational perspective these theories combine some 'good news' with some not so 'good'. They make useful contributions by considering the symbolic value of behaviour and the fact that through the interpretation of organizational activities social realities are constructed. Against this, they continue implicitly to understand leadership as an issue of individuals, their cognitions and their behaviours. They also give prime focus to the problem of a leader influencing the perceptions, interpretations and reality constructions of the followers. Who constructs organizational realities becomes a central question in these accounts of leadership.

There has been recent and increasing interest in leadership practices such as teamwork, enabling, empowering or coaching. However, such texts of leadership are likely to continue the fundamental meaning of someone in charge and someone as follower. This will be so if leadership continues to be referenced to the implicit assumptions regarding self as subject, other as object, relationships as those of influence and manipulation or, more generally, to the assumptions of the masculine culture. In other words, the larger implication is that the prevailing narrative of leadership, and the contextual narratives it references, severely restricts what is thinkable and doable. In a relational perspective questioning, and so making explicit, the taken for granted narratives is central and opens the possibility for radical change as contrasted with what otherwise would turn out to be more of the same.

Possible narratives of leadership in a relational perspective Within a relational epistemology one cannot specify the contents of leadership, such as certain attributes of leaders. To do so would again reflect an entitative perspective as is happening, for example, in talk about feminine leadership or questions about successful and unsuccessful leaders and how they differ in their leadership behaviours. Rather, a relational perspective invites very different questions. It invites questions about the social processes by which certain understandings come about and represent the social reality with reference to which certain behaviours make sense and not others. A relational perspective of leadership cannot ask questions about 'what' (content) without asking how (process) certain communally held knowledge is created and given ontology. This means that the central question becomes how the 'social' in the social construction of reality is to be understood. As a result, our understanding of relations in leadership needs to be reconsidered.

So, for example, now we may ask how, that is by what social construction processes, a particular enactment of leadership has been socially constructed. Questions need to be asked about the communally agreed upon enactment of leadership (e.g., cooperative leadership) and what it means. Is it simply another name for something that still has a basic meaning of someone in charge, who now thinks it motivating for the followers to be asked about their opinions and have some of them integrated in decisions at the discretion of the leader (cf. Dachler & Wilpert, 1978)? Other questions relate to the degree to which a particular understanding, held within a language group, makes sense with respect to a particular project. One needs to ask whether a particular understanding of cooperative leadership is helpful in more creatively dealing with the current project. Alternatively, the question becomes whether the implicit understanding of 'cooperation' in leadership requires a redefinition by making reference to other kinds of narratives about cooperation, e.g., cooperation in terms of accepting others perspectives as equally legitimate in finding a common understanding of some problem.

From a relational perspective narratives of gender relations play a crucial role in all social-relational processes, including leadership. In science and public life the narrative of gender relations has been told nearly exclusively by the masculine voice, muting possible narratives told by the feminine voice (Gilligan, 1982; Harding, 1986). From the privileged masculine-cultural standpoint care work is given less importance, less (economic) value than world structuring work. In this context the dominance model of relationships also is given privileged ontology in differentiation from the partnership model, a narrative of the feminine culture. Clearly then, the way self, other and relationship are understood in the text of leadership cannot be understood without referencing the narratives created in gender relations.

In a partnership model identity is constructed from being in relationships, being connected, as contrasted with the masculine construction of identity through separation and competition (cf. Gilligan, 1982). The feminine life experience has emerged from care work so that relationships between different but equal partners are a constituting aspect of relationships. Moreover, relationships are understood as caring. This means sharing responsibility for oneself and for others and respecting other standpoints, giving central voice to the issues of team working and cooperation in the sense of all interacting actors sharing responsibility for their interrelationships; we have more to say about this later.

Of course it follows from the assumptions of the relational epistemology that the partnership model of relations is a social construction like any other. We are persuaded that dominance and partnership are narratives that are socially constructed in gender relations - at least in recent western history (see Eisler, 1990). However the point that is central to our present purposes is that the partnership model of relations cannot be seen as meaningful from the epistemological perspective of possessive individualism. Partnership does not make any sense with reference to understandings of self as subject, other as object, and a subject-object model of relationships; dominance, not partnership fits a subject-object model of relationships. The partnership model can only make sense by reference to the fundamental epistemological assumptions of the relational perspective.

These are examples of the kind of process questions that can be asked about leadership from a relational perspective. It is important to notice, however, that such questions, while clearly implying normative priorities, are above all concerned with how certain understandings of leadership come about and how they are given privileged ontology (Berger & Luckmann, 1966). Moreover the question is no longer which narrative of leadership is correct. This question only makes sense if we assume knowledge has truth value relative to the contours of the world. Instead narratives of leadership are evaluated in terms of the extent to which they 'enlarge the world' (Knorr-Cetina, 1989) by allowing understandings that up to now have been hidden or muted in the prevailing masculine culture. This also implies that whether a particular text of leadership is given privileged ontology, i.e. has 'epistemological profit' (Knorr-Cetina, 1989 p.94) depends on the extent to which that narrative allows coordinated movement with respect to a particular, commonly understood and valued project.

To pursue this line of argument for a moment, consider the recent strategic reorientations of companies, reducing hierarchy, emphasising team work and cooperation rather than competition. Given such projects, it becomes essential to examine the extent to which the entitative narratives within the masculine culture actually allow the kind of social relations implied by team work and cooperation. Many a company has attempted to change leadership through, for example, new visions of management, e.g., managers become coaches and subordinates are called associates. Many also have failed. A relational perspective suggests that this is because they have not questioned and changed the taken for granted assumptions or the 'dominant logic' (Prahalad & Bettis, 1986). What usually gets ignored are the social processes by which leadership is constructed and constantly in the making.

The text of leadership, in the context of a relational epistemology, becomes a question of coordinated social processes in which an appointed leader is one voice among many. Within a relational perspective appointed leaders share responsibility with others for the construction of a particular understanding of relationships and their enactment (Dachler & Dyllick, 1988). The issue can no longer be whether it is the brilliance of the leader or the lack of motivation showed by the co-workers that is the reason for the leader dominating the process and outcomes of his/her relationships with others. Rather, leaders and those with whom they interact are responsible for the kind of relationships they construct together (Brown & Hosking, 1986). This implies that besides the content questions raised in discussions, possible differences in understandings of self, others, and relationships, need to be explicitly addressed and negotiated. It is worth emphasising that for someone to raise questions about the ongoing relational processes, for example, of leader-member relations, would be viewed from an entitative perspective as, at best irrelevant, and at worst, taboo. It is simply taken for granted that the relational processes make sense, as they do but only by implicit reference to the dominance model of relationships. However, it is only through multiloguing about the taken for granted assumptions about self, other and relationship that it is possible to construct a common understanding of the relational context with reference to which the content questions in part derive their meaning. Moreover in trying to understand how certain common understandings emerge one could say that the involved actors are participants in co-constructing the 'choreography' (Knorr-Cetina, 1989) in which joint action 'enlarges the world'. The appointed leader's attention shifts to multiloguing, negotiation, networking and other social means of narrating texts concerning the possible meanings of individual and collective actions.

Narratives of networking and negotiating

Possessive individualism and the narratives of networking and negotiation
Much of what we have said about entitative conceptions of leadership is equally true of the prevailing treatments of networking and negotiation in the literatures of management and organization. This is to be expected since their meaning is constructed with reference to the same epistemological assumptions and in relation to the same sociocultural narratives. We will proceed by analysing each of these referents. We will start with the implicit understandings of subject, object, and subject-object relations. However, at the same time we show that these are understood in crosscutting reference to management, organization, and hierarchy. The implicit understanding of social relational processes then is unpacked to show that they are understood from the subject's point of view as more or less instrumental for collecting information and creating social order; negotiation receives extended discussion at this point. Finally, relations are shown to be understood with implicit reference to prevailing masculine cultural narratives and the dominance model of relations.

First, we may examine the ways in which a knowing, active subject is assumed in narratives of networking and negotiation. In the literatures of management and organization, networking and negotiating are understood as acts performed by an individual, and the person so considered usually is an appointed manager. The networking, negotiating manager is implicitly understood as active: 'moving around', making 'contacts' and building 'contact networks' (e.g., Kotter, 1982; Stewart, 1976). The activity involves talking to others. Of course such talk is not just about anything, or with just anyone, rather it is understood as talk that is strategically linked to the subject's purposes or goals as a manager. In other words, just as with leadership, the act of networking is understood in relation to its implications for managerial effectiveness. One illustration of this general line of argument, lies in the claim to have found that the more skilled manager has larger 'contact networks' (a possession comparable to leadership style), and networks 'more aggressively' (Kotter, 1982), than other, less effective managers. It should be noted that while it is one thing to identify activity as making contact and talking, it is quite another to identify the relational processes implicated in networking. So, for example, when a manager is observed to be spending much time on the phone is this wasting time as some have claimed (e.g., Luthans & Lockwood, 1984) or is it useful networking? It is perhaps ironic that those who study managers and their networks have realised that they cannot easily get at the 'content' of networking (e.g., Kotter, 1982; Stewart, 1976) and yet, at the same time, have failed to consider that this might be because knowledge is not information resident in the text but meaning created in text-context relations.

Second, the underlying assumption of a passive object goes together in text-context relations with the above narratives of the networker/negotiator as subject. The subject's point of view is assumed in references to other as a contact. This linguistic tool reflects the underlying taken-for-granted that other is fundamentally passive. Other is discussed as one who is contacted, but not one who contacts; other is the chosen object of networking but cannot choose; other is never considered as one who moves around. As an object of the subject's regard, the meaning of other is confined to being a contributor to the size of the managers' contact networks (e.g.,Kotter, 1982).

Third, we come to the understandings of relations as subject-object relations. The term relationship building is usually offered as a broad interpretation of what making contacts means. However the enormous numbers reported to makeup managers' networks (e.g., Kotter, 1982) make it hard to see how managers and their contacts could together build wide-ranging relational histories in and about their social relations with one another. Apparently they do not; it is taken-for-granted that it is only the networker who is building the relationship. Furthermore, this activity is considered for its potential instrumental value to the networker. There are several interrelated themes each of which reflect this underlying one-way treatment of the relationship. It is the networking manager who defines the purposes of making contact and who is understood to collect information from contacts. By building such relationships it is assumed that the networker can better understand how things really are (knowledge that) and can act, based on better known facts, to structure objects in the world (achieve power over). These last two themes are central to how relationships are understood in entitative treatments of networking and negotiation; we will elaborate each in turn.

Networking generally is understood as a process in which the manager can collect 'live information' (Mintzberg, 1973). In the entitative account of networking information is understood as knowledge about the world. Only factual knowledge is considered. In addition, information is considered 'live' when it is current or timely and, by implication, is thought more likely to be true, relevant and useful to the networker. Live information is understood to be instrumental in relation to the assumed purposes of the manager as subject, namely: for identifying and selecting policies; to know better how some selected policy should be interpolated, and to facilitate effective implementation. For example, managers are said to use their networks to: 'receive' and 'gather information' (Kotter, 1982, p.63); to 'keep (their) information live and accurate' (Wrapp, 1984, p.8); search or scan as a means to identify issues, policies or problems (e.g., Wildavsky, 1983), or for decision recognition and diagnosis (Mintzberg, Raisinghani & Theoret, 1976). By seeking information 'more aggressively', managers are said to make best use of the 'incredible information processing systems' (Kotter, 1982, p.78) that their networks provide.

Through networking, the mind contents of managers are assumed to be more comprehensive; through moving around their contexts they are understood to better know what is real (e.g., Neisser, 1976) and good. However, the comprehensiveness is actually severely limited since what is thought of as real and good is restricted to data that are considered factual. Implicitly networkers are understood to collect, and act on the basis of, data that reflect objective reality, that is, refer to how the world really is. As a result, all other kinds of data are thought to be subjective, are thought of as myths, or as fictions of the imagination. By being unable to consider other kinds of data as the bases and outcomes of networking then networkers remain blind to other kinds of truths. So, for example, left out of account is the cultural context that gives some event a particular meaning rather than another.

The knowledge base, achieved through networking, allows managers better to know what and who they must influence including the perspectives of their subordinates, organizational practices, structures and policies. This line of argument is reflected in references to managers shaping network members (Kotter & Lawrence, 1974), getting the right vision and personifying it (Bennis & Nanus, 1985), managing meanings, and using networks to help them execute (their) agendas. Again we see the underlying narrative of possessive individualism: the knowing subjects use their knowledge to structure/form the external world of objects - including other people. Of course this is why writers tacitly take the point of view of the subject, taking it for granted that this standpoint is objectively given as discovered in empirical studies.

Power, when referenced to the narrative of networking, is understood to be created and mobilised in live, face-to-face relations rather than, for example, through impersonal written rules and procedures. Furthermore, hierarchy is implicitly referenced in that networking relations are confined to lateral and external (to the organization) contacts, that is, to non authority relations. Networkers are understood to mobilise influence through a variety of influence strategies and, most importantly, through what is called either bargaining or negotiation (e.g., Sayles, 1964; 1979; Wrapp, 1984). Consistent with the narratives we have outlined, negotiation is understood as an individual act. Attention is directed to managers and to negotiation as an activity they may choose when they are unable to use the formal authority of their hierarchical position and/or when that authority seems insufficient. In other words, networking to achieve influence, and negotiating as an influence strategy, are understood as complements to hierarchy and to power based in hierarchy. They supplement hierarchy; they are processes in which managers fill in the gaps, so to speak - gaps left by insufficient authority and inadequacies of formalised organization structures (e.g., Sayles, 1964, 1979; Dalton, 1959).

Negotiation is viewed as a means for the networking manager to win the consent (Sayles, 1979) of others. The meaning of negotiation lies in removing or getting around multiple perspectives and not in what we have called multiloguing. So, for example, negotiation is described as trading, compromise, give and take (Sayles, 1964); it is exchange, mobilising resources 'to negotiate a trade' (Kotter, 1982, p.73) and to remove trade barriers between individuals (Kaplan, 1984). In addition, the wider meaning of networking and negotiation is understood with reference, not just to influencing individuals but, by forming individuals as objects, to creating what variously is known as culture or social order. Through individual acts of networking, negotiating and the like, leaders are understood to be able to create strong cultures (e.g., Deal & Kennedy, 1982; Peters & Waterman, 1982). In other words, organizations are treated as 'designer goods...fashioned by leaders' (Hosking, 1990, p.182).

We have shown that the texts of networking and negotiating, like that of leadership, are made meaningful in relation to an interwoven texture of referents including subject-object relations and culturally located narratives concerning managerial work and effectiveness, organization and hierarchy. Finally, it is possible to make the connection, again as we did with leadership, to masculine cultural narratives and the dominance model of relations. For example, the social- relational processes of networking and negotiating are understood as functional for: individual achievement and prominence; making oneself separate from and better than others, and; creating social order that is, world structuring - themes that earlier were described as central to the dominance model. Given the present-day connection between dominance and socio-cultural constructions of masculinity, it is probably no coincidence that studies of networking and negotiation typically have focused on male managers - after all, the prevailing western conception of gender relations is that the male is active and the female passive (e.g., Hubbard, 1983). The crucial point here is that the possible meanings of networking and negotiation are seriously restricted by being referenced to the narratives of possessive individualism and the masculine culture. In contrast, a relational epistemology, by asking questions about the processes by which particular meanings are made, opens-up the possibility for networking and negotiation to be referenced to other contexts and so take on new meanings.

Possible narratives of networking and negotiating in a relational perspective
The relational epistemological assumptions we have outlined direct attention: to ongoing processes of meaning making rather than to the acts of knowing and structuring networkers; to processes of multiloguing and not to the monologic of talk, making contact, and bargaining, and; to processes understood as ongoing constructions of multiple realities, not to individual acts of gathering information as fact and negotiating to remove differences in perspective. Investigations undertaken from a relational perspective do not take a restricted view of knowledge as only factual, as information about how the world is really, as mind stuff. Instead it is assumed that what is thought of as knowledge is local and temporal, changing with variations in text-context relations.

Our central concern is now to show what the narratives of networking and negotiation could be when referenced to relational epistemological principles. However we must emphasize that, on the basis of relational epistemological principles, it is not possible to say what such processes look like in terms of specific content. This is because knowledge now is viewed as meaning and meanings change with changes in text-context relations. It is relational processes of meaning making that are of interest and particular examples, available as content for analysis, must be analysed in terms of the underlying relational processes. We will give illustrations of how relational epistemological principles lead to different kinds of questions about networking and negotiation. We show that new meanings can be created when networking and negotiation (as texts) are referenced to changed contexts of management, leadership, organization and hierarchy.

Let us first consider what it might mean to view networking as a conversational process of meaning making. Here, managers who network may be regarded as seeking to understand the meanings of the others' conversational contributions. To do so, they would have to give up the assumption that they and others necessarily mean the same thing by the same linguistic term or expression. A manager, when networking, would be asking questions that invite others to make explicit what is usually left implicit. This could include narratives concerning their identities as certain kinds of professionals (engineers, marketing manager and so on), their concepts of career and advancement, what they define as leadership, and so on. In other words, networking is understood as 'moving around' the narratives that others are referencing for meaning making.

Of course, from a relational perspective, networking is no longer viewed as a one-way street, so to speak. Instead, meaning making is regarded as a joint activity. Further, it is a process of coordinating action on the basis of multiple perspectives. Imagine then, a consultant who is acting from relational assumptions. S/he would have to ask questions about the processes by which the networking manager and others come to know and respect each other's perspective. The processes could be such that, for example, each believes they know the other's different perspective, but do not. Alternatively, each might believe they share the same understanding when, because they are implicitly referencing different contexts, they do not. Equally, the processes might be such that the conversational participants come to agree particular contexts for meaning making. The consultant's task would be to ask questions that lift the networkers on their implicit narratives. Suppose, for example, that in conversation a manager speaks of motivation, with implicit reference to a narrative of self who energizes others and a narrative of others as needing to be activated and controlled. Others might understand the manager's talk of motivation very differently, for example, by referencing narratives of shared responsibility, equal status, and collective empowerment. Only by being lifted on what is usually left unaddressed is it possible for participants to know what each defines as real.

These examples of how networking can be understood from a relational perspective suggest how negotiation takes on a new meaning. Negotiation now is viewed as a process of multiloguing. Instead of trading away differences, so to speak, negotiation is a process in which manager and others may come to know each other's perspectives and construct shared understandings in and about their relations. Relational epistemological principles suggest that negotiating be viewed as an ongoing process of narrating with self and other referencing interrelated narratives to the point that each can reconstruct the other's narratives. In this way, each comes to know the context to which the other references their texts for meaning making. Of course the progression of A's understandings of B's narratives also constitutes a changed context for A's own text; text-context relations are an ongoing change for each participant as together they create some shared understandings in the sense of knowing what the other means by their story. What emerges is a more or less local reality characterised by at least some shared understandings of what is real and good.

In the above sense, negotiating is a process that allows managers and others seriously to discuss and agree aspects of their relationship with one another including related aspects of their wider contexts. For example, management and staff representatives may participate in a process of dialoguing in relation to management's proposal to initiate a system of appraisal. Management may reference the proposed change to narratives of equity (e.g., differential pay for different competencies), efficiency and flexibility. Management may also implicitly reference an understanding of other as in need of incentives and self as the source and controller of these instrumentalities. On the other hand, staff may reference the proposed appraisal scheme to narratives of rivalry and competition. They may view management (other) as manipulative and construct themselves as self directed and self controlling. Processes of negotiating in the sense described, are processes in which the participants' multilogue, their understandings changing in text-context relationship, creating shared understandings that are emergent. In this way changed texts (such as appraisal) may actually change their meaning because the contexts also are changed through negotiating. This is a very different process from one in which participants argue about the correct meaning of a text without realising that they are implicitly referencing the contexts they have always referenced and therefore are constantly reproducing more of the same, that is, the same meanings.

It is vital to appreciate the implications of this line of investigation: social order, rather than being constructed through 'power over', becomes understood as a social process of relating on the basis of conversation, negotiating shared understandings in the very special sense just described, agreeing particular text-context relations and particular ways of relating out of the many possible relations that could be constructed. No longer is it necessary implicitly to assume that people need to be organized. In other words, it no longer is necessary to assume that a management-subordinate relation is required for this purpose. Instead, relational epistemological assumptions lead to questions about self organizing and the ways in which this is achieved. It then becomes possible to ask questions about organizing, networking and negotiating wherever there are ongoing social-relational processes, rather than just in connection with formal organization and hierarchy.

Similarly, a relational perspective makes it possible to ask questions about the meanings of networking and negotiating in relation to the differing projects of participants. Such projects could include, for example, enjoying a particular way of being in relation, such as partnership relations, in a masculine context where dominance is the norm. So, for example, it becomes possible to consider the ways in which women's groups (Brown, 1992; Brown & Hosking, 1986) or extended families of relatives and partners, aunts, sisters and the like (Grieco, 1992; Grieco & Hosking, 1987) act as self organizing systems in relation to a variety of projects such as gaining employment, supporting the family, performing ongoing social relational processes in which they can enjoy certain ways of being in relationship.

Just as with the entitative perspective of networking and negotiation, the relational understanding of these processes has meaning with reference to the narratives in the feminine culture, especially those that Eisler (1990) and others have called the partnership model. With reference to the partnership model, the meanings of networking and negotiating are socially constructed through their differentiation from the separation and being different that is implied by hierarchy and the masculine-cultural narratives. Networking and negotiation then are seen as processes that produce and reflect connectedness and interdependence as egalitarian relations, and as processes that construct collective authority and responsibility. In the context of partnership, networking may be meaningful in the sense of giving voice to the multiple perspectives of participants, making it possible to negotiate in the sense described above and, in this way, to seek out, recognise and respect differences as different but equal.

In this connection, there have been studies of non-hierarchical ways of organising as they characterise the social practises and values of autonomous women's organizations. The story of women organising, told by a participant observer (Brown, 1992), seems to have many connections and similarities with the narrative themes of partnership and with the above meanings of networking and negotiation. In the women's groups described, one pervasive local-cultural narrative was the negative valuing of stable status hierarchies as formalised hierarchies of power and values and an abhorrence of individual prominence and individual leaders. Instead, leadership was understood as a shared responsibility for relationships and for the ongoing production and simultaneous enjoyment (consumption!) of a certain kind of social order (Brown & Hosking, 1986). Networking and negotiating were prominent social-relational narratives, meaningful in relation to the above conception of leadership and the rejection of hierarchy. So, for example, they organized non-hierarchically and collectively, negotiating relationships to produce agreed (often explicitly) meanings and related social practices. They gave close, continual, reflective attention to how they were socially relating with one another and to how they organized themselves in relation to the cultural narratives of the women's movement. Networking and negotiating were meaningful in relation to narratives of equality, being in (something like) partnership relations, shared responsibility for relational processes, and for enabling all participants in relation to their shared and different narratives (see Brown, 1992). In a social world of local realities there is always the possibility socially to construct partnership rather than dominance.

With these examples we do not want to be understood to imply that women's groups, by being made up of women, are necessarily less hierarchically organized and necessarily will create social realities through reference to partnership. This would imply a characteristic that women possess, in contrast to men, an assumption that makes sense only in the context of possessive individualism. The crucial point of our arguments draws attention to the social construction of a feminine culture born out of the life experiences of women in the course of western history. Since, within the current practices of gender relations, women are more likely to be involved in care work than men, it is not surprising that we find women's groups whose practices reference epistemological assumptions of the relational perspective and feminine cultural narratives. However, it is the general principle that we want to stress which is that through referencing relational epistemological assumptions a truly generative (Gergen, 1993) alternative to the meaning of networking and negotiation is possible.

References

Allport, F.H. (1955), *Theories of Perception and the Concept of Structure*, Wiley, New York.
Argyris, C. (1982), *Reasoning, Learning, and Action*, Jossey-Bass, San Francisco.
Belbin, R.M. (1981), *Management Teams: Why they Succeed or Fail*, Heinemann, London.
Bennett, W.L. & Feldman, M.S. (1981), *Reconstructing Reality in the Courtroom*, London, Tavistock.
Bennis, W.G. & Nanus, B (1985), *Leaders*, Harper & Row, New York.
Berger, P. & Luckmann, T. (1966), *The Social Construction of Reality*, Penguin, New York.
Brown, H. & Hosking, D.M. (1986), 'Distributed leadership and skilled performance as skilful organisation in social movements', *Human Relations*, 39, p.65-79.
Brown, H. (1992), *Women Organising*, Routledge and Kegan Paul, London.
Calas, M.B. & Smircich, L. (1988), 'Reading Leadership as a Form of Cultural Analysis', in Hunt, J.G., Baliga, B.R., Dachler, H.P. & Schriesheim, C.A. (eds.), *Emerging Leadership Vistas*, Lexington Books, Lexington, MAS.
Cicourel, A.V. (1974), *Theory & Method in a Study of Argentine Fertility*, Wiley, New York.
Clark, B. (1972), 'The organizational saga in higher education', *Administrative Science Quarterly*, 17, pp.78-84.
Culler, J. (1988), *Dekonstruktion. Derrida und die poststrukturalistische Literaturtheorie*, rororo, Reinbek.
Dachler, H.P. (1988), 'Constraints on the Emergence of New Vistas in Leadership and Management Research: An Epistemological Overview' in Hunt, J.G., Baliga, B.R., Dachler, H.P. & Schriesheim, C.A. (eds.), *Emerging Leadership Vistas*, Lexington Books, Lexington, MAS., pp.261-286.

Dachler, H.P. (1992), 'Management and Leadership as Relational Phenomena' in Cranach, M.v., Doise, W. & Mugny, G. (eds.), *Social Representations and Social Bases of Knowledge*, Hogrefe & Huber, Bern/Göttingen, pp.169-178.

Dachler, H.P. & Wilpert, B. (1978), 'Conceptual dimensions and boundaries of participation in organizations: A critical evaluation', *Administrative Science Quarterly*, 23, pp.1-39.

Dachler, H.P. & Dyllick, T. (1988), 'Machen und Kultivieren: Zwei Grundperspektiven der Führung', *Die Unternehmung*, 4, p.283-295.

Dachler, H.P. & Enderle, G. (1989), 'Epistemological and ethical considerations in conceptualizing and implementing human resource management', *Journal of Business Ethics*, 8, pp.597-606.

Dachler H.P. & Hosking, D.M. (1993), 'Relational processes: A social constructionist perspective', *11th EGOS Symposium*, Paris.

Dachler, H.P., Pless, N. & Raeder, S. (1994), 'Von der Dominanz zur Kooperation', *Psychoscope*, 15, p.7-10.

Dalton, M. (1959), *Men who Manage*, Wiley, New York.

Deal, T.E. & Kennedy, A.A. (1982), *Corporate Cultures*, Addison-Wesley, Reading, MA.

Dinnerstein, D. (1976), *The Mermaid and the Minotaur*, Harper & Row, New York.

Eisler, R. (1990), *The Chalice and the Blade*, Unwin, London.

Feyerabend, P. (1978), *Against Method*, Verso, London.

Flax J. (1987), 'Postmodernism and gender relations in feminist theory', *Signs*, 12, 4, pp.621-643.

Garfinkel, H. (1967), *Studies in Ethnomethodology*, Prentice Hall, Englewood Cliffs.

Gergen, K. (1993), *Toward Transformation in Social Knowledge*, 2nd edition, Sage, London.

Gilligan, C. (1982), *In a Different Voice*, Harvard University Press, London.

Glasersfeld, E. von (1985), 'An Introduction to Radical Constructivism', in Watzlawick, P. (ed.), *The Invented Reality*, Norton, New York, pp.17-40.

Grace, G.W. (1987), *Linguistic Construction of Reality*, Croom Helm, Beckenham.

Grieco, M. (1992), *Keeping it in the Family*, Routledge, London.

Grieco, D. & Hosking, D.M. (1987), 'Networking, exchange and skill', *International Studies in Management and Organization*, XVII, pp.75-87.

Harré, R. (1979), *Social Being: A Theory for Social Psychology*, Basil Blackwell, London.

Harding, S. (1986), *The Science Question in Feminism*, Open University Press, Milton Keynes.

Harding, S. & Hintikka, M. (1983), *Discovering Reality*, Reidel, London.

Hollway, W. (1991), *Work Psychology and Organisational Behaviour*, Sage, London.
Hodge, R. & Kress, G. (1988), *Social Semiotics*, Polity Press, Cambridge.
Hosking, D.M., (1988), 'Organizing, leadership, and skilful process', *Journal of Management Studies,* 25, pp.147-166.
Hosking, D.M. (1990), 'Leadership Processes: The Skills of Political Decision making', in Wilson, D.C. & Rosenfeld, R. (eds.), *Managing Organisation: Text, Readings and Cases,* London, McGraw Hill.
Hosking, D.M. & Morley, I.E. (1991), *A Social Psychology of Organising*, Harvester Wheatsheaf.
House, R.J. & Mitchell, T.R. (1974), 'Path-goal theory of leadership', *Journal of Contemporary Business*', 3, pp.81-97.
Howard, G.S. (1991), 'Culture tales: A narrative approach to thinking, cross-cultural psychology and psychotherapy', *American Psychologist,* 46 (3), pp. 187-197.
Hubbard, R. (1983), 'Have Only Men Evolved?' In Harding, S. & Hintikka, M., *Discovering Reality*, London, Reidel.
Kaplan, R. (1984), 'Trade toutes: The manager's network of relationships', *Organization Dynamics*, Spring, pp.37-52.
Knorr-Cetina, K. (1989), 'Spielarten des Konstruktivismus; Einige Notizen und Anmerkungen', *Soziale Welt*, 40, pp.86-96.
Kotter, J.P. (1982), *The General Managers*, Free Press, New York.
Kotter, J.P. & Lawrence, P. (1974), *Mayors in Action: Five Studies in Urban Governance,* Wiley, New York.
Luthans, F. & Lockwood, D.L. (1984), 'Measuring Leader Behavior in Natural Settings', in Hunt J.G., Hosking, D.M., Schriesheim, C.A. & Stewart, R. (eds.), *Leaders and Managers: International Perspectives on Managerial Behavior and Leadership*, Pergamon Press, Oxford, pp.117-141.
McCall, J.G. & Simmons, J.L. (1978), *Identities and Interactions*, Free Press, New York.
Mannheim, K. (1936), *Ideology and Utopia*, Routledge & Kegan Paul, London.
Mannheim, K. (1952), *Essays on the Sociology of Knowledge*, Oxford University Press, New York.
Marshall, J. (1993), 'Viewing organisational communication from a feminist perspective: A critique and some offerings', *Communication Yearbook*, vol. 16.
Martin, J. (1982),' Stories and Scripts in Organizational Settings', in Hastorf, A.H. & Isen, A.M., *Cognitive Social Psychology,* Elsevier, Oxford.
Mead, G.H. (1934), *Mind, Self and Society,* University of Chicago Press, Chicago.

Mintzberg, H. (1973), *The Nature of Managerial Work*, Harper & Row, New York.
Mintzberg, H., Raisinghani, D. & Theoret, A. (1976), 'The structure of 'unstructured' decision processes', *Administrative Science Quarterly*, 21, pp.246-75.
Morgan, G. (ed.) (1983), *Beyond Method*, Sage, Beverly Hills, CA.
Morgan, G. (1986), *Images of Organization*, Sage, London.
Neisser, U. (1976), *Cognition and Reality*, Freeman, San Francisco.
Neuberger, O. (1990), *Führen und geführt werden*, Enke, Stuttgart.
Orr, J.E. (1990), 'Sharing Knowledge, Celebrating Identity: Community Memory in a Service Culture', in Middleton, D. & Edwards, D., (eds.) *Collective Remembering*, Sage, London.
Peters, T. & Waterman, R.H. (1981), *In Search of Excellence*, Harper & Row, New York.
Pfeffer, J. (1981), *Power in Organizations*, Pitman, Boston.
Potter, J. & Wetherell, M. (1987), *Discourse and Social Psychology*, Sage, London.
Prahalad, C.K. & Bettis, R.A. (1986), 'The dominant logic: A new linkage between diversity and performance', *Strategic Management Journal*, 7, pp.485-501.
Sampson, E.E. (1985), 'The decentralization of identity', *American Psychologist*, vol 40, 11, pp.1203-1211.
Sampson, E.E. (1985),' The debate on individualism', *American Psychologist*, 43, 1, pp.15-22.
Sayles, L.R. (1964), *Managerial Behaviour: Administration in Complex Organizations*, McGraw Hill. New York.
Sayles, L.R. (1979), *Leadership: What Effective Managers Really do and how They do it*, McGraw Hill, New York.
Schattschneider, E.E. (1960), *The Semi-sovereign People: A Realists View of Democracy in America*, Holt, Rinehart and Winston, New York.
Schein, E.H. (1985), *Leadership and Organizational Culture*, Jossey-Bass, San Francisco.
Schutz, A. (1962), *Collected Papers*, Nijhof, The Hague.
Shotter, J. (1980), 'Action, Joint Action and Intentionality', in Brenner, M. (ed.), *The Structure of Action*, Blackwell, Oxford.
Smircich, L. (1983), 'Concepts of culture and organizational analysis', *Administrative Science Quarterly*, 28, pp.339-358.
Smircich, L. & Morgan, G. (1982), 'Leadership: The management of meaning', *The Journal of Applied Behavioural Science*, 18, pp.257-73.
Stenner, P. & Eccleston, C. (1994), 'On the textuality of being', *Theory & Psychology*, 4, 1, pp.85-103.

Stewart, R. (1976), *Contrasts in Management: A Study of the Different Types of Managers' Jobs, their Demands and Choices*, McGraw Hill, New York.

Szmatka, J. (1989),' Holism, individualism, reductionism', *Int. Soc.*, 4, no. 2, pp.169-186.

Vaassen, B. (1994), *Die narrative Gestalt(ung) der Wirklichkeit, Grundlinien einer postmodern orientierten Epistemologie für die Sozialwissenschaften*, Dissertation Hochschule St.Gallen, Difo-Druck, Bamberg.

Watzlawick, P., Weakland, J.H. & Fish, R. (1974), *Change: Principles of Problem Formation and Problem Resolution*, W.W. Norton, New York.

Watzlawick, P. (ed.), (1984), *The Invented Reality*, W.W. Norton & Co, London.

Weick, K. (1979), *The Social Psychology of Organizing*, Addison-Wesley, Reading, MA.

Wildavsky, A. (1983), 'Information as an organizational problem', *Journal of Management Studies,* 20, pp.29-40.

Winograd, T. & Flores, F. (1986), *Understanding Computers and Cognition: A New Foundation for Design*, Ablex, Norwood, N.J.

Wittgenstein, L. (1963), *Philosophical Investigations* (G. Anscombe, transl.), Macmillan, New York.

Wrapp, H.E. (1984), 'Good managers don't make policy decisions', *Harvard Business Review,* July-August, pp.8-21.

Notes

1. Mannheim (1936, 1952) invented the term 'relationism' to contrast with 'relativism'; see e.g., Berger & Luckmann (1966), Stenner & Eccleston (1994).

2. We shall use these terms interchangeably; one term is sometimes more helpful than the other to bring out the particular point we wish to make.

3. We are not offering a detailed critique of epistemological assumptions or related treatments of 'content' concerns; the interested reader may find these elsewhere (e.g., Gergen, 1993; Szmatka, 1989; von Glasersfeld, 1985; Feyerabend, 1978; Morgan, 1983; Harding, 1986; Flax, 1987)

4. Garfinkel (1967, p.30) refers to 'intersubjectively used grammatical scheme(s)' or 'rules' which participants invoke to understand what was said.

5. These authors deconstructed the leadership literatures to show that they implicitly embrace masculine cultural narratives.

2 Relational theory and the discourses of power

Kenneth J. Gergen

If only the ruler and his people would refrain from harming each other, all the benefits of life would accumulate in the kingdom. Lao Tzu Tao Teh Ching.

Although rich in evocative imagery and ripe with pragmatic potential, the concept of power has been a fruit not readily plucked by many social analysts. For example, organizational theorists, social psychologists, systems analysts, therapeutic specialists and educational theorists, all of whom might readily feast on its potential, have displayed an uncommon reticence to developing or applying the concept to ongoing social processes. In part this reluctance may be traced to the historical residues carried by the term. The concept of power is rhetorically hot; it is suffused with the revolutionary energies of countless diatribes against inequality, oppression, and domination. Thus, the social scientist who is reasonably at home with the exiting state of affairs may have little need for the term. To thrust it into the centre of analysis is to raise a red flag, suggesting that existing arrangements are replete with oppression and inequity, and that fundamental change is required. For the organizational theorist to characterize the business firm as a domain in which the powerful enslave the weak is to suggest revolutionary change. For a social psychologist to paint a picture of human relations as a continuous struggle for domination is to threaten the liberal ideology so central to the discipline's history.

There are important exceptions to this general tendency. There are, for one, a substantial number of theorists within the Marxist and critical school tradition (Lukes, 1974; Habermas, 1971) whose analyses are specifically aimed at social critique and change. Further, there are theorists whose analyses of power either redefine it in such a way that it loses much of its evaluative edge (e.g. Parsons, 1969; Giddens, 1984), or who attempt to show how power distribution in western society is more equitable or more pluralist than generally believed (e.g.

Dahl, 1961). However, in spite of their potential, the language of power continues to remain in the penumbra of social analysis.

In recent times even the classic theories of power have come under critical scrutiny (see for example, Clegg, 1989; Wartenberg, 1990). As social analysts have become increasingly aware of the textual or constructionist turn within the academy more generally, of the extent to which theoretical categories engender the putative objects of analysis, they have turned reflexively on their own conceptual implements. Under this kind of scrutiny, it has become increasingly difficult to take power seriously. Thus, Marxist critics may inveigh against the current distribution of power in contemporary culture, pointing out the hegemonic and oppressive character of the capitalist ideology. But, it is now asked, to what extent are such critiques to be trusted; are they accurate assessments of social life, as the analysts claim? For if the accounts of the critical analyst, no less than the bourgeois liberalist, are dominated by class interests, rhetorical tropes, and the negotiated agreements of a particular subculture (in this case Marxist), then on what grounds are such accusations justified? Are they not mystifying in their effects? Or, in terms central to our present colloquy, is the concept of power not a social construction, used by theorists in this case as a rhetorical hammer for inducing social change? And if power is not a fact in the world, but an artifact of discourse, then in what sense should we take power relations in contemporary society as a topic about which serious discussion is demanded?

Although I am quite compelled by this line of reflexive critique, I find myself simultaneously unsettled. There are two primary sources of my concern. The first is a general dismay over the future of social analysis. For, if this kind of deconstruction becomes the dominant intellectual posture, social analysis itself is slowly debilitated. If all that we have previously taken to be objects of study become, through such de-entification, nothing more than locutions in discursive space, then we are left, in the Derridian sense, with nothing of text. Social analysis ceases to inform us about the world, for the object of discourse is none other than discourse itself. If the object of theoretical discourse is thus deconstructed, the function of social analysis is simultaneously impugned.

My second concern is more specific to the concept of power. Many within the constructionist fold are exploring possibilities for reconstituting the character of scientific inquiry. In particular, as the empiricist program begins to wane, and with it the belief in an ideologically neutral science, the door is open to legitimating social analyses of a distinctly valuational nature. That is, social constructionism invites the scientist to view professional actions in their full personal and political consequences. In this context, societal critique and reconstruction become central challenges for the human sciences. Thus, for example, feminist critics have condemned various institutional hierarchies for their androcentric biases, and have attempted to coalesce around the attempt to alter the existing structure of power (see for example, Smith, 1987; Lipman-Bluman, 1984). Similar critiques have been mounted by various ethnic minorities, children's rights advocates, and women against sexual and physical aggression. In each case the concept of differential power has been pivotal. Thus, to reduce the concept of power to that of mere construction is simultaneously to undermine the constructionist legitimation of social critique and reconstruction.

How is this dilemma to be resolved? How, on the one hand, can we recognize the concept of power as cultural construction, and at the same time objectify the term within a program of societal critique? What place are we to give the concept of power in future social analysis? It seems to me that there are two primary options to be considered here. First, we may agree that the concept of power is simply one among many symbolic implements for analyzing and criticizing existing states of affairs, and that it, like any other concept used for such purposes, is subject to various forms of deconstruction. Regardless of such de-entifying maneuvers, it may be said, the term will probably retain a good deal of its rhetorical or illocutionary capacity, and we can continue to use it for the foreseeable future. To put it otherwise, we can scarcely abandon concepts because they fail to be accurate descriptors; this would be to jettison virtually all propositional language. At the same time, one can scarcely speak without presuming some sort of world independent of language, to which the language is, by convention, referentially related. And, should sources of anguish be located within the space of existing conventions, then terms within the existing vernacular may be serviceable as pragmatic means of inducing change. There is nothing about constructionism that denies cultural participation.

There is much to be said for this option, and for extending the range of rhetorical resources available for moral and political purposes. However, it is to a second possibility that I am drawn in the present paper. In important respects, social constructionist theory operates as a scientific metatheory. That is, like logical empiricism and critical rationalism, for example, it attempts to offer an account of the scientific process, a theory of scientific theories. At the same time, constructionism as a metatheory is neutral with respect to what form scientific theories should take. Unlike its competitors, it does not require that the theories of human action spawned within the sciences support or vindicate its suppositional network.[1]

In this sense, we can thus discriminate between two forms of theoretical (and practical) work, that which opposes constructionist metatheory as contrasted with that which lends support. It is the second of these alternatives I wish to explore in what follows. This is first because there are many respects in which constructionism seems superior to existing alternatives. To hammer out conceptual tools by which the metatheory is vivified, is to augment its potentials.

In addition, as I shall hope to show, the major treatments of power currently extant are uncongenial to constructionist metatheory. Thus, to explore possibilities for a constructionist theory of power may enable new conceptions of power to emerge, and new conceptual resources to enter the cultural lists.

Invited, then, is a formulation of power that is consistent with, or which lends rhetorical legitimacy to, a constructionist orientation to theory and social life. In the remainder of this paper, I shall thus open discussion on what may be termed a relational theory of power, and finally treat several implications of this particular option for issues in organizational and social life more generally.

Discourses of power

> In loving your people and governing your state are you able to dispense with cleverness? Lao Tzu Tao Teh Ching

One of the most intuitively compelling ways of conceptualizing power is in terms of the macro social order. One speaks easily of the power of such institutions as the church, government, military force, industry and so on. Marxist theory of class conflict and Parsonian functionalism represent formal articulations of the intuition. However, as debates on power have proceeded during the past 20 years, the macro-social orientation has met with significant difficulty. For one, it is difficult to comprehend social life without recourse to the individuals who make up the broad structures. Yet, once individuals are recognized, the theorist falls into a problematic dualism, with individuals on the one side and institutions on the other. Yet, the phenomenal sets are fully conflated; remove all the individuals and there is nothing left over to be called an institution, and vice versa. Such theories also favour a problematic determinism. We are forced, as it is said, by the power of institutions to behave as we do. Yet, if the theory is to be emancipatory, it must simultaneously plump for voluntary resistance against the institution. (Thus, the Marxist incitement, 'workers of the world unite.') In the inducement to resist, the presumption of institutional determinism is undone.

For these and other reasons many theorists have relocated the cite of power at the individual level. Even for theorists such as Lukes (1977) and Giddens (1984) who attempt to integrate concepts of both social structure and the individual into the same theory, the strong emphasis is placed on the latter as opposed to the former (see Barbalet, 1982; Layder, 1987). Most pervasive are definitions of power in terms of personal characteristics. Consider, for example the definitions of Dahl, 'A has power to the extent that he can get B to do something B would not otherwise do.' (1957, p.203); Lukes, 'power ...

presupposes human agency ... although agents operate within individually determined limits, they none the less have a relative autonomy and could have acted differently (1977, p.6-7); and Giddens 'to be an agent is to be able to deploy (chronically, in the flow of daily life) a range of causal powers, including that of influencing those deployed by others' (1984, p.14). To these definitions analysts typically add a range of additional processes, capacities, or characteristics at the psychological level. Thus theorists variously explain processes of domination in terms of individual wants, needs, choices, real interests, and the unconscious.

While I see no compelling reason for returning to the macro social level of analysis, I am not wholly sanguine either with the further elaboration of the individual accounts, or with the integration of such accounts into a constructionist metatheory. There are, in my view, a number of serious problems inherent in the psycho-centered analysis of power, and at least three of these deserve attention in the present context. At the outset, post-empiricist and post-structuralist critiques of recent years make it increasingly difficult to sustain the assumption of individual minds, capable of registering events in the world, contemplating these events on a rational basis, and acting on the basis of rational decisions. As it is argued, there are no viable accounts of either the means by which real world events could be converted to abstract ideas (in the head), nor the means by which abstract ideas (or rational process) could be converted into concrete action (see my 1989 discussion). Further, should individuals possess independent minds, there would be no means by which others (including scientists) could determine their meaning or intent (see Fish, 1980), that is by which they could decipher the public code in such a way that intentions could be revealed. As Rorty (1979) concludes in his Philosophy and the Mirror of Nature, the presumption of individual minds, reflecting and reflecting on an independent nature, creates a host of unnecessary and principally insoluble riddles. There is good reason for abandoning the obfuscating dualisms of mind and nature, subject and object, inner and outer.

Second, by placing mental characteristics in a pivotal explanatory position, theorists place themselves in a problematic position vis a vis the culture more generally. For as we find, the analyst's assertions about people's intentions, wants, needs, and unconscious are without compelling grounds for justification. Not only is it impossible for the analyst standing external to the individual, to fathom the true nature of the individual's mental states, but there are no respectable reasons for assuming that individuals can turn introspectively on themselves to accurately perceive their own mental condition (see Lyons, 1986; Gergen, 1994b). Given the shaky character of the analyst's assertions, then any statements about who does or does not possess power loses its substantive base. Assessments of current imbalances in power, oppressive conditions, and injustices based on such mentalist attributions lose their warrant. The analyst claiming dispassionate grasp of the realities of social life thus appears either to be acting in bad faith or out of naive conventionalism.

Finally, I am compelled by the arguments of Sampson (1978), Bellah et al. (1985), Schwartz (1986) and others concerning the inimical consequences of individualistic orientations for cultural life. The rhetoric of individualism, including the presumption of individual minds, rationality, intentionality, and the like, lends itself to forms of social life that, in my view, ultimately endanger the species (if not all life on the planet). For as this perspective suggests, each of us in essentially independent of the other, operating on the basis of our own powers of reason and volition, fundamentally opaque to others, and fundamentally bent on enhancing one's own being. Unless individuals are curbed from seeking their own private ends, life is a war of all against all. And, because individuals are fundamentally alone, relationships are products of artifice, unnatural and usually temporary. Such a view of social life lends itself to alienation and divisiveness. Individualist theories of power additionally invite the public to see their social world in terms of domination and submission. We must, then, be attentive to the possibility of alternative formulations.

Toward a relational theory of power

As we find, there are important shortcomings inherent in both the macro-social and individual approaches to power. If we abandon the traditional accounts, what alternatives are available? Most important in the present context, how may we articulate a theory of power congruent with a constructionist metatheory? One moves with trepidation at this point. For, on the one hand, there is no univocal agreement concerning the nature of the constructionist standpoint. No one can properly claim to speak for the range of interlocutors more generally. Rather, we must envision a range of constructionist accounts with no single entry privileged in its position. In addition, the term power is widely used both within the social sciences and without. Its meanings and uses are many and varied. As one moves toward a reformulation, many of the previous meanings are discredited, altered or destroyed. In this sense, any new minting of the term threatens a range of social patternings sustained and supported by the previous meanings. As outlined, I do believe the previous conceptualizations of the term have inimical consequences for society. At the same time, there are many contexts in which I would heartily endorse the critical manner in which the term is used; I would favour the kinds of patterns sustained or advocated by the term in its traditional form. Thus, while I believe a constructionist refiguration of the concept could open new and potentially significant modes of action, I do not thereby wish to favour yet another totalizing discourse.

With these caveats at hand, there is at least one critical site at which the articulation of a constructionist theory of power can commence. It is the site of the privileged ontology. Unlike individual theories of power (in which the individual mind serves as the originary source), and in contrast to macro social theories (in which large-scale collective structures are presumed), most constructionist accounts begin with the presumption of human relatedness. Both the focus of concern and the explanatory fulcrum within a constructionist frame are episodes, processes or patterns achieved by ongoing processes of human interchange (Gergen, 1994a). It is the conversation which is perhaps most emblematic of the constructionist orientation, for the conversation is the product of neither an individual nor an institution, but of face-to-face, mutually contingent relationships. Further, it is from this nexus of joint-action (Shotter, 1980) that language ensues, and from language the vast array of ontological assumptions, including such assertions as individuals exist, and institutions control our lives.

Beginning with relatedness as the central ingredient, I am also drawn by certain aspects of Foucault's (1979; 1980) discussions of power. Foucault also shares a discontent with the traditional macro social view. As he argues, this essentially feudal form of power (juridico-discursive in his terms) has largely been replaced by what he terms disciplinary power. In the juridico-discursive case, specific rule systems, backed by the equivalent of a police force, demanded obedience. However, in the disciplinary context of the Panopticon, techniques were developed which led to the incorporation of belief systems within subject populations. Suppression was replaced by internalization. Central for present purposes, among the most important sources of disciplinary power are discursive or disciplinary regimes, roughly organized bodies of discourse and associated practices that serve both to engender beliefs and to rationalize their own existence. As the system of discourse, often taken to be truth or knowledge by its advocates, becomes the argot of everyday activity, seeping into the capillaries of the normal or taken for granted, so does the aggregate become complicit in its own subjugation.

While Foucault generally avoids the question of defining power[2], his analysis is congenial in certain respects with the constructionist emphasis on relatedness. Because of the centrality of discourse to his analysis, and the inherent relational quality of language, Foucault's analysis is primarily concerned with relational processes. The chief focus is the emergence and extension of power within micro-social processes (e.g. the confessional, the doctor-patient relationship) Or, as Foucault (1980) writes, 'power means a more-or-less organized ... coordinated cluster of relations' (p.198). Additionally promising is Foucault's emphasis on the capillary diffusion of power. Rather than seeing power as inherent in vast centralized structures, or within the capacities of charismatic individuals, power relations are distributed throughout the society. Further, for Foucault, relations of power are not travesties on the normal or the valued. Rather, in certain respects they are essential to social life, and productive of its most valued institutions.

Yet, while drawn by certain aspects of Foucault's writings, it is difficult to locate anything resembling a fully developed perspective in this work. Ambiguities regarding the character of power and oppression are pervasive. Further elaboration is thus invited. In carrying out such an elaboration, I am guided by certain aspects of Bakhtin's (1981) discussions of language and social process. Of particular interest, Bakhtin argues persuasively for the fragmented character of cultural languages. That is, our common languages are seldom unified, guided by an integral and inclusive set of rules. Rather, we inherit a multitude of linguistic usages, a legacy of long and complex relations among various cultural and sub-cultural groups. And, as we move through the novel demands of multitudinous contexts, so are we forced to borrow, patch, elide, and so on. Language is in a continuous state of multiple transformations (or heteroglossia in Bakhtin's terms). When paired with Foucault's emphasis on discourse, we might conclude that no society is bound to a singular discursive regime. Rather, we must entertain the possibility of multiple, fragmentary and partial regimes, of power relations as heterogeneous and ever changing.[3] We shall return to these themes shortly.

In the present analysis there is no attempt to define power in terms of a set of behavioral, psychological, or material coordinates. Rather, the focus will be on discourses of power, their emergence in relationships, and their consequences as they come to possess a lived validity. As I shall propose, within particular contexts of relatedness, discourses of power come to have functional significance. Two analytic moments may be distinguished, the first in which persons in relationship may come to view themselves as possessing the power to act in various ways. In a second set of relational conditions, a discourse of power over is invited.[4] The primary ingredients of this view are contained in four inter-related theses:

The formation of relational nuclei

For present purposes I will assume that human beings exist within an array of relationships (both to other human beings first, and further to the environment more generally). They do not commence life as single, unitary or self-contained monads but gain their very capacity to exist in such apparent states (what we call states of individual identity) by virtue of their relatedness. In this sense we are always already in relationship (social and otherwise). However, to gain conceptual clarity regarding the genesis of power in a constructionist frame, it is useful to explicate more fully the emergence of interdependence within a dyad, what we may call an elementary relational nucleus. Although face to face relationships will ordinarily entail the mutual coordination of bodily movements, sounds, focus of gaze, facial configurations, and so on, let us focus on what will prove a critical element in our analysis, the linguistic construction of meaning.

Language essentially derives its meaning (or capacity to communicate) by virtue of the coordinated activities of two or more persons. In this sense, the utterances (or other actions) of a single individual are not in themselves meaningful. For example, the utterance of a selected morpheme (e.g. ed, to, at) does not itself possess meaning. Standing alone, the morpheme fails to be anything but itself; in the Derridian sense the morpheme operates as a free standing signifier, opaque and indeterminate. Lone utterances begin to acquire communicative potential when another (or others) coordinate themselves to the utterance, that is, when they add some form of supplementary action (which may or may not be linguistic). The supplement may be as simple as an affirmation (e.g. yes, right) that indeed the utterance succeeds in communicating. It may take the form of an action, e.g. shifting the line of gaze upon hearing the word 'look'. Or it may extend the utterance in some way, e.g. when, 'the' is uttered by one interlocutor is followed by ,'end', uttered by a second. Thus the basic unit of linguistic meaning may be viewed as action-and-supplement. The formation of meaning within the primitive nucleus thus depends on the mutual privileging of language (and other actions). If others do not recognizably treat one's utterances as meaningful, if they fail to coordinate themselves around such offerings, one is reduced to nonsense.

In this regard, virtually any form of utterance may be granted the privilege of being meaningful, or conversely, serves as a candidate for absurdity. The other may invest profound significance in the simplest groan or monosyllabic grunt, or may respond with an opaque stare to the most perfectly formed sentence. The fate of the speaker's utterance is in the other's hands. As we find, the initial language unit does not, in pristine form, demand any particular form of coordinated action. In principle, an utterance may be taken to mean anything (see Gergen, 1994a). The act of supplementation thus operates in two opposing ways. First, it grants a specific potential to the meaning of the utterance. It treats it as meaning this and not that, as entailing one form of action as opposed to another, as having a particular illocutionary force as opposed to some other. At the same time, as it grants specific meaning, it simultaneously acts to constrain alternative possibilities of the utterance. Because it does mean this, it cannot mean that. In this sense, while others' actions invite us into meaning, they also act so as to negate our potential. From the enormous array of possibilities, only a limited array are made possible. And, as others both open and constrain, so do our subsequent actions serve the same functions with respect to them.

The creation of a local ontology and value system

Of course spoken language is only one form of coordinated action, and it may be that the linguistic account just outlined could provide a useful metaphor for the development of all forms of relatedness. In effect, all may require action-supplement sequences that define and constrain. Yet, for analytic purposes it is useful in the present context to distinguish between two outcomes intrinsic to most attempts to coordinate actions through language. In the first instance, to the degree that given patterns of coordination are to be sustained within a nucleus, language usage must be reiterative. Sequences of words-and-supplements must be replicated (or nearly so) under particular conditions. Thus, for example, employees in an office setting may coordinate their actions around such terms as boss, the mail, balance sheets, and the like. In order to carry out the tasks that we generally call getting the job done they will employ such terms on a repetitive basis. In doing so, however, the group succeeds in developing a local ontology. The terms in conventional usage come to establish a localized reality. The vocabularies essential to coordination of the participants take on the sense of a palpable order: what the world is made of in this case. Terms such as boss, the mail, and the like cease to be merely the syllables uttered under certain conditions, but come to serve as literal descriptions of what occurs. They become sedimented or entified.

The second byproduct of linguistic coordination is a valuational (moral, ethical) reality. To the extent that an utterance is indeterminant, open to multiple meanings, coherent patterning is disrupted. That is, established patterns of coordinated action (repetitive action-and-supplements) are threatened. If coordinated action within a group is to be sustained, it is thus essential to seal off the potential of the signifiers. Means must be found of delimiting the range of possible supplementarities. (For example, if he is not the boss but our slave or a vicious exploiter, then the typical patterns of action are difficult to sustain.) Means are invited, then, of restricting the process of signification (or preventing, what in other terms is called unlimited semiosis). At least one common means of doing so is by developing an ancillary language of valuation, a language that both places a positive value on existing patterns of action and impugnes all deviations.[5]

Such valuational supports may take many forms. In many instances groups have claimed certain patterns (e.g. democracy, charity, heterosexuality) to have inherent value. Or, strong appeals are made to the valuational authorities, to God, the Bible, wise men, poets, and so on. In many quarters reliance is placed on good reasons, as embodied in folk tales and axioms, or in volumes on methodology or philosophical foundations. Typically, each of these languages is also fortified by practices of approbation, means of discrediting the deviant and rewarding those remaining within the ontology and its implicature. In each case, however, the existing ontology and its underlying array of coordinated actions is buttressed by a valuational discourse that discredits deviation and sanctifies tradition.[6]

The condition of centripetal power

> By not exalting the talented you will cause the people to cease from rivalry and contention. By not displaying what is desirable, you will cause the people's hearts to remain undisturbed. Tzu Tao Teh Ching

Tendencies toward coordinated action also establish the conditions for what may be termed centripetal power. Consider here a condition (idealized for analytic purposes) in which varying groups succeed in stabilizing valued patterns of coordinated activity. The local ontologies are embraced and the valuational discourse functions so as to sustain the common reality. In effect, by the internal standards of the group, they function in an effective way. Centripetal power is achieved within a group when they can achieve their own goals according to their own definitional terms. They are empowered from within their own conceptual configuration. Illustrative, for example, is a couple who believe they have control of their lives, and can live in a reasonably stable and fulfilling way. Or, centripetal power is exemplified by an organization that sees itself as achieving its goals, expanding, profiting, and innovating in just the ways it defines as valuable. In effect, we are not speaking in this instance of a power over, but the sense of power to achieve specific goals.[7] It is also important to reiterate that the concept of power is not objectified on this account. That is, I am not speaking here of the actual capacity of a relational unit to achieve its ends. Rather, the concept of power operates in this case as a discursive vehicle for those within the relationship, a means of indexing a particular configuration of coordinated action. It is manifest in attempts, for example to label such coordination as achievement, or to see the interaction as possessing a goal which is being fulfilled.

The concept of centripetal power enables us to open several lines of discussions occluded by classic treatments of the subject. First, on the present account, we may see the culture as one in which local coordinations are everywhere under development. Thus, rather than a singular hierarchy, as suggested by much classic work on power, we find a multiplicity of groups, each of which may define power and its attainment according to different ontologies and value systems. In principle, with each movement toward coordinated action within a dyad or group, there are corresponding possibilities for centripetal power. To the extent that persons participate in multiple groups, with different conceptions of the real and the good, configurations of power are multiple. To the extent that the terms of the real and the good are negotiable, such configurations undergo continuous transformation.

The present perspective also acts as an antidote to common tendencies to define power in terms of a singular dimension, commodity, or criterion. The analyst standing outside the culture is not free, on this account, to render a general characterization of the source of power (e.g. capital, military might, freedom of action). Rather, in the present case we find that attributions of power, powerlessness, and oppression must always take account the local character of power ascription. Each group may come to see itself as coordinated around certain ends or goals, and these ends or goals may be as varied as there are differences in vocabulary. At the same time, any group may come to see other groups, those who fail to share their forms of coordinated action, as inferior, lacking judgement, lacking motivation, and powerless. This is to say that attributing power to those in executive positions, with high income levels, occupying political office, reaching championships and the like, is to join the interpretive systems of the particular groups in question. It is to capitulate to the apparent objectivity and valuational systems of the local realities, raising these constructions to the level of fundamental ontology. The valued coordinations of any given group may either be devalued or considered irrelevant within the local ontology of other groups. For the Buddhist monk, those bent on economic gain are pitied; they are running dogs. For those valuing the simple life, close to community and nature, high office is tedious and pressurized; and for communities devoted to intellectual or aesthetic ends, team championships exact a form of slavery. The present conception of centripetal power, then, acts to inhibit broadscale or unilateral critiques of existing power imbalances. Such critiques always presume some standpoint; their problem is in generalizing their ontology across all sectors of society.

Further, the present analysis also militates against knee-jerk condemnations of exclusionary practices, often viewed as expressions of power. As people consolidate communities, school systems, private clubs, and the like in such a way that entry is difficult or forbidden by others, we are quick to criticize. Such actions seem to be raw and unfair exercises of the powerful to exclude all others, to sustain their own positions of superiority while denying others the right to participate. Yet, as the present analysis suggests, groups whose actions are coordinated around given constructions of reality risk their traditions by exposing them to the ravages of the outliers. That is, from their perspective, efforts must be made to protect the boundaries of understanding, to prevent the signifiers from escaping into the free-standing environment where meaning is decried or dissipated. In this sense, unfair or exclusionary practices are not frequently so from the standpoint of the actors. Rather, they may seem altogether fair, just and essential to sustain valued ideals against the infidels at the gates. This is also to say that we may anticipate, on these terms, perpetual struggles against oppression. For centripetal forces within groups will always operate toward stabilization, the establishment of valued meaning, and thus the exclusion of alterior realities. Exclusive communities, private schools and secret societies are simply the most flagrant manifestations of a process that operates at all levels of social life. From international negotiations, to the whispered gossip of daily relationships, processes of coordination and exclusion are in operation. Let us consider a second site of power ascription.

Counter-reality and the emergence of centrifugal power

> When all the world recognizes good as good, this in itself is evil. Indeed, the hidden and the manifest give birth to each other. Lao Tzu Tao Teh Ching

As the present analysis suggests, all those practices taken to be unfairly exclusionary or oppressive are only so by virtue of a particular ontology. Outsiders to a group would fail to experience exclusion, except for the fact that they have come to accept the ontology and related values of a particular group. If members of a bridge club hold a closed tournament, there is no outcry of discrimination by the local bowling league. Outcries of injustice and discrimination are the result of generalizing the ontology and related value system of a particular group beyond its borders, and possessing a rationale by virtue of which this condition is held to be wrong (i.e. unjust, inhumane).

Of course, daily life is seldom so tranquil as at the borders of France and Switzerland or between those who prefer bridge as opposed to bowling, both instances of centripetal power processes at work in relatively independent groups. Rather, we confront widespread fears of power imbalances, accusations of inequity, and attributions of exploitation. Unions are created to curb the self-serving tendencies of management; feminists work to right the balance of power in the workplace; and the 'have not' nations express resentment and contempt for the hegemonic tendencies of the 'haves'. To understand such actions our analysis must press beyond the condition of centripetal power. More specifically, the prevalence of intergroup conflict requires an understanding of the transformation from conditions of centripetal power to those of centrifugal power. Rather than viewing a group as possessing power to (as in the case of centripetal power), we must explore the conditions in which the sense of power over becomes dominant.

The critical transformation in this case has its origins in the production of counter-reality. As we have seen, participants in a continuing relationship will tend toward a stabilized ontology. Physicists will agree, for example, that the world is fundamentally material, and idealist philosophers that it is fundamentally mental. Yet, in moving centripetally toward a stabilized reality, the interlocutors simultaneously set in motion an opposing tendency. For in generating agreeable assertions concerning what is the case, in effect a positive ontology, the soil is also prepared for the growth of a an oppositional discourse, a negative ontology This is so because the intelligibility of any assertion is only made possible through contrasts, differences, or negations. That something is the case can only stand as an informative assertion against the backdrop of an alternative or a contrary. To specify that Joan is the boss stands as meaningful only if the world contains non-bosses; to declare profit to be a 'good' is only significant if there are other outcomes that are not good.

To press further, in the creation of the positive ontology possibilities for its own subversion are generated. As participants in a relationship come to organize themselves around discourses of the real and the good, they set the conditions for disorganization. This is so because the terms of the discourse have no fixed context of application; they may be applied over a broad arena. And as 'language goes on holiday' (in Wittgenstein's terms, 1953), any object of one naming becomes a candidate for another. Any proclamation stands subject to question. If there are the rich, then there must be the poor; and if there are the poor by what rights are certain persons granted status as the former and not others? On what grounds are the designations made? Could the reverse be possible? And if there are justifications for the present arrangement, let us say in terms of rights, then the possibility is simultaneously created for a concept of wrongs. And questioning is again invited: Why are certain conditions granted the status of right or proper, and others designated as wrong or unjust? Is it possible that what now stands as just could be its opposite? Without the creation of the positive ontology, there would be little means of challenge; to question or criticize one must possess an intelligible discourse of counterclaims. Without version there is no role for subversion.

We thus find that participants in a relationship exist in a state of continuous threat. In creating a given ontology and its rationalization, they also generate grounds for doubt. Their very proclamations of what is the case simultaneously assert the possibility of their negation. In this sense, the process of assertion feeds upon itself. For to begin the process is also to create tendencies toward opposition. In turn, the threat of opposition invites a further strengthening of the network of assertions. Thus, for example, to create an arsenal for purposes of superior might is simultaneously to create the possibility that one is not superior. The possibility instigates further arms development, which again raises the question of sufficiency. The quest for power incessantly feeds upon its own doubts.

More central to our purposes, as the negative ontology is articulated, and critique becomes possible, the conditions are established for centrifugal power, an emerging sense of inside vs. outside, we vs. them, and most focally, the power of one over the other.[8] This is to say that the ascription of power over, is importantly dependent on a language of critique. If a manager gives a raise to an employer, or a policeman apprehends a criminal, we are not likely to speak in terms of power. So long as these are creditable aims, we are not likely to see one as manifesting power over the other. However, if the manager gives a raise far beneath what the employee deserves, or the apprehended individual has committed no crime, then ascriptions of power are apposite. The critique separates subject from object, us from them; and because they do not succumb to critique (their patterns remain obdurate) it is possible to see them in terms of having power over. It is the result of the negative ontology that the concept of power acquires the moral force with which it is often embued.

Let us consider the emergence of such attributions in diachronic dimension. It is not simply the potential for critique that evokes claims of power discrepancies. The stage must be properly set; a particular array of relational scenarios is implicated. Consider first the development of 'power over' within a given nucleus. As relational nuclei expand and develop over time there is a tendency toward differentiation, with different individuals carrying out different tasks with different results. In effect, no organization or society is constituted by homogeneous living conditions. With variation in such conditions, and the availability of a negative ontology, the stage is set for questioning and critique. Why are outcomes distributed in just this way; why are they privileged and we are not; why am I positioned in this inferior way? The mounting of questions and critique, in turn, commonly evoke a posture of defense and counter-critique on the part of others. And, as I have outlined elsewhere (Gergen, 1992), the rhetorical process of argumentation, at least within the Western tradition, is typically accompanied by progressive tendencies toward isolation (with each group turning increasingly inward toward those with whom coordination of language and action is most easily accomplished), and antagonism (with each group locating forms of evil within the other, and acting on these assumptions). Those under attack thus become invested in defending and reinforcing the traditions, while those engaged in critique seek means of change. As such efforts are thwarted in various ways, so do attributions of power become relevant.

These attributions may be intensified by the existence of other, adjoining groups. In the earlier account we spoke first of a hypothetical condition in which each nucleus developed its own reality, independent of all others. However, as the thesis unfolded we found social life more properly viewed as a plurality of nuclei, ever shifting, ever interpenetrating. In this sense, instances of an independent nucleus should be rare. Rather than a single ontology and its negations, there are multiple ontologies and valuational discourses (and their antitheses) available to most relationships. Such cases occur most frequently as members of one group become functional in other groups, the family member is also a student, the executive a marriage partner, the worker a union member, and so on. The greater the complexity of society, the more porous the boundaries of a group's reality.[9]

Most important for present purposes, these alternative realities become available to those in contention. Thus, any group embarking on critique is likely to find available a host of supplementary rationales for bolstering its case; likewise, those on the defensive can make use of many ambient rationalities. The sense of boundaries between, and power over intensifies. Further, and most interestingly, as the various bodies of signification begin to interpenetrate, the stage is set for what may be termed contrapuntal conflicts. In this condition, members of differing groups come to share conceptions of valued ends, but carry out critique in terms of local vernaculars, each but dimly understood outside the confines of the group. Groups view themselves as contending for particular resources, but the grounds for the claims are carved from different intelligibilities. The government of Iraq shares in the common value placed on economic resources, but the rationale for the invasion of Kuwait fails to be rhetorically compelling outside the Arab community; similarly the US government's claims to the injustice of the invasion fail to be understood within Iraq. As the rhetorics are converted to acts of brutality, the relationship is indexed in terms of power differences.

As a general surmise, it may be said that both centripetal and centrifugal forces are always at work within the culture. As relationships form, friendships, colleagueships, partnerships, and so on, actions will be coordinated, outcomes will be invested with significance, and efforts will be made to stabilize and exclude. Simultaneously, doubts are created in the existing coordinations, and the complex configurations of normal society will work toward their questioning. To the extent that memberships within these complex configurations equip people both to value and to doubt, the stage is set for ascriptions of power differences, exploitation, and injustice.

Consequences of the configuration

These remarks outline an orientation to power consistent with certain aspects of a constructionist metatheory, namely its assumption of fundamental relatedness and its focus on the discursive structuring of the social world. As I have tried to argue, we may envision two major moments in the emerging construction of power. The first derives from the capacity of groups for self-organization, and the concomitant moulding of local realities. With local conceptions of fact and value in place, groups may come to see themselves as possessing power in various degrees. This concern with local conceptions of power enabled us to view power as a comparative concept, differentially established, variably distributed and continuously changing. The second moment in the construction of power derives from the generation of a negative ontology, the necessary counterpart to the group's construction of reality. With this conception at hand we were prepared to treat the moral dimension of power differences, the prevailing sense that power is corrupt and oppressive.

Although it is possible to assess the proposal in a variety of ways, I wish in closing to confront one important critique and then to explore several implications of the analysis. The critique is that of the realist who may find little of value in the present account. Does the present analysis not deny the evidence of power in the capacity of large armies to rampage across helpless lands, the capacity of wealthy nations to control the outcomes of the poor, or the ruthlessness of dictators in silencing the people through threat and torture? These are the realities of the world, the realist proclaims, and the fact of power is undeniable. Of course, this is a rhetorically compelling critique, and in certain walks of daily life I might well speak of power in realist terms. But the critical point is the situated character of such speech acts. For under other circumstances, I might also intelligibly speak of the power of a beautiful face, the power of an infant's cry, or the power of a magnet. The meanings here are clearly different from the initial examples, but how should we distinguish between the more and less accurate meanings? And if we are free to negotiate about such matters, then by what particular authority does the concept of power necessarily apply to armies, wealth and tyrants? Are there not other and different means of describing these same conditions, ways for example that might be used by the actors themselves? And if taking a scholarly stance, would it not be possible to demonstrate the metaphoric character of the concept of power, its problematic assumption of linear and efficient causality, and the incapacity of analysts to locate specific referents? As Lukes (1974) proposes, the concept of power is essentially contested, and it is that essential ambiguity which the present proposal attempts to embody. Let us turn, then, to two realms of implication.

There are a number of important implications of the present analysis for issues of organizational management. Chief among them is the challenge posed for the hierarchical model of power. The traditional view of organizational structure, with a CEO as senior in command, followed by various levels of managers, workers, and the like proves problematic on a variety of grounds outlined above. Further, as suggested within the present analysis, what are termed achievements within organizations are first and foremost the result of coordinated activities. There most certainly are individuals we single out as high and low level managers and the like. However, such labels should not obscure the extent to which their actions are embedded in patterns of reciprocity. Those who lead only do so by virtue of a shared system of understanding in which others agree to do what is called following. The labels could be switched with no ontological consequences; leaders might be viewed as victims of their underlings, and followers as the true power behind the office. Further, the extent to which all such patterns are sustained depends on the extent to which participants keep the borders of meaning secure.

As the present account also suggests, the attempt of organizations to achieve effective outcomes takes place in highly tenuous circumstances. As languages of efficacy are developed, so do they engender a local sense of reality that is at once self sustaining and self-justifying. Thus, the world looks different within an organization than it does to those outside, and those within one sector of the system come to see reality as different from those within another. And the sense of what is the case in any of these sectors comes to seem correct and superior. Further, because the viability of a business organization depends on the realities outside itself, and the functioning of each organizational sector is vitally affected by functioning in another, then the strong tendency toward local ontology works against the longterm vitality of the organization. As each organization or sector within the firm forms its realities, necessary for effective action, so do they unleash the forces for their own undoing.

This latter outcome is hastened in some degree by the creation of the negative ontology. As the firm establishes a definition of the good and the powerful, so do they lay the groundwork for challenging their local ontology. Yet, in the end, the health of the organization may depend on a sensitive listening to the counter-reality. For as the alternative realities are given credence within the firm, so is the firm more fully coordinated to the surrounding environment. As the firm listens to the angry voices of those who accuse of them of exploitation, environmental pollution, unfair employment practices, immoral or insensitive practices of takeover, and the like, they stand to gain. If they do not use such instances to bolster the validity of their internal realities, and incorporate these languages into their own, then they may increase their capacity to co-exist in a larger world of coordinated interdependence. Success may require the undoing of effective patterns of action within the organization, but from the present standpoint, the only viable organization is one in which there is a continuous process of organizing and disorganizing.

Power, values, and constructing society

Within a constructionist perspective, one of the most important questions to be put to a theory concerns its ramifications for lived vocabularies. That is, rather than asking whether a theory accurately reflects life as it is, (an obfuscating question in itself), the constructionist asks, what are the social implications of a given system of theoretical intelligibility should that system be incorporated into ongoing social life? In this respect, the present analysis has several implications I take to be of promising proportion.

First there is an important sense in which the present analysis can soften existing tendencies toward ascendent or competitive striving. As we have seen, conceptions of power arise within particular groups, and are embedded within various forms of social practice. Mutually annihilating competitions come about largely through the broad dissemination of a single reality system. It is the unquestioned assumption that wealth, victory, high office and so on are valuable and important that moves people to competitive action. As the present analysis suggests, such assumptions of the effective and the good should always be placed in question. The grounds for question are always there, born of the negative ontology. Thus, rather than joining the bandwagons of the culture (e.g. striving for increased income, placing children in competitive sports programs, purchasing the latest electronics, etc), the present analysis suggest a scanning of alternative realities. For as the oppositions become apparent, the glitter can be removed from the prevailing goals.

In a similar vein the present account also dulls the edge of absolutist critiques of unfairness and injustice. Traditionally, critiques of this kind recognize only a single reality. There are the oppressors and the oppressed, the exploiters and the exploited, and so on. The former are deemed evil, the latter good, and where evil was, good shall now prevail. In effect, in their one-world myopia, such critiques are highly devisive, exacerbating conflict and galvanizing resistance. From the present standpoint, such accusations are considerably softened. One is instead invited to expand the range of relevant perspectives, to explore the realities of the dominating groups, as well as those of still other groups whose realities may differ. This is not to negate the moral force of existing accusations of inequity and exploitation. Such accusations are fully legitimate within the ontology of the exploited group. But rather than unleashing unilateral attacks in the name of righteousness, the present urging is for a co-mingling of perspectives.

References

Arendt, H. (1969), *On Violence*, Harcourt Brace Jovanovich, New York.
Bakhtin, M.M. (1981), *The Dialogic imagination*, University of Texas Press, Austin.
Bellah, R.N. et al. (1985), *Habits of the Heart*, University of California Press, Austin.
Clegg, S.R. (1989), *Framework of Power*, Sage, London.
Cousin, M. & Hussain, A. (1984), *Theoretical Traditions in the Social Sciences*, St. Martin's Press, New York.
Dahl, R.A. (1961), *Who Governs? Democracy and Power in an American City*, Yale University Press, New Haven.
Dahl, R.A. (1957), 'The concept of power', *Behavioural Science*, 2, pp.201-205.
Fish, S. (1980), *Is There a Text in this Class? The Authority of Interpretive Communities*, Harvard University Press, Cambridge.
Foucault, M. (1979), *Discipline and Punish: The Birth of the Prison*, Random House, New York.
Foucault, M. (1980), *Power/Knowledge*, Pantheon, New York.
Gergen, K.J. (1989), 'Social psychology and the wrong revolution', *European Journal of Social Psychology*, 19, pp.731-742.
Gergen, K.J. (1992), 'The Limits of Pure Critique'. In H. Simons & M. Billig (eds.), *The Future of the Critical Impulse*, Sage, London.
Gergen, K.J. (1994a), *Realities and Relationships*, Harvard University Press, Cambridge.
Gergen, K.J. (1994b), *Toward Transformation in Social Knowledge*, 2nd ed., Springer, New York.
Giddens, A. (1984), *The Constitution of Society*, Polity, Cambridge.
Habermas, J. (1971), *Knowledge and Human Interests*, Beacon, Boston.
Laclau, H. & Mouffe, C. (1985), *Hegemony and Socialist Strategy*, Verso, London.
Layder, D. (1987), 'Key issues in structuration theory: Some critical remarks', *Current Perspectives in Social Theory*, 8, pp.25-46.
Lipman-Blumen, J. (1984), *Gender Roles and Power*, Prentice-Hall, Englewood Cliffs.
Lukes, S. (1977), *Essays in Social Theory*, Macmillan, London.
Lukes, S. (1974), *Power: A Radical View*, Macmillan, London.
Lyons, W. (1986), *The Disappearance of Introspection*, MIT Press, Cambridge.

Parsons, T. (1969), 'On the Concept of Political Power', in R. Bell, D. Edwards & R. Wagner (eds.) *Political power: A Reader in Theory and Research*, Free Press, New York, pp.251-284.

Pitkin, H. (1972), *Wittgenstein and Justice*, University of California Press, Berkeley.

Rorty, R. (1979), *Philosophy and the Mirror of Nature*, Princeton University Press, Princeton.

Sampson, H.H. (1978), 'Scientific paradigms and social values: Wanted - a scientific revolution, *Journal of Personality and Social Psychology*, 36, pp.730-743.

Schwartz, B. (1986), *The Battle for Human Nature*, Norton, New York.

Shotter, J. (1980), 'Action, Joint Action and Intentionality', in M. Brenner (ed.) *The Structure of Action*, Blackwell, Oxford.

Smith, D.H. (1987), 'Women's Perspective as a Radical Critique of Sociology', In S. Harding (ed.) *Feminism and Methodology*, Indiana University Press, Bloomington.

Wartenberg, T. (1990), *The Forms of Power*, Temple University Press, Philadelphia.

Wittgenstein, L. (1953), *Philosophical Investigations*. G. Anscombe, trans., Macmillan, New York.

Notes

1. As I have outlined elsewhere (Gergen, 1994a) most behaviourist theory in psychology represents a recapitulation at the theoretical level of the suppositions built into the empiricist metatheory guiding the research.

2. As Cousins and Hussain (1984) summarize, 'there is in Foucault's writings no theory of power, not even a sketch of such a theory' (p.225). However, as they see his more positive contribution, Foucault offers an invaluable tool-kit for the anlaysis of power relations.

3. Influenced by Derrida's analyses of the undecidability (continuous deferral) of meaning, much the same conclusion is reached by Laclau & Mouffe (1985).Arguing against the Marxist view of power as essentialist, they are concerned with the ways in which meanings are distributed across relationships and altered in usage.

4. In distinguishing between the power to take action vs. the power over other, the present theory reflects what many theorists (see, for example, Pitkin, 1972) take to be a central distinction in the description of power. However,

where most view the distinction as primarily referential, the present analysis is concerned with its performative potential.

5. It is within the development of these local ontologies of the true and the good, that individual actors also become identified as such and furnished (discursively) with various attributes (e.g. emotions, intention). For Foucault, this process would be seen as one of subjectification. Yet, while the process of subjectification (let us say, by a given regime of knowledge) would be viewed by Foucault as a power relation, in the present analysis power is an ascriptive implement growing out of relational forms. There are, on the present account, discursive relationships, and the resulting discourse may include accounts of power (attributed to groups, individuals, material, etc.).

6. It is the attempt to fix meaning within the group that constitutes the moment of power for Laclau and Mouffe (1985).Thus, 'in a given social formation there can be a variety of hegemonic nodal points ... some of them may be highly overdetermined: they may constitute points of condensation of a number of social relations and, thus become the focal point of a multiplicity of totalizing effects' (p.139). In contrast, in the present analysis it is not the self-organizing process that itself constitutes power. Rather, such self-organization sets the context for a particular discourse of power.

7. It is in this respect that the present account is in accord with Arendt's (1969) view of power as a consensual (rather than imposed) outcome. As Arendt argues, power refers to the ability of a group to realize its own ends through cooperation. In the present case, the concern is not with actual capacities, but the group's construction of what they take to be such capacities.

8. I have borrowed the concepts of centripetal and centrifugal forces from Bakhtin's (1981) discussion of forces in the organization and disorganization of cultural languages. However, where Bakhtin views such disorganization as naturally derived from the varied demands made on language (thus forcing multiple uses), the present analysis focuses on the inherent potential for conflict within any ontological aggregate.

9. See also Bakhtin's (1981) discussion of dialogized heteroglossia, a term referring to the subtle and self-consciousness undermining of a language system (its beliefs and suppositions) as it interacts with other languages.

3 Constructing power: Entitative and relational approaches

Dian-Marie Hosking

Overview

Contributions to this volume offer relational approaches to organising and to bracketed topics such as management and change; power is one such topic and is addressed head on, so to speak, in Ken Gergen's chapter. Gergen starts by suggesting that social scientists have shown a marked reluctance to theorise power as an ongoing process. He argues that power 'has been a fruit not readily plucked by many social analysts', and that this is so because the concept of power is 'rhetorically hot'. I will take up these points, examining them in relation to the mainstream literatures on organization. The present analysis supports Gergen's suggestions and adds another reason why power is relatively ignored. In brief, I will argue that entitative narratives of organization place severe constraints on the possible meanings of power. Power is made a non issue by the individualistic separation of cognitive, social, and political processes; power is made invisible by the rhetoric of structural-functionalism and its emphasis on technical rationality, organization structures and control.

Second, and on the basis of the above, I suggest some of the (changed) narratives which characterise relational approaches. Some of the ways these have been developed in existing social constructionist writings are briefly examined. Then I return to Gergen's argument that the concept of power has been relatively ignored. However, this time it is considered in the context of existing relational approaches. Again, I add another reason why power may be ignored suggesting that constructionist approaches, by seeing power everywhere, demand more than is possible from one concept. Explicit talk of power is replaced by an extensive mesh of interrelated concepts dealing with the many social processes through which definitions of reality are socially constructed. Third, I turn to the details of Gergen's own relational theory of power to consider his central arguments and to suggest what might be some of the consequences of moves he makes. I comment on some of his theoretical moves, suggesting they are less helpful than they might be in getting him where he wants to go, and suggesting others that might be worth exploring. Additional lines of enquiry also are suggested, lines that fit with his journey but which he left unexplored. I finish by drawing attention to a major problem of which I am sure Gergen is aware: the limiting effects of assuming that interdependence is located in shared constructions of reality. Probably he readily would agree that people can act jointly on the basis of quite different language games in which case perhaps this line of argument needs further refinement. Perhaps the restrictions could be lessened by locating interdependence in ongoing social-relational processes, whether or not self believes that other shares the same construction of their relationship.

Introduction

Entitative taken for granteds

Gergen means something very special by a relational theory and to understand what this is it may helpful to start where he starts. He describes two discourses of power. One he calls psycho centred in that it focuses attention on the individual, and treats power as a personal characteristic. The second locates power at the macro social level, for example, in organizations, institutions, and/or cultures; this level is understood as macro, compared with the individual, and as the independent context of individual behaviour. These two approaches have been variously described in the literatures (e.g., Allport, 1963), as has the perspective they share (e.g., Sampson, 1993); I shall refer to the latter as an 'entitative' perspective. When evaluated from the position of a contrasting, relational perspective, we see that entitative taken-for-granteds create a very particular starting point for theory. Briefly, person and context are treated as entities each having their existence separate and independent of the other. Further, these entities are seen as characterised by physicalist properties. Relations are understood as relations between entities - viewed as either subject or object. The subject is understood to act by gathering 'knowledge that' (other has certain characteristics) and to achieve 'influence over' other (as object) (see Hosking & Morley, 1991; Dachler & Hosking, this volume).

The meanings of relational

Rejecting entitative assumptions For some theorists, and Gergen certainly is one, the point of departure for a relational approach must lie in changing the above pre-theoretical premise concerning person, context, and their relations.

Sometimes theorists focus on epistemological issues, disputing entitative taken-for-granteds about how we know the world around us (see e.g., Dachler & Hosking, this volume; Gergen, 1982). Equally, they sometimes focus on the entitative perspective's implicit ontological assumptions of what reasonably can be claimed to exist in its own right, disputing entitative claims about the separate and independent relations between the person and the world. In the chapter presently under consideration, Gergen focuses his critique on what he calls the attribution of a privileged ontology. He argues that both person and culture are treated as if they had their existence independently of the other. His relational alternative is to shift the ontological assumption to a new location, that is, to relational processes. Relational processes are made the unit of analysis so to speak, and therefore are made the vehicle by which both person and culture are produced and reproduced. Later I shall turn to how precisely he does this. For the present, the point I wish to emphasise is that once this pre-theoretical move is made, subsequent theoretical talk about person and context must be understood in a very special way. The terms cannot be treated as if they referred to independent entities; they must be understood as references to ongoing constructions that vary in different cultural settings and historical periods. This kind of relational theory focuses on conversations or discourse more generally. It does so to show how meanings (descriptions) are (re)constructed through discourse, and to identify what constructions (e.g., what kinds of understanding of person) are produced.

Relations between entities   Of course the literatures embrace other meanings of relational and this can create considerable confusion; relatively few go as far as Gergen to consider and change their pre-theoretical assumptions. So, for example, theories of power that explicitly emphasise relations (rather than individuals) immediately come to mind as examples of a relational approach to power. For example, Cartwright & Zander, when introducing the topic of power and influence, and speaking of the work of theorists such as Dahl, March, and Thibaut & Kelly, observed the following relational themes. First, 'most theorists assume that influence should be viewed as a relationship between two social entities such as individuals, roles, groups or nations...' (Cartwright & Zander, 1953, p. 215). Next they stressed the contextual nature of power, noting that a social entity might be able to achieve influence in some relationships and not in others, for example, with respect to certain issues. Part of this argument was the assertion that whether or not A influences B depends on the relationship between their different points of view. In addition, they drew attention to certain reciprocal qualities of influence relations: in any given social relationship both parties may influence the other, for example, with respect to different issues.

The above themes of contextualism and the like seem very fitting to a relational perspective. However the key point, from a position such as that taken by Gergen, is that although relations are emphasised, the starting point assumes that person and context are entities existing independently of each other. This makes them individualistic; the meaning of relations is restricted to relations between entities.

Looking ahead

This entitative understanding of relations is characteristic of the literatures on organization and, therefore, the understandings of power they embrace. We will conduct a relational analysis of the network of implicit and explicit narrative themes that together create the context in relation to which the text of power has been understood. In so doing we can illustrate and affirm Gergen's assertion that power has not been theorised as an ongoing social process, at least not in the mainstream literatures of organization. In addition, we show that the narratives of organization and people in organization effectively marginalise any talk about power. This suggests that power does not have to be 'rhetorically hot' to be ignored. Rather power, or indeed any construction, may be ignored because it is not thinkable in the context of certain taken-for-granteds, certain kinds of story.

Narratives of organization and their implications for power

Entitative treatments of social, cognitive, and political processes

The concept of organization is more or less explicitly developed in the literatures of organisational behaviour (OB), human resource management (HRM), and organizational analysis (OA). To discuss these literatures and the understandings of power they embrace analytical distinctions will be made between three aspects of organization: social, cognitive, and political. In discussing these it will become clear that each is understood as though it were a separate characteristic of independent entities, and relations are understood as relations between entities. Apparently power is not theorised as an ongoing process (cf. Gergen); moreover it becomes clear that it could not be. This is true, not just of power, but of the wider narratives to which it is referenced: the entitative pre-theoretical assumptions and narratives make this impossible.

Social aspects of organization Examination of the literatures of OB, OA, and HRM, shows that the social aspects of organization are reduced to inputs from person; they are not theorised relationally. They are constructed, on the one hand, as social needs and, on the other, as their behavioural inputs to social interactions. The former are viewed as properties or characteristics of person, but have been most often considered as characteristics of certain kinds of person, that is, non- managers. This is illustrated, for example, in interpretations of the Hawthorne studies and in managerial practices connected with these, the so called social man approach to group working, supportive supervision and so on (see, for example, Schein, 1980). The latter, that is social interactions, are reduced to behavioural inputs contributed by individuals. These inputs are understood as objective characteristics of the performer, as for example, socio- emotional, or task- oriented, supportive and so on.

The meaning of behavioural inputs to social interactions is further constructed with reference to entitative narratives about characteristics of organization. Two are crucial: the assumption of an organization wide shared logic, and the assumption of organization wide structures (e.g., Meyer & Associates, 1985); these characteristics are assumed to limit and guide individuals' behavioural inputs/social processes. Turning first to the assumption of an organization wide logic, different versions of structural-functionalism implicitly assume that the organizational whole has functional unity. Further, they locate the standards by which functionality is judged in the organization's environment, understood as independent of the organization and as characterised by physicalist brute facts, so to speak. This being so, individuals' behaviours and social interactions (social processes) are defined as rational (or irrational) in relation to the brute facts, the seeming facticity of organizations' goals, values, and what is taken for granted as functional. This rules out of court any questioning of the standards and the practices they legitimise: the organizational mission, values, goals are placed beyond question. This underlying narrative of knowledge as fact effaces its narrative alternative which is that power is implicated in what is defined as a fact. Talk about facts effaces other potentially relevant narratives, for example, a narrative of political processes as processes in which different constructions of the 'real and the good' are constructed on the basis of discourse.

Turning to the assumption of organization wide structures, these are understood rationally to limit and guide social processes in the service of the organization wide logic. By implication, power is understood to be located in organization structures and relations between structural positions. However, what is interesting is that the language of power rarely is used. Instead we find talk of authority viewed, for example, as rational-legal (Weber, 1947) and as legitimate in relation to hierarchy, a dimension of structure. Similarly, the language of control is used to refer to influence achieved on the basis of structures such as written rules, procedures and standards - understood as impersonal characteristics of organisation. Influence is understood to characterise social relations but, given the assumed organizational characteristics, is understood legitimately to be achieved through the acts of superordinates (behavioural inputs, sic) in relation to subordinates. Here we find social relations reduced to talk about managerial behaviours and effectiveness; the rhetoric of leadership is especially favoured for talking about the ways superordinates may achieve power over subordinates. In sum, entitative narratives of organization that, in turn, reference a narrative of 'social' as inputs from person, efface the alternate narrative of power.

Cognitive aspects of organization Entitative narratives of organization treat cognitive as separate from social. The latter we have seen are understood as individual needs and behavioural inputs to social interactions: nothing cognitive there. No, cognitive is located elsewhere, treated as it were, inside the head, as mind operations so to speak. Cognition is viewed as a fundamentally solitary, unsocial activity. It is activity in which the subject is understood to perform computations on information about internal and external nature, understood as facts in the world. On the basis of these and other taken for granteds many have supposed that organisational structures can be designed. So, for example, it has been thought possible to allocate to managers thinking tasks so to speak, understood as a cognitive activity; non-managers could be assigned doing tasks, understood as no cognitive activity. As an illustration, consider Taylor's & Weber's assumption of the existence of technical knowledge (knowledge that) and their emphasis on its significance for the rational structuring of organisation. Taylor urged that the workers 'rules of thumb' be acquired by management, that is, be taken out of the heads of workers and designed into jobs and organisation structures (see Hosking & Morley, 1991). Presumably theorists understood this as a rational means for management to achieve power over others. However, as with understandings of social processes, theorists employed a discourse of rationality, of design based on knowledge, not on power.

The above understandings of cognitive processes imply a sharp separation from social and political processes and from power. Since cognitive operations are understood to concern the facts of nature they are viewed as technical, as issues of right and wrong. In the context of these narratives, departures from rationality are explained in two ways: as individual errors in mind computations/operations, &/or as an unfortunate intrusion of political processes resulting from the expression of social needs and social interactions. As far as cognitive processes are concerned, managers can safely be left to make decisions, to design structures, that is, to organize for the good of all: questions of power are made irrelevant when knowledge is a matter of right and wrong, when organizations are viewed as more or less rational in relation to the facts of nature.

Political aspects of organization   The above analysis of cognitive and social narratives of organization reveals a very restricted context with reference to which the text of politics may be understood. To expand, the narrative of social aspects means that politics must be understood as individual behaviour reflecting social needs, or as social relations; politics messes-up what otherwise would have been a rational process. Similarly, the narrative of cognitive aspects invites a view of politics as the result of faulty information processing. And what of the narratives of organization? Organization wide structures are understood rationally to direct behavioural inputs and decision making on the basis of power, defined in terms of authority and related concepts. This narrative constrains the potential meaning of politics, seeing it as resulting from structures that are badly designed; badly designed structures fail to integrate differentiated functions in relation to the assumed organization-wide logic. The assumption of an organization-wide logic invites the definition of behaviours as political if they deviate from standards of functionality. These standards are taken for granted as matters of fact. It is assumed that they can be defined by senior management, that is, by those whose job it is, who are assumed most competent, as it were, to read nature and to translate it into strategic purposes. A moments consideration will reveal that these interwoven narratives locate politics in inter-individual and inter-departmental competition and conflict. Rather than being viewed as intrinsic to social- relational processes, politics is understood as the malign and illegitimate mobilisation of power. Political behaviours are peripheral to the legitimate structures and functions of the organization; they are a source of noise that may disrupt what otherwise would be its rational functioning.

In sum, the narratives of cognitive and social processes place massive restrictions on how politics may be understood. Politics reflects cognitive incompetence, social needs and faulty structures; political behaviours constitute the abuse of power in relation to the facts of nature. In these ways a veil is drawn over other narratives that join power and politics in talk of ongoing social relational processes: as emerging constructions of the real and the good, some of which become sedimented and many of which do not.

Narratives of organization and the construction of power   Our analysis has shown that questions of power are made hard to raise by being glossed through talk about organisational characteristics, managerial behaviour, and leadership: goals are organizational goals and not, for example, the goals of those who can make their definitions stick; structures are understood as facts of nature rather than, for example, constructions reflecting power relations; managers are managers because of their superior knowledge and achieve some degree of effectiveness on this basis; what could be more rational? The story is clear. When (i) facts reign supreme, rather than constructions, when (ii) social, cognitive and political processes are separately theorised, and when (iii) relations are reduced to relations between entities, then power is separated from politics, politics are of marginal significance, and power is not an issue.

In developing his arguments to construct a relational theory of power, Gergen writes of discursive or disciplinary regimes. These reflect, create, and rationalise certain beliefs about what is true and why. I suggest that the above may be an example of such a regime in social scientists' discourses about organizations: certain kinds of stories make sense and certain kinds of rhetoric are constructed to legitimise those stories. This being so, other kinds of story become hard to tell, to oneself (thinking), or to others. However, I should add that it's not just the discourse of social scientists. Managers in contemporary western organizations tell similar stories: the scene[1] is described as being one in which the facts of the market, global competition...demand structural/cultural changes; the lead actor is the knowing and powerful hero who struggles with less knowing and less competent actors; agency is achieved by the individual actor, mobilising power over others based on their more accurate and more extensive knowledge; purpose is rational 'world making' (Dinnerstein, 1976, p. 202) for the good of all.

To conclude, discourse can be viewed as constructing a view of what is true, rather than reflecting truths dictated by the facts of nature. When considered as a 'disciplinary regime' the above construction of social, cognitive, and political processes can be seen to impose serious limitations. To summarise: 'social' cannot be considered as an ongoing relational process that is both the locus and continuing production of cognitive and political processes, and power cannot be understood as an ongoing construction on the basis of, and about these processes. It seems that power can only be theorised as an ongoing construction if the wider set of referents in relation to which it makes sense are themselves changed. The first and most fundamental requirement will be to change the meta-theoretical assumptions of the entitative perspective and, as it were, start somewhere else. I shall continue with a brief sketch of alternative narratives, variously described as interpretive, textual, or constructionist and go on to see how, on the basis of these, constructionist approaches have theorised power. I shall again address Gergen's observation that the concept of power has been a fruit not readily plucked by social scientists.

The emerging relational perspective

The narrative space of relational theories

Gergen observes that there is no general and definitive agreement concerning the nature of the constructionist standpoint. Rather, there is a 'range of accounts'. Since his primary concern is to develop his relational theory of power he says relatively little about that range, either at the metatheoretical level or at the level of particular theories. He tells us what, for him, is crucial: to abandon the presumption of individual minds performing computations and 'acting on the basis of rational decisions', and to abandon the objectivist presumption. To fill this out a little here, the foregoing would involve abandoning the 'transcendental' view of an external reality (Billig, 1987, p. 49) which the mind more or less accurately mirrors. This removes what might be called the pre-theoretical rug from the continued pursuit of: facts as empirical statements about the world as it really is; generalizations based on the presumptions of universal and cumulative knowledge, and; explanations based on the 'laws' or 'forces' assumed to characterise nature, defining what is and can be real (e.g., Rorty, 1980). The 'transcendental' view of an external reality may be replaced with the assumption of multiple, socially constructed realities: with meanings and meaning making rather than facts and fact taking. The presumed possibility of generalisation is replaced by the assumption that beliefs about what is real, being constructed in social relational processes, are better understood as 'local knowledge' (e.g., Geertz, 1983). What makes up a particular local knowledge system or culture is understood to be open to investigation in terms of content; here the interest is in 'knowledge that'. However, more important to a relational perspective are the ongoing social processes by which particular meanings (rather than others) are constructed and reconstructed, and how particular constructions are explained and justified with reference to particular cultural themes. When we turn to the details of Gergen's theory we will find him tackling just these issues, using narratives of power to talk about the processes in which people construct a 'local ontology' (cf. local knowledge, local reality ...) creating a sense of 'power to' whilst, at the same time, creating relations of 'power over' competing constructions of what is real and good.

The above shifts lead directly to the question of how meaning making processes may be conceptualised in a relational perspective. They cannot be located inside the head; they cannot be considered as right or wrong in relation to standards set by nature; they must be located in social-relational processes. We are led to a radically changed view of thinking and cognition: no longer in the mind and therefore solitary and private but now 'an overt act' (Geertz, 1973, p. 83), 'social and public', whose 'natural habitat is the house yard, the marketplace, and the town square' (Geertz, 1973, p. 45; also Gardner, 1991). Perhaps nothing is more social and public in the town square than conversation. Conversations then become understood as ongoing social processes in which participants' re(construct) meanings, referencing past conversations and anticipating future conversations. Knowledge is understood as that which we are justified in believing and justification is seen as a social phenomenon; for example, 'we understand knowledge when we understand the social justification of belief and thus have no need to view it as accuracy of representation', when we view it as 'a matter of conversation and social practice' (Rorty, 1980, pp. 170 - 171).

But how is power now understood? We turn next to examining power in the context of existing constructionist theories. We will find that there is a sense in which relational theories also may have found the concept of power to be 'a fruit not readily plucked' (Gergen, sic), ironically perhaps because of the changed narratives of cognitive processes and related arguments about knowledge. Relational approaches, in different ways and to varying degrees, consider meaning making processes as processes in which contrary views are expressed (multiple realities) and explored in some way. Such processes produce and reproduce relations and ways of relating which are sedimented in recurring social practices and artifacts of human activity. However such lines of argument seldom make explicit reference to power.

Relational approaches to power

Once in the realm of relating on the basis of language, power now is seen as 'present in every symbolic[2] interaction, whether as a physical shove or honey - dipped words of persuasion' (Weigert, 1983, p. 186). To put it briefly, knowledge and power are closely linked because what is counted as knowledge: is socially constructed; is to some extent socially shared; is socially distributed; is supported and sustained by its seeming facticity, by explanations and justifications, and by what Berger & Luckmann (1966) referred to as the intrinsic controlling character of institutionalization (see also Schutz, 1962).

Lets see how the above can be developed in a little more detail by examining those (relatively) few discussions of power which are clearly located in a social constructionist perspective. Given the wider perspective, power is considered to be a fundamental feature of how we know and how reality is defined. Put at its most general, and to borrow Gergen's useful form of words, power is apparent in the what people reciprocally define/act out as 'the real and the good' (Geertz spoke of the 'struggle for the real', 1973, p. 316) and how they come to do so. Weigert seems to me to make the argument exceedingly elegantly and I will quote him at length.

From the paradigm of social reality as a process of communication and interaction, we see fundamental power as that which defines what an object, person, or event is and how it is to be interpreted. In addition to the 'what' question, there is the 'how' question, how do I interpret or make sense of this? Socially meaningful power affects us first through the stock answers to the 'what' and 'how' questions. Our use of language, our unspoken assumptions, and our routine forms of interaction are the first effects of power in our lives... they underline the importance of viewing power as cognitive, that is, as affecting the way in which we know and interpret reality. We must understand power as 'knowledge', or 'cognitive power' (Weigert, 1983, p. 187).

The above seems to me representative of a relational/social-constructionist position, indeed, Weigert references Berger & Luckmann, and Schutz, when making it. This said, the language of power doesn't stand out in their discussions of these processes; Weigert is unusual in this respect. We can quickly overview Berger & Luckmann's (1966) main lines of argument to illustrate this point. In their talk about language they observe, amongst other things, that language has coercive effects. By this they mean that what can be counted as knowledge is restricted by vocabulary, grammar and syntax: for example, there are some things I can think and say in French but not in English. Moving on to talk of conversations and face to face interactions as the 'prototypical case of social interaction' (p. 43), the language of 'typifications' is used; typifications are effectively taken as the fundamental building block of social worlds. The ongoing 'social reality of everyday life is...apprehended in a continuum of typifications' (pp. 47-48). The social world is said to be 'institutionalised' whenever there is a 'reciprocal typification of habitualized actions by types of actors' (p. 72).

It is at this point in their argument that a vocabulary of power and related concepts begins to be used: an 'institutionalised' world (in their very special sense of the word) is shown to be a world of power relations. Three general lines of argument can be distinguished. First, 'control' is said to be inherent in institutions to the extent that alternative patterns of action/meaning are made difficult to construct in the context of these particular habitualized (repeated) actions and associated reciprocal typifications. As a result, institutions such as the law effect 'coercive power' by virtue of their seeming facticity (power as a social construction), that is, without intention. Second, 'control mechanisms' are constructed to limit deviance. Institutions are characterised by differentiation: of types of actors, for example, judges, jurors, accused...; of reciprocal patterns of action, for example, the judge enters and the court stands; and associated 'stocks of knowledge', that is, 'reciprocal typifications'. The latter is what Schutz was referring to when he said knowledge was socially distributed - we don't all have the same knowledge stocks. Third, differentiation poses problems of conflict and competition and poses issues of integration. These problems are handled through 'legitimations', (chapter 2) understood as socially constructed 'machineries of universe maintenance' (e.g., p. 127): machineries which offer justifications and explanations.

To comment, it seems that power, being 'present in every symbolic interaction' (Weigert, sic.), ends up being a small word with a big job to do. As a result, a whole 'vocabulary' (Mills, 1940) of cross cutting, interrelated terms has to be constructed so as to theorise its many-faceted involvements in the construction of the real and the good. This may be one reason why the concept of power does not stand out even in constructionist approaches. Another reason may lie in the disciplinary, discursive regime(s) to which Gergen referred. So, for example, constructionists have built a vocabulary in which they talk of knowing, sense-making, shared meanings, reciprocal typifications and the like. It may be that the coercive effects (Berger & Luckmann, sic) of this vocabulary are such that we lose sight of power precisely because of its close connection with knowledge. As a result, we neglect explicitly to consider the ways power is implicated in the social processes of sense-making. In sum, perhaps we are forced to conclude that, even when working from a social constructionist perspective, many theorists may have found power 'a fruit not readily plucked' (Gergen, sic). Lets now turn to the details of how Gergen does so.

Gergen's relational theory of power

A relational starting point

Gergen lays his metatheoretical ground by noting that he starts with the presumption of human relatedness. Few psychologists would disagree with this as put. However, Gergen means something rather special by this in that he is not speaking of relations between entities. Instead, he wishes to make relating, understood as ongoing processes of human interchange, both the focus of interest and locus of explanation. This leads him to talk about conversation, theorised relationally as 'face to face, mutually contingent relationships'. This is a relational starting point in that conversations consist of (at least) two interrelated contributions which are interdependent in that neither has meaning or existence independently of the other (see Flax, 1987).

Gergen develops this relational starting point through talk about the 'emergence of interdependence' in conversation. For the purposes of explication this is first discussed with reference to the simple, idealised case that is, relations in a dyad, viewed as an 'elementary relational nucleus'. 'Interdependence' is said to be created through the construction of units of linguistic meaning. These consist of an action, for example a linguistic utterance such as someone saying 'look', plus some kind of supplement such as looking or saying 'oh yes'. The action plus supplement is claimed as a 'basic unit' of meaning on the basis of a further argument, namely, that the supplement grants a 'specific potential' to the meaning of the action: 'treats it as meaning this and not that', thus 'constrain(ing) alternative possibilities'.

The work that Gergen is doing at this stage of the argument is simply to create the relational foundation, or building block, on the basis of which he then can develop his further arguments about ongoing processes and power. At a minimum, this requires establishing some unit of coordinated or joint action which provides a sufficient basis for participants to continue socially to relate to one another. However, by doing some more work at this stage, clarifying the arguments and developing certain specifics, Gergen could make more plain what it is that he intends; this would benefit his later arguments about processes.

We can begin with the issue of clarification. Gergen's definition of the basic building block is open to at least two, importantly different, interpretations. I think that what he intends is perhaps best signalled by his reference to others 'treat(ing) ones utterances as meaningful': a reference to the listener's act of supplementing the speakers action. It might be helpful to underline and extend this by noting that ongoing relational processes are made possible to the extent that each conversational participant believes (construction) that the other understood their utterance, and supplemented it on this basis, such that it makes sense to the speaker to make a further utterance; this is all that is required - the response (any supplement) of the listener to the speaker.

However, a second and importantly different interpretation of what he means by his basic building block also is possible. It is suggested by his talk about 'the basic unit of linguistic meaning', the 'formation of meaning', and supplements which 'grant a specific potential to the meaning of the utterance'. These formulations could lead one to suppose that Gergen is proposing that specific meaning is granted to the action, achieving 'closure' of meaning in each action plus supplement. However there are a number of reasons why shared meanings are not a good place to start. First, it would be to start rather a long way down the track, so to speak, leaving untheorised the question of how meanings came to be shared. Second, Gergen wants to theorise ongoing relational processes and power as quality of the same. This demands that 'supplements' be understood as limiting the range of possible meanings, rather than specifying only one, since the latter would close the meaning making process. Third, to assume shared meanings would be to subvert subsequent arguments about one of the possible 'outcomes' of relating, that is, constructing difference on the basis of which critique and challenge are made possible. Last, as constructionists have found, theorising the meaning of shared meaning relationally is neither easy[3] nor, it seems, a necessary basis for joint action. On the latter, it seems clear that people are able to relate, to sustain some kind of joint performance on the basis of language, when they do not share the same meanings, that is, when they are playing quite different 'language games' (Wittgenstein, 1953; see, for example, Bateson, 1993). Just as an example, Tannen's work on men and women in conversation shows how ongoing relational processes can continue to be ongoing even when each participant is constructing radically different meanings of the other's text (Tannen, 1991).

Gergen's formulation of the basic unit of interdependence as action plus supplement invites certain lines of enquiry. For example, it would be possible ask questions about participants internal conversations so to speak, viewing these as part of what is ongoing in ongoing social processes. This would be a way of re-theorising cognitive processes: not as mind operations, but as relational processes in which participants silently dialogue a range of possible supplements for the purposes of meaning making, including wider cultural narratives, doing so on the basis of past and anticipated conversations. Another possible area for further elaboration would be to unpack the synchronic aspects of conversations. This would require important changes to traditional approaches to conversation analysis since these do not embrace a relational perspective. Instead, conversations would be examined as running texts in which any action plus supplement (relational unit) is understood as both text, and as context for previous text, such that participants are understood to be engaged, on line so to speak, in ongoing processes of (re)constructing possible interpretations. This then would invite investigation of ongoing conversational processes as characterised by multiple potential meanings, as processes of arguing, negotiating, justifying, criticising..., as processes from which emerge ongoing constructions of what is shared and what is understood as different.

The outcomes of meaning making

Having established the fundamental relational unit (action + supplement), Gergen goes on to consider what follows from this. He outlines two 'outcomes' which he regards as 'intrinsic to most attempts to coordinate actions through language'. The first outcome is the creation of a 'local ontology' or 'localized reality' achieved through continuing repetition of the basic units. In other words, participants in a particular conversational community, idealised as a dyad but later spoken of as a group, come to share a sense of order. This argument does the same kind of job as that achieved by other theorists using concepts such reciprocal typification and institutionalization (Berger & Luckmann, 1966), or 'sense of social order' (Cicourel, 1973, p.31) and concerns part of what Geertz refers to as 'local knowledge' (Geertz, 1973). Gergen speaks of a 'local ontology' to underline that conversational participants, in the course of constructing their interdependence, socially construct a view of how the world is and these constructions become 'sedimented or entified' or, as others have said, their constructions are 'objectified' (Berger & Luckmann, 1966). In other words, those who together construct a local ontology assume that the world exists as they understand it, independently of their sense making: they attribute ontological status to their constructions.

The second outcome Gergen describes as 'valuational': means are sought to sustain existing meanings, ruling out alternative supplements; an 'ancillary language' of valuation emerges. Appeals to 'good reasons' and to authorities such as God and the like are used to sanctify the existing ontology and to discredit alternatives; social practices emerge to reward those who stay within the ontology and to punish deviations. More usually valuations in this sense are regarded as part of what is counted as 'local knowledge' (Geertz, sic) that is, form part of the local ontology. Presumably Gergen has separated these outcomes for analytical purposes so that he can discuss the ways in which one set of outcomes (valuations) support the other (repetitions of basic units) and limit alternatives.

Earlier it was noted that similar arguments and concepts have been developed by others for related reasons. The potential strength of Gergen's formulation lies in its ability to capture and pose questions about relating as an ongoing process, local ontologies and valuations as ongoing productions, and power as a central theme of these processes. At this stage Gergen is still constructing the backcloth for his later arguments about centripetal and centrifugal power as the warp and weft of these processes, so to speak, and so is holding back his detailed arguments. This said, I suggest it would be more helpful at this stage to note that alternative, competing constructions of reality, as it were, run alongside the often repeated coordinations of the local ontology. This then would set up later arguments about both centripetal and centrifugal power instead of just the former. In addition, a more processual language might help to theorise running stabilities, so to speak, as they are interwoven with running potentials for subversion and constructions of counter realities.

More generally, it may be said that there is considerable room for further elaboration of specifics at this stage of the argument. Work of this sort would have the advantage of opening up more possibilities for theorising the diverse and interwoven textures of ongoing processes. So, for example, the present discussion of meaning making leaves unconsidered the role and relevance of a person's constructions of other(s) with whom they are in relationship, on the basis of conversation, constructions which are interrelated with their own self understandings and their constructions of their relationships. These constructions are crucial since they are part of what any conversation is about at a meta-level, and are very relevant to the issue of which particular meanings become part of the local ontology and which do not. In addition, discussion of this sort might help to introduce some finer interweaves using concepts such as arguments and justifications, legitimations and negotiation. The small groups literatures, though generally lacking a relational stance, include findings and arguments which could be re-theorised from a relational perspective, making salient the involvement of power in constructing particular definitions of the real and the good, that is, in constructing particular social identities, social orders, and intergroup relations.

Conditions of power

We have seen that Gergen sets up arguments about the creation of basic units of meaning, which, through repetition, emerge as a local ontology (what is real), buttressed and defended by various kinds of valuational support (what is real is good). These arguments are further developed to bring power into the picture. Two ongoing productions are distinguished: 'centripetal' and 'centrifugal' power, each being discussed in turn.

Centripetal power   First, Gergen takes up the existence of local ontologies arguing that these create the 'conditions' for centripetal power. Briefly, once a local ontology is established then the group, simply an expansion of the idealised relational nucleus, is said to function in an 'effective way' according to their own, socially constructed, standards. He elaborates on what he means by this but leaves open a variety of importantly different interpretations. Further, the language of effectiveness may not be the best for his purposes. I think the key to Gergen's intended meaning may be found in the connection he makes with 'power to', speaking of the groups self understanding as having a '*sense* of power to achieve specific goals' (emphasis added). He adds that he is not speaking of the actual capacity so to do, but to the group's use of language to label their coordinations as valuable/instrumental in the pursuit of certain goals. Presumably then a group's language of valuation, previously discussed as a linguistic tool for legitimising or crediting the existing ontology, now is being shown to be a matter not just of buttressing particular knowledge claims and associated practices, but also to implicate considerations of power.

Gergen is grappling with a problem which confronts all relational theorists who want to theorise ongoing processes, that is the problem of developing an appropriate and helpful language. Talk of 'conditions' and 'goals' may not be so helpful inasmuch as these terms typically are employed with reference to entitative distinctions between processes and outcomes and reference, implicitly or explicitly, an understanding of goals as ends, as the outcomes of (some now stopped) processes. Further, the language of goals directs attention to outcomes and their value (e.g., in terms of effectiveness) and, in this way, fails to invite attention to the valuing of processes as good or not so good (by local definitions) ways of being in relationship. This missed opportunity is serious since it represents a line of questioning which uniquely follows from a relational perspective. When ways of being in relationship are brought into focus then 'power to' is seen to include the sense of having the 'power to' enjoy certain ways of relating (see e.g., Brown & Hosking, 1986).

The above constitutes an elaboration of Gergen's arguments about power to but fits with his interest in ongoing processes. It opens up questions about processes, questions which can only be asked when ongoing relational processes, and not entities, are assumed, are given prominence and given conceptual bite. In addition, attention to different ways of being in relationship, the associated valuations and sense of 'power to' opens up the possibility to go beyond the dominance model of relations endemic to entitative perspectives. This point is worth some brief amplification. Our earlier discussion of power and organization showed the former to be understood as a characteristic of entities in hierarchical relation. Power could only be understood as power over, that is, as either an organization's power over people as achieved on the basis of organizational goals and structures, or as one person's power over another on the basis of hierarchical position, more and better information (viewed as knowledge) and so on. A relational theory of power is potentially able to make an extremely important contribution, one which would not be possible from an entitative perspective. Power, when theorised in a relational perspective, can embrace power to be in non-hierarchical relations, where different is viewed as different but equal, including differences in what is claimed as knowledge. These issues will be returned to in the following discussion of centrifugal power.

Centrifugal power   The processes of creating a local ontology and a sense of 'power to' also are said to be characterised by implicit and explicit constructions of reality which 'contrast' with, 'differ' from, or directly 'oppose' the local ontology. At this stage of the argument it becomes clear that in the processes through which a local ontology emerges there also is 'contrast', 'difference', and 'opposition'. In other words, the processes of constructing a local ontology also create the conditions for centrifugal power - an 'emerging sense of 'inside vs. outside, we versus them, and most focally, the power of one over the other'. This is discussed as an intergroup relation, and as a relation of conflict, but its origins are located in within group dynamics.

To comment, it seems that there is again an opportunity to go beyond the dominance model of relations which characterises the entitative perspective. Gergen's elaboration of his conception of centrifugal power emphasises 'opposition', 'conflict' and 'power over'. When he speaks of relations between groups characterised by differing ontologies his examples only concern negative valuing of one group by another, the other being seen as inferior, lacking judgement and so on. A relational perspective uniquely allows the possibility that intergroup relations may be other than negative. For example, what of the possibility of group A viewing group B as different, by definition because of their different ontologies, but equal, not better or worse? Perhaps Gergen might give more emphasis to difference as the fundamental intergroup construction and give space to the possibility that difference can be constructed as different but equal. Of course this then means that centrifugal power is not necessarily power over and a broader conception of this kind of power relation is invited.

Concluding comments

A relational perspective seems to permit and invite broader conceptions of both centripetal and centrifugal power than Gergen has so far attempted and a broader conception seems more consistent with his interests. Further, moves of this sort invite attention to conversational processes as yet undeveloped in Gergen's analysis. For example, a widened conception of centrifugal power invites attention to processes of dialoging between differing ontologies, relating in ways which acknowledge each group's power to, without constructing power over. This line of inquiry could open up some more serious exploration of negotiation as a social relational process. Whilst Gergen referred to the possibility that 'the terms of the real and the good' might be 'negotiable' he left the possibility unexplored. He is in good company. Other theorists of varying constructionist positions also have suggested that social order is negotiated, rather than imposed by nature, but have done little to theorise what negotiation might mean in this context (e.g., Berger & Luckmann, 1966); the negotiation of meanings and valuations has yet seriously to be explored from a truly relational perspective. In the case of intra-group relations this seems likely to involve talk of dialoging to reach agreement concerning particular relational units and their value. In the case of intergroup relations the term negotiation might provide a useful linguistic tool for discussing processes of dialoging in which A and B come to understand the others' cross cutting references which make sensible their particular meanings, in this way creating a changed context for their own text, seeking ways of relating which enable those different but equal ontologies.

Finally, we have seen that a relational perspective assumes multiple, socially constructed realities, and locates their construction in the social processes of discourse. Attention shifts to meanings, to local knowledge, and to ongoing meaning making processes. If we return to our themes of social, cognitive, and political processes, we can see what they now might mean with reference to our changed assumptions and interests. These now are seen as fundamentally interrelated, ongoing processes which are (i) social in the sense of being conducted through and with reference to social relations, conversations being a major vehicle of socially relating; (ii) cognitive as processes of socially constructing realities in and on the basis of conversations[4]; and (iii) political processes in which multiple realities emerge, only some of which are entified in local cultures, processes in which are constructed relations of power.

References

Allport, G.W. (1963), *Pattern and Growth in Personality*, Holt, Rhinehart, & Winston, London.
Bateson, M.C. (1993), 'Joint performance across cultures: Improvisation in a Persian garden', *Text and Performance Quarterly*, 13 (2), pp. 113-121.
Bennett, W.L. & Feldman, M.S. (1981), *Reconstructing Reality in the Courtroom*, Tavistock, London.
Berger, P. & Luckmann, T. (1966), *The Social Construction of Reality*, Penguin, NY.
Billig, M. (1987), *Arguing and Thinking: A Rhetorical Approach to Social Psychology*, CU, Camb.
Brown, M.H. & Hosking, D.M. (1986), 'Distributed leadership and skilled performance as successful organization in social movements,' *Human Relations*, 39, pp. 65-79.
Cartwright, D. & Zander, A. (1953), *Group Dynamics: Research and Theory*, 3rd ed, Tavistock, London.
Cicourel, A.V. (1973), *Cognitive Sociology*, Penguin, Harmondsworth.
Dachler, H.P. & Hosking, D.M. *'The Primacy of Relations in Socially Constructing Organizational Realities'*, this volume.
Dachler, H.P. & Hosking, D.M. (1991), *'Organizational cultures as relational processes: Masculine and feminine valuations and practices'*, 10th EGOS Colloquium, Vienna, July.
Dahl, March, and Thibaut & Kelly
Dinnerstein, D. (1976), *The Mermaid and the Minotaur*, Harper & Row, NY.
Flax, J. (1987), 'Postmodernism and gender relations in feminist theory', *Signs*, 12 (4), pp. 621-643.
Gardner, H. (1991), *The Unschooled Mind*, Basic Books, NY.
Geertz, C. (1973), *The Interpretation of Cultures*, Basic Books, NY.
Geertz, C. (1983), *Local Knowledge*, Basic Books, NY.
Gergen, K. J. (1982), *Toward Transformation in Social Knowledge*, Springer-Verlag, NY.

Hosking, D.M., & Morley, I.E. (1991), *A Social Psychology of Organizing*, Harvester Wheatsheaf, Hemel Hempstead.
Meyer, M., Stevenson,W. & Webster, S. (1985), *Limits to Bureaucratic Growth*, Walter de Gruyter, NY.
Mills, C.W. (1940), 'Situated actions and vocabularies of motive', *American Sociological Review*, 5, pp .904-913.
Rorty, R. (1980), *Philosophy and the Mirror of Nature*, Basil Blackwell, Oxford.
Sampson, E.E. (1993), *Celebrating the Other*, Harvester Wheatsheaf, Hemel Hempstead.
Schein, E.H. (1980), *Organizational Psychology*, 3rd ed., Prentice Hall, Englewood Cliffs, NJ.
Schutz, A. (1962), *Collected Papers*, (1962), Nijhof, The Hague.
Tannen, B. (1991), *Thats Not What I Meant*, Virago, London.
Weick, K.E. (1979), *The Social Psychology of Organizing*, Addison-Wesley, Reading, Mass.
Weigert, A.J. (1983), *Social Psychology: A Sociological Approach Through Interpretive Understanding*, University of Notre Dame Press, Notre Dame, IN.
Weber, M. (1947), *The Theory of Social and Economic Organization*, Oxford University Press, Oxford.
Wittgenstein, L. (1953), *Philosophical Investigations*, Basil Blackwell, Oxford.

Notes

1. The structure of narratives has been conceptualised in different ways by different authors. This terminology comes from Bennett and Feldman,1981.

2. 'Symbolic' being a reference here to language-based interaction.

3. It cannot be done in terms of 'content' as it would be in an entitative perspective. Rather, from a relational perspective it must be theorised in terms of the referents to which each relates a given text for the purposes of meaning making (see, for example, Garfinkle, 1967).

4. Billig (1987) is interesting on this. He suggests that thinking, rather than being viewed as a private and silent process, can be understood as conversation, as 'public argument', as 'dialogic' rather than 'monologic' (see p.111).

4 The social construction of grievances: Organizational conflict as multiple perspectives

Paul Salipante and Rene Bouwen

Introduction

This chapter explores implications for the organizational sciences of studying grievances as a social construction process. Occurring regularly, grievances have cumulative effects that bear heavily on the tension between conflict and cooperation in an organization. This makes them highly relevant to research in industrial relations, human resource management, managerial policy, organization development, and organization theory. Employees' grievances concerning their superiors or organizational policies go to the heart of the psychological contract between member and organization. They are peak opportunities for individuals to reinterpret organizational events and construct new meanings and beliefs (Gray, Bougon, & Donnellon, 1985) that guide their future actions.

The social construction paradigm suggests a broader conceptualization of organizational conflict and of organizing than currently guides most conflict research. Rather than casting a grievance as due to the most evident substantive source of a conflict, for example a disciplinary action, the social construction approach points to the history of past social interaction and the complexity of current experience that give meaning to a grievance conflict. Rather than direct investigation of the consequences of parties' actions in conflict or negotiation situations, social construction emphasizes the conceptualization (or formulation) of grievances, and the negotiation of those formulations among individuals. In the course of our research on grievances, we, the authors, were persuaded of social construction's appropriateness by the ubiquity of differences across individuals in the interpretation of the same events. This paper proposes that such conflicting interpretations and the differing perspectives that underlie them are the essence of organizational conflict. Based on our research findings, we begin with a discussion of conflict conceptualization and evidence that conflicting parties hold differing formulations. We continue by exploring some insights that the social construction paradigm offers to understanding organizational conflict and action and the paradigm's implications for research. We go on to present a model of perspectives and a generative metaphor, along with some data on perspectives; we conclude by outlining a number of implications for the study of conflict.

The neglect of conflict formulation

Although a long neglected topic in conflict research, the formulation of conflict is a key to understanding the social construction of reality in organizations. As noted by Kenneth Thomas (1976), parties' formulation of conflict provides the second phase in a four-step process model of dyadic conflict: frustration, conceptualization, behavioural interaction, and outcomes. Based on a review of the conflict literature, he remarked that 'surprisingly little psychological theorizing and research appear to have been done on the conceptualization of conflict by the parties involved' (Thomas, 1976, p. 896). Similarly, Meryl Reis-Louis (1977) noted that her six-step model of conceptualization was the first to examine conflict from the individual's viewpoint. Since their remarks, little has been published that would change these assessments. A few researchers have produced findings and concepts that can be cast as relevant to the conceptualization of conflict. For example, Deborah Kolb (1983) observed that labour mediators attempt to restructure conflict situations to use their preferred mode of intervention; we would say that a mediator's perspective of the proper way to solve a conflict is relatively fixed. Another source of literature on understanding conflict is that which advocates the efficacy of negotiating by identifying needs rather than positions (c.f., Walton, 1969; Filley, 1976) and separating interpersonal issues from substantive issues (Fisher & Ury, 1981). We suggest that these ideas can be viewed as dealing with conflict formulation, however, they are discussed in terms of actions rather than with reference to formal theories of formulation. In contrast, the newly emerging literature on the framing of conflict (c.f., Shepard, Blumenfeld-Jones & Roth, 1989) offers great promise by directly addressing conflict formulation. However, the continued viability of such research depends upon the acceptance and more widespread application of the interpretive, or social constructionist paradigm.

The arguments and concepts presented here result from a research program investigating grievances. We took as a grievance any breakdown of the psychological contract between employee and organization. More narrowly, we defined a grievance as any complaint - concerning a superior, or an organizational policy or procedure - made manifest by a subordinate, even by as minimal an action as discussing the situation with a peer or family member. Grievances so defined offer a convenient way to investigate the formulation of organizational conflict.

Rather than focusing on formulation, research on grievances and organizational conflict has concentrated on procedures, interventions, and outcomes. In the field of industrial relations, for example, research has dealt with the number and type of grievances formally filed and the characteristics of grievance systems and complainants; however, this research has lacked a theoretical base (Gordon & Miller, 1984). Walton & McKersie's (1991) behavioural concepts of social negotiation and conflict resolution have been influential, and recent research on grievances by Lewin & Peterson (1988) has responded to the call for greater utilization of behavioural analyses in the field of industrial relations (Strauss, 1982; Lewin & Feuille, 1983). However, a base in social theory has yet to be established for understanding the genesis and progression of grievances. Social construction promises to be such a base. Exploring its insights into grievances provides a first contribution toward an understanding of organizational members' conceptualization of conflict.

Traditional grievance research has labelled conflict as falling into unambiguous single categories such as wages and discipline, as if conflict were a characteristic of the situation rather than of individuals' constructions of it. Our research program started from this orientation but eventually found it wanting. For example, grievances, as described by the principal parties involved, could not be classified into a single category in any reliable fashion. The difficulty with the traditional approach was that researchers looked for the bases of conflict in what they regarded as objective realities. With this orientation, only one construction of reality can be considered the truth at a given moment in time. In contrast, a view that recognized the multiple perspectives of the various parties was found essential in understanding the emergence and dynamics of a conflict experience.

Emerging evidence for a multi - perspective view

The difficulty of classifying a grievance into a single category directly reflects the essential aspect of conflict, that is, the various parties form differing perspectives of the situation. The very diversity of their formulations, rather than being seen as a measurement or coding error, should be understood as a given of conflict situations.

The importance of multiple perspectives in formulation was made clear by initial efforts at content analysis of summarized interviews with actual grievants. The research started by categorizing the sources of conflict as reported by the grievant and found that nearly all grievants saw their conflict as complex, stemming from multiple sources (causes) of conflict (Salipante & Bouwen, 1990). In cases where two parties reported on the same grievance, even the use of broad categories of sources of conflict revealed differences between the two parties' formulations. For example, in one company where we studied the grievances filed during one year, one type of grievance involved employees accusing management of a planned unwillingness to pay overtime. The employees' formulation focused on the substantive aspect of the situation, that is, the amount of pay and the number of hours to be counted. Managers, arguing that overtime could only be paid when planned for and agreed upon in advance, defined the problem as miss - communication between workers and managers, a relational source of conflict in our categorization scheme. Although managers and their subordinates talked about the same organizational events, the two groups framed the situation in different ways (Deutsch, 1973). In consequence, the proposed actions and desired outcomes were very different.

A later phase of our research centred on three-party cases in order to investigate differences in parties' formulations. The stories of each actor were kept separate and coded as parallel views emerging from a particular event. Upon examining these views, we concluded that each individual's view reflected that person's particular framing of past interactions. Each person relied upon a historically developed perspective to select and interpret organizational events that were personally meaningful. Consider as an example the following shortened reconstructions of the stories in one multi-party case. Alex, a male worker in a chemical facility, will first describe his view of the events.

> As I was filling a tank, a safety valve failed and some of the chemical spilled on the ground. When I saw what was happening, I quickly alerted the other workers, and we rapidly cleaned up the spill, just as we have been trained to do. As soon as we finished, my boss Pam started yelling and swearing at me, right in front of all my friends, shouting that I hadn't been paying attention. If she hadn't been a woman, I think I would have punched her. Instead, I straightened her out by telling her that I was watching the filling gauges. I stressed that no safety alarm had sounded, like it should have, and that we have a serious equipment problem here. She must have ignored that, because then she tells me that I am suspended for five days! Who does she think she is, anyway? It's bad enough that she is the facility manager with her limited experience, but then she flies off the handle, becoming all emotional. How can we continue to work for a person like that? I'm challenging this suspension. I'm not going to take it lying down!

Pam, the manager of this facility, saw things differently.

My office is on the second level and overlooks the work area. I was doing some paperwork when I looked out my window and saw the liquid pouring out of the top of the tank. Who knows how long it had been spilling! Alex was sitting down at the control panel on the other side of the tank, not even seeing the chemical streaming out. I rushed out of my office and to the top of the stairs. Just as I was going to alert Alex, he noticed the spill and called to the other workers. I stayed out of the way until they had it cleaned up, then went down to discuss things with Alex. I knew that I had to do something dramatic with these guys, to make sure that this wouldn't happen again. I impressed on Alex that if he had been observing the tank like he was supposed to, instead of sitting down, none of this would have happened. He gave me some kind of excuse. Then I suspended him. You know, for the last few months I have been trying to get his group to follow proper safety procedures with this hazardous chemical, but they just ignore me. The workers better start listening to me and giving me some respect. They think I am too young, but I am in authority and I know how to make this facility safer.

Each of these two parties relied on a different perspective to formulate the situation. As an experienced worker who felt like he knew how to do his job properly, Alex initially emphasized the substantive issue of the failure of the equipment. Then, in reaction to what he saw as Pam's impulsive action of berating him in public, Alex's perspective shifted to the emotional aspects. This was not the way he wanted to work with a boss. As a young female manager of a male crew, Pam's perspective reflected her past interactions with the men and emphasized the need for them to respect her authority. Here was her opportunity to express this need by requiring proper attention to safety procedures. Her concern with authority led her to act in a dramatic manner that she describes as calculated, but which Alex interpreted as emotional, shifting him to the same type of expressive perspective that he saw in Pam.

In this situation, two others found themselves enmeshed in the evolving conflict. The first was Tom, the union representative at this facility.

> Alex came to me and told me how Pam had yelled at him and then suspended him. He was very worked up about it. I tried to get him to see things more calmly, because I knew that Pam had not followed proper procedure. While she is indeed the manager of this facility, she is not the direct manager of this work group. We are all employed by a firm that staffs this facility for Pam's company, and Jim is our boss. According to the union contract with our own company, Jim is responsible for any discipline. Procedurally, Pam cannot suspend Alex.

Jim had been visiting another work site when the spill occurred, but he heard about it from both Tom and Pam when he returned.

> My first reaction was that I needed to keep things from going out of control. My firm cannot afford to lose the contract with Pam's company. So, I needed to smooth out the relationships among all these people. I talked with everybody concerned and got them calmed down. We discussed the proper procedures for a suspension and also the need for all the workers to follow the safety rules. After this, Pam agreed to withdraw the suspension and Alex returned to the job.

Tom and Jim saw the expressive nature of Pam and Alex's views, but adopted other perspectives that fit their roles in handling conflicts. Tom was concerned with procedural fairness, and Jim with restoring relationships to a workable level. Starting from these perspectives, they could interact with Alex and Pam and turn the discussion to the more organizationally legitimate issues of procedures and rules, eventually negotiating a settlement.

As typified by this case, in grievance conflicts there exists no single, objective formulation, only the formulations of various individuals. In multi-party cases we consistently found different parties relying upon different perspectives to formulate their interpretations of and give meaning to the conflict. The most striking observation was that each party to a grievance holds to his or her own private formulation with conviction. As Rogers (1965, p. 8) describes it, people feel 'I am right, you are wrong. You are unfortunately mistaken and inaccurate in your view and analysis'. While many individuals are uncertain about some possible causes of the problem situation, they are quite fixed on the rightness of their basic views. People's schemes of mental categorization have a morally binding quality to them (Durkheim, 1915; Barrett, 1990). This strengthens their confidence in the correctness of their own views, and the vigour with which they state them in social interactions concerning the grievance.

Grievants typically do not accord much legitimacy to perspectives which differ significantly from their own. However, they implicitly recognize the existence of multiple perspectives by striving to develop arguments that will influence people holding other perspectives, as did Tom and Jim in the chemical spill case. Indeed, dramatic differences were found between individuals' private formulations of the sources of conflict, as expressed to friends who interviewed them, and the public formulations that they expressed to opposing parties (Salipante & Bouwen, 1990). A grievant's public formulations are often designed to fit the organization's desired construction of reality. As an organization attempts to create a negotiated order (Gray, Bougon, & Donnellon, 1985) and to manage meaning (Morgan, 1986; Smircich & Stubbart, 1985), its key figures can create a dominant paradigm - such as safety in a chemical facility - within which discourse about social reality takes place. Without necessarily accepting that paradigm, an individual can use knowledge of it to state public formulations that appear more acceptable to others, although they deviate from his private constructions.

There is a highly dynamic quality to grievances and their public formulations. Since many grievants make several attempts to convince others to act on their complaint, most grievances go through several episodes (Bouwen & Salipante, 1990). Each of these episodes reflects distinct action strategies on the grievant's part. Each episode brings new interactions and opportunities for the parties to restate views on the grievance and negotiate new realities. The changing nature of any one grievance over time may explain why individuals tend to see a particular grievance as highly idiosyncratic, when it may actually be part of a broader, long-term pattern of new reality construction.

Let us review the points to which our research has led us. They can be summarised as follows: most grievants perceive several sources of conflict underlying a single grievance; many grievants deviate from their private formulations when they define the grievance publicly; any given grievance is formulated differently by the various parties involved, each formulation seeming self-evident to its holder; and, most grievances go through several episodes, bringing into continuing interaction individuals' differing formulations. Because of this interaction of formulations and the changes over episodes in action strategies, particular grievances appear to those involved as unique, as idiosyncratic.

Given the complexity of grievance formulation and the changes that can occur over time in the formulation of a grievance, organizational records that classify each grievance into a single, objective category are highly misleading, as is any research that then relies on such records and categories. For example, any one label such as 'safety' or 'discipline' fails to convey several important pieces of the chemical spills case. Despite starting from a deterministic perspective in which we sought objectively to categorize grievances, our methodological struggles and research findings led us to the view that the key characteristic of grievance formulation is the variation across individuals in their perspectives on the situation. It is exactly this variation that underlies the observed grievance characteristics of complexity, multiplicities, dynamism, and apparent idiosyncrasy. Variation in perspectives is the very essence of grievance that needs to be captured in conceptual representations, leading to new explanations for previously identified effective actions and to new ideas about conflict management.

New paradigm thinking

How can we think and theorize about organizational conflict when its essential element is a multiplicity of perspectives? In line with new paradigm or social constructionist thinking, we started to rephrase the problem, shifting attention from organization to organizing.

The process of conflict formulation draws attention to the crucial role played by the experiencing of subjective reality. This experiencing involves a crucial point of intense discussion in the history of social science: how can we deal scientifically with subjective realities and yet make an objective analysis of the social environment. Allport asserted: 'The way a man defines his situation constitutes for him its reality' (Allport, 1955, p. 84). However the full consequences of this idea were only recently brought into organizational theory by Karl Weick and his students (Weick, 1979). Social science promoted the ideal of the impartial and distant objective observer until some authors took up this issue and made it the subject of inquiry. Following the tradition of Allport, Kelly (1955) developed a psychology of personal constructs. In sociology, influenced by phenomenology, Berger & Luckman (1967) developed their theory of the social construction of reality.

Recognizing the multiplicity of perspectives is, increasingly, the post-modern approach in social sciences. Kenneth Gergen (1985) sees social constructionism as having parallels in all fields of social and cultural life. For example, anthropology speaks of 'local knowledge' (Geertz, 1983), literary criticism tells of readers' perspectives, and writers in the tradition of hermeneutics refer to forestructures of understanding (Gadamer, 1975). Semiotics understands symbols as able to signify several alternate meanings (Eco, 1976). The phenomenological approach in philosophy, exemplified by Husserl, provides the underpinning for this new thinking in various fields. Even in the physical sciences, so called new paradigm thinking calls for recognition of alternate perspectives as legitimate, with Capra (1982) arguing the importance of the scientific observer's viewpoints and methods. In the biological sciences, Prigogine's theory of dissipating structures (Prigogine & Strengers, 1985) challenges determinism by pointing to the self organizing and constructing forces that operate in nature.

Each of these approaches emphasises both the primacy of perspective in guiding human scientific activity and the problems of valuing any single perspective over another. The social constructionist approach to social interaction recognizes the perspectives of all participants as equally valid and emphasizes the discourse that develops.

Grievances change constructions of reality

The social construction view holds that organizations are not objective entities but socially constructed phenomena. To understand organizations we must understand the intersubjective meaning held among organizational members and the processes by which these meanings coincide, are reaffirmed and lead to conjoint action by members (Gray, Bougon & Donnellon, 1985). A single social reality is no longer considered as a given.

> Social actions appear to carry little in the way of intrinsic meaning; the conceptual categories or meaning systems into which they are placed appear primarily to be products of social negotiation. The fact that a given stimulus pattern falls into the category of...depends not on the intrinsic properties of the relevant pattern but on the development of a community of agreement (Gergen, 1978, p. 1350).

These statements describe both the general processes of sense-making in a group and the conflict processes in which disputants disagree about some topic and attempt to reach a common understanding. In the chemical spill case mentioned above, the involved parties' diverse ways of framing and attributing meanings both created the grievance and led to a dynamic of interactive reality construction.

Social construction helps us analyse organizational conflict in a new way by implying a continuous striving for coincident meaning by parties having differing views. Is not conflict in an organization simply the result of one or more parties sensing that a diversity of interpretations of the situation is emerging and that the social negotiation process is failing to create an acceptable meaning?

Discourse is the usual means for seeking coincident meaning. Gergen (1986) speaks of the issues involved in interpreting text or attempting to determine the intent behind an observed action, as in the spill case. He argues that innumerable interpretations are possible and that a social interpretation is negotiated through discourse. If an agreement concerning interpretation is reached, it is not due to the compelling nature of the events interpreted but to the negotiation of linguistic terms. Furthermore, several forms of relationships are available in discourse, and each interchange has at its disposal a certain range of scenarios from which it can draw. During the interchanges occurring in a grievance, then, one of several scenarios can be followed, depending on how the parties conceptualize the negotiated reality. This view of discourses and alternate scenarios implies that the formulation of a conflict has significant consequences for the organization. This is because it represents a choice point for different action scenarios.

For example, Alex's coworkers in the spill case might decide that the young manager acted irrationally, suspending Alex due to an argument she had with a different worker the previous day. Alternatively, they might agree that the manager yelled in her typical way, but was concerned primarily with their own safety. Through discourse an interpretive frame emerges which labels the manager's actions, and attributes them to one specific cause out of the many possible. Such negotiating over motives and meaning is continuous in the organization, occurring in a 'changing web of interactions woven among its members' (Day & Day, 1977, p.132). The consequences of the emerging interpretive frame are significant for day-to-day functioning. One scenario has Alex and his coworkers avoiding contact with Pam as much as possible, while another frame and scenario has them more closely attending to Pam's views of safety.

Grievances can change conceptions of reality on several dimensions. One, as just noted, concerns the attributing of motives and intentions to others (Reis-Louis, 1977). Another concerns the judgment of someone's moral integrity (Salipante & Fortado, 1989). As an example in the chemical spills case, Alex may lower his moral judgment of Pam if he interprets her actions as an attempt to get even with any one of her subordinates for the fight she had the previous day with another work group member. A third interpretive dimension, strongly affected by many grievances, is the individual's sense of whether a superior values the individual as a worker. Pam's harsh tone and lack of acceptance of Alex's arguments may be discussed by Alex and his coworkers as showing lack of appreciation for his (and their) efforts and expertise.

As with motives a wide range of alternate interpretations on each of these dimensions can be made from a particular set of experiences, often influenced by discourse with coworkers and friends. Interpretations are dynamic and socially influenced, yet ultimately individualistic. An individual may fail to accept the socially negotiated interpretation of a group, or prefer one group's interpretation over another's. Concerning dynamics, present interpretations are built on past interpretations, but can be changed through discourse concerning recent events. In turn, current interpretations shape future behaviour. Grievances are significant to organizations, not because they can temporarily disrupt smooth functioning, but because their effect on interpretations such as motives, integrity and one's value to the organization can strongly influence individuals' entire constructions of their organizational reality. These constructions affect members' continuing commitment to the organization and associated decisions of participation and production.

Reconceptualizing organizational conflict

A fundamental question is how organizations function effectively when coincident meaning is not attained by their members. We have posited that individuals strive for, but do not necessarily attain, shared interpretations. How can the operation of multiple perspectives and divergent interpretations continue in organizations that are supposedly cooperative systems? Various writers have treated this question of divergence in organizations. Cyert & March (1963) focused upon goal coalitions as a mechanism for managing divergent interests, and Cohen, March & Olsen's (1972) garbage can model is founded upon diversity.

Building on these ideas, and emphasizing conflict formulation and the multi-perspective view, leads to a reexamination of the view that organizations are fundamentally cooperative systems. Nearly twenty years after its initial formulation, Louis Pondy (1992, p.259) revised his classic theory of organizational conflict in precisely that fashion.

> The central flaw...is...the assumption that organizations are cooperative, purposive systems that occasionally experience conflicts or breakdown in cooperation. Suppose that we treat organizations as arenas for staging conflicts and managers both as fight promoters who organize bouts and as referees who regulate them...Far from being a breakdown in the system, conflict in this alternative model is the very essence of what an organization is.

Organizations provide a forum for confrontations from which action can eventually emerge. Several scholars, Weick (1979) most prominently, have observed that organizations consist of many pairs of opposing tendencies (e.g., innovation vs. stability, risk-taking vs. risk aversion). The interaction of individuals with differing perspectives may be seen to produce such polarities, with attendant variation in interpretation of events and irregularities in decisions and courses of action.

In previous theories conflict was something to be avoided or eliminated through a resolution process. Most research efforts were therefore directed to identifying actions leading to resolution. A point gaining increasing favour is that conflict can have positive effects. However, seeing organizations as arenas for conflict requires that we move even beyond the view of conflict as positive. Rather, conflict and the negotiation of meaning may be seen as the core organizational process. That is, understanding conflict as the interaction of multiple perspectives leads to a better understanding of organizations themselves. Following this line of thinking, diversity in the meanings attributed to critical events becomes more important to understanding the organization than the tangible outcomes of a conflict. Multiple perspectives are at the heart of organizational conflicts, and deriving meaning through the interaction of perspectives is what organizations are all about. A useful focus, for organizations then, would be to examine their conflicts in order to understand the arenas of meaning that are in flux and their portent for the future.

A new aim and model for research on organizational conflict

When organizations are seen as cooperative systems, the ultimate goal of research on organizational conflict is to learn something valuable about resolution and cooperation. The above reconceptualization of organizational conflict as contributing to ongoing sense-making can free researchers from the constraining assumption that organizations need be cooperative, thereby promising wider sets of knowledge. Key research issues that can be investigated from this freeing reconceptualization include the following. First: what are the sources of divergence in perspective; what personal histories of interpretations are carried into the present, and how are they triggered; why do different types of conflict problems trigger different perspectives in the same individual? Second, how do organizational members interactively view and label situations where their perspectives and interpretations differ? Third, how do differing perspectives and interpretations interact to affect the continuing life of the organization?

Pursuing the second research question requires a cultural deconstruction of the phenomena labelled as conflict. In a particular situation, consider which party first uses the label and means by it the need to restore cooperation. Pondy (1992) asserts that it is the in group, the establishment, which most strongly supports cooperation, but on its own terms. An employee may label the situation very differently, not even using the term conflict in situations sensed as frustrating. Even personal awareness of frustration can be too low to be recognized, let alone expressed to others (Freire, 1981), if the power distance is so imbalanced that parties do not engage in renegotiating their relationship. Organizationally, such situations lead to what Brown (1984) calls situations of too little conflict. The label of conflict, in the sense of an active interference with another's position (Schmidt & Kochan, 1972), is used by a person who is aware and feels strong enough to act. Conflict indicates an organizational situation where the diversity of perspectives on important issues can be expressed openly and acted upon. Recognition of conflict requires that the parties are willing to bring their diversity of perspectives into discussion. By deconstructing the term in this way, we can see that research on conflict should extend beyond cases where individuals feel powerful enough to act, by exploring the differing perspectives and interpretations held by organizational members, even by those not labelling their differences as conflict.

The key assumptions of the social construction paradigm that provide insight into the third research issue (the role of divergence of perspectives in organizational life) are that people strive to attach meaning to their situation and that they attempt to reach social agreement concerning that meaning. Weick (1979) distinguishes three core processes in the interpretation of organizational events: enactment, selection, and retention. Applying these processes to organizational conflict, we conceptualize them as referring, respectively, to decisions and actions, interpretation, and perspectives. Each individual selects certain features of communicated and experienced events and interprets their meanings according to a perspective formed in prior social interactions. The individual's interpretation influences their publicly-stated formulation of the problem, which provides an entry point for interactive formulation with the others involved. These individuals then negotiate with each other through discourse, though no agreement on interpretation need necessarily occur. Some coincident actions can emerge from this process, as can divergent actions. The discourse and any resulting actions are then interpreted by each individual. Any number of subsequent rounds of public formulation, discourse, action and interpretation may occur. When actions are interpreted very differently, it is very likely that another episode will occur, in a new attempt socially to negotiate meaning.

In this framework, one's perspective is composed of the current interpretations and the retained aspects of prior interpretations. Therefore, a perspective carries the individual's history of past social interactions and represents a repertoire of possible interpretations. Over a succession of grievance episodes, interpretations of new social experiences modify the individual's perspective.

In many grievances this modification process is a critical one that changes the individual's basic views about organizational actions and decisions. The changes can be so fundamental that they threaten the continuation of the individual's relationship with the organization. Since (according to this scheme) the person never needs to reach a shared interpretation with others, the key behavioural action for the individual is simply remaining a member of the organization. In the spill case, for example, Alex may significantly lower his evaluation of Pam and continue to interpret events very differently from her, yet choose to remain and do the job according to his own standards.

These concepts can be applied to conflict and non conflict situations alike. Organizational conflict emerges from those negotiation episodes which fail to achieve the minimally shared meaning required for an action to be accepted - in the sense of not being actively challenged and resisted with opposing action.

Given a particular pattern of divergent perspectives among specific parties, there will be certain types of actions that are particularly likely to provoke divergent interpretations and lead to active interference. Also, for a given pattern of divergence in perspectives, active interference is more likely when an individual fails to accord some legitimacy to another's perspective.

In sum, we propose that the most important elements to understanding organizational conflict, the dynamics of organizational action, and the nature of organizing itself are:
a   the perspectives that individuals rely upon to interpret organizational events,
b   the expressing of these perspectives through social interaction,
c   the degree to which individuals accept others' perspectives as legitimate,
d   the resulting convergence or divergence in individuals' interpretations and actions.

Identifying perspectives

Drawing on the social construction paradigm, and key writers on organizational sense-making and organizational conflict, the above discussion builds a base for new types of research on organizational conflict. Since individuals' perspectives are central to their interpretation of organizational events, investigating perspectives is an important task for research. Several researchers have recently begun to study the perspectives that individuals use to frame organizational events and conflict (Gray, 1989; Pinkley & Northcraft, 1989; Shepard, Blumenfeld-Jones & Roth, 1989). In the next two sections we develop first, a model of grievance perspectives and second, outline a metaphor we found useful in analysing our grievance cases; the concepts are meant to apply only to the grievance type of organizational conflict.

The model and metaphor were developed to match the characteristics of grievances observed in the analysis of interview cases referred to earlier, namely: multiple perspectives; complexity; the seeming self-evident nature of one's own view; dynamism resulting from the interaction of various parties' formulations; and, the apparent idiosyncrasy of a specific grievance. The model consists of four alternative perspectives upon which grievants can draw: substantive or content, relational or processual, procedural, and expressive. We propose that each individual's interpretive frame for a particular grievance is comprised of a particular combination of these perspectives. Differences across parties in the combination of perspectives gives rise to differing interpretations of the situation, that is, to the grievance. Differences in perspectives can arise from belonging to different groups.

The substantive perspective

This traditionally is used by arbitrators and by many other industrial relations specialists. People using the content viewpoint attempt to define a problem according to an existing legal standard or contractual rule. Organizations set rules and norms through work design, work place regulations, and organizational structures. According to the content perspective, individuals must live up to these established standards and rules, so the question of blame and of who is right is always in the air.

In the chemical spill case, it was clear to Alex, who had a content perspective, that the safety equipment was at fault and that he and his coworkers had followed the rules by quickly and expertly instituting the proper cleanup procedures. Employees who adopt a content perspective feel they can rely on rules and norms, on individual and collective contracts, and on legislation to bound the arbitrariness of organizational or managerial action. Managers with this perspective similarly emphasize the rules and norms proscribing certain behaviour by subordinates. Many technically trained people use the content perspective, at least if we go by the judgements of students who typically emphasize the physical aspects of the situation when they read the chemical spills case. Those who use the content perspective classify grievances into categories such as work rules, wages, job environment, working conditions, job evaluation, sickness regulations, and discipline.

The relational perspective[1]

Those trained in organizational behaviour tend to use this viewpoint. When using this perspective, an individual assumes that something is wrong in the relationships among the parties to a grievance. Communication problems are seen as especially likely causes of the conflict. In the chemical spill case Jim, the other manager involved in the dispute, felt that there was a sensitive boss-subordinate relationship between Pam and Alex. In Jim's view, Pam's youth and eagerness to prove her managerial ability clashed with the subordinate's experience and conviction that he knew better than his new manager how industrial work should be done. Focusing as it does on relationships and processes, the relational perspective leads to a preference for integrative problem-solving (Walton, 1969; Schein, 1973; Filley, 1976), and to a concern with employees' desires for development and growth. The relational perspective encourages one to confront others about underlying conflicts to begin a communication process for resolving interpersonal problems.

The procedural perspective

At its core are the use and development of due process (Evan, 1961; Aram & Salipante, 1981) - something of special concern to union officials and many legally trained individuals. When considering the source of a grievance, people drawing on this perspective ask whether procedures designed to assure fair decisions existed and were followed. When dealing with the grievance itself, they are concerned with the procedures that should be followed to handle it (Scott, 1965; Rowe & Baker, 1984; Salipante & Aram, 1984). In the chemical case they would ask, as did the union representative, questions such as: 'was a serious investigation of the spill's circumstances made before the manager suspended the worker; could the first manager (Pam) act independently of the worker's direct supervisor (Jim) on such a matter; could a suspension be given without advance notice to the union?'

The expressive perspective

This last perspective focuses on expressive action in which issues of power and authority are central. Those who are interpreting a situation from this viewpoint are concerned with taking a stand and making a point. They are disposed to act forcefully and often rather rapidly and impulsively. Conscious formulation itself is sometimes cursory. The impulsive actions that then follow become part of the problem, as emotions are rubbed raw. The chemical facility manager, Pam, concerned with establishing her authority, typified this perspective by impetuously and publicly blaming the subordinate and using a direct threat in the presence of Alex's peers. Her anger impeded any probing to establish the content (the facts) of the case. An expressive action perspective is reflected in literature relating grievances to the power of work groups (Kuhn, 1961; Sayles, 1958) and theories of power distance (Mulder, 1976). In traditional industrial relations terms, all forceful actions such as strikes, lockouts, and sit-ins, show this perspective. In these situations the formulation is not impulsive but calculated. The concern is with doing harm to the other party or asserting and strengthening one's position. If one party to some grievance acts from an expressive action perspective, the attention of other parties is directed to power issues. As did Alex, they may then adopt the same perspective and become concerned with protecting themselves. Therefore, use of this perspective has a self-fulfilling quality to it.

In the model, content, relational, procedural, and expressive are the base perspectives upon which individuals draw to understand a grievance situation. Each perspective can be seen as a dominant paradigm that invites discourse based on the same paradigm. Each party can use more than one perspective simultaneously, as will be illustrated later.

Metaphors as semiotic carriers of process knowledge

Since semiotics deals with means for transferring intended meaning, it can provide insight into to social processes of reality construction. Every communication process between human beings presupposes a signification system (Eco, 1976). Consistent with the earlier discussion of discourse, we see organizational realities as having no existence independent of the parties involved. People create their reality while interacting, and they need a shared system of representation to communicate and come to some understanding (Searle, 1984). Metaphors, being important to organizational symbolism (Pondy, Frost, Morgan & Dandridge, 1986), are semiotic vehicles that carry meaning to facilitate the creation of a common reality among organizational members. 'From a situation that is vague, ambiguous, and indeterminate, a metaphor selects and names different features and relations...' (Schon, 1980, p. 264). Through a process of naming and framing, Schon argues that a metaphor can help individuals restructure their views by integrating conflicting perspectives without sacrificing the simplicity required for action. Conflict researchers can concern themselves with metaphors in at least two ways: by creating metaphors that describe reality construction processes during conflict; and by studying the metaphors which conflict participants themselves use to describe conflict experiences. Certain of these metaphors can be generative for practitioners, by encouraging them to see the diversity of views from which a rich, multifaceted set of actions can be drawn.

We propose a specific generative metaphor useful in understanding and acting on grievance phenomena. The four perspective model presented above is static. A metaphor that carries meaning about dynamics can be a useful way to represent knowledge about grievance processes. The metaphor that we propose is that of turning a kaleidoscope. As Barbara Tuchman (1962, p.442), commenting on the writing of history, has put it:

> ...truth is subjective and separate, made up of little bits seen, experienced, and recorded by different people. It is like a design seen through a kaleidoscope; when the cylinder is shaken the countless coloured fragments form a new picture. Yet they are the same fragments that made a different picture a moment earlier.

Consider the experience of a child peering for the first time into a kaleidoscope, seeing light reflected from many pieces of coloured glass. The view is complex, but with some effort the child perceives a symmetry to the scene. The combination of complexity and symmetry seduces the viewer into a high degree of certainty concerning the reality of what is seen, corresponding to the seemingly self-evident nature of a grievance and correctness of one's own view. Now consider a group of children passing around a kaleidoscope. The physical movement randomly distributes the pieces of glass, so each child sees a somewhat different scene. Only through repeatedly turning and peering into the kaleidoscope does each child learn that there is not a single picture. Each member of the group soon learns that there is not one view that is correct. What is less evident to any one viewer is that there are many ways to interpret the symmetry that results from a kaleidoscope's particular construction. That is, after turning it and understanding the alternative pictures possible, different viewers will focus on different elements as figure and as ground. The parallel to turning the kaleidoscope in a conflict would be when one begins to see the beauty of the multiple aspects and interpretations possible in the situation, while realizing one's own tendencies to emphasize selected aspects and de-emphasize others.

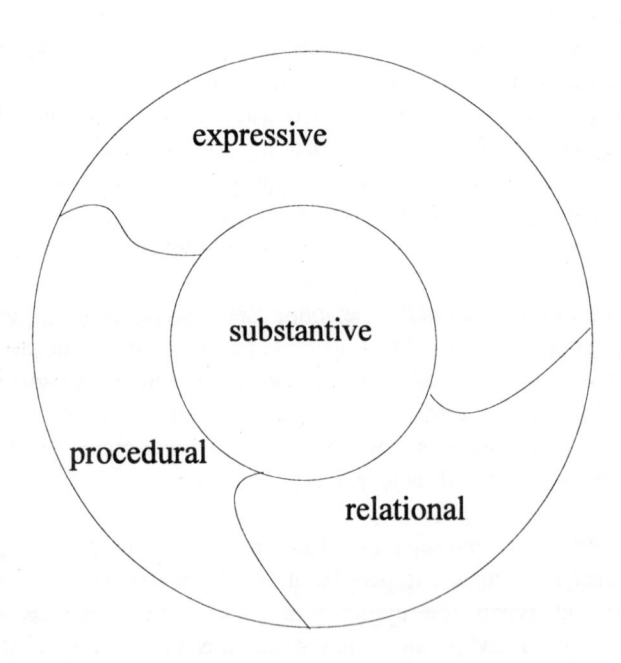

Figure 4.1   **A kaleidoscope model of grievance perspectives**

In instructional situations we have had participants role play the chemical spills case, each person adopting the view of one of the four actors and interacting with the three others. In such situations, and when combined with the four perspective model, the kaleidoscope-turning metaphor is generative. If its introduction is properly timed, it leads conflicting parties to be sensitive to the differing constructions of reality held by the different actors. It alerts them to the potential value of combining a multiplicity of elements, each drawn from a different reality construction, into a practical action plan. Thus, the kaleidoscope-turning metaphor serves as a semiotic representation of conflict reformulation.

The semiotic representation of conflict concepts, through metaphors such as the above, conveys process-oriented knowledge rather than the component knowledge typical of traditional grievance research. An example of the latter (drawing on the four perspective model) would be 'relational conflict has a lower resolution rate than substantive conflict'. Such component knowledge conveys little about conflict processes, whereas generative metaphors such as the kaleidoscope not only convey process knowledge, they also stimulate the individual to conceive of the situation in a new way and provide conflicting parties with a common image (the particular metaphor) to guide their discourse.

Process knowledge concerning the social interaction associated with various patterns of perspectives would help practitioners choose a process, and perhaps a metaphor, for guiding a particular conflict. Yet, we have little such knowledge. What differentiates between patterns of perspectives where convergent vs. divergent actions emerge? We may presume that when most members of an organizational unit share a common perspective, socially agreed - upon interpretations emerge, followed by jointly - accepted action. However, it is also possible for discourse to lead to joint action even when members hold differing perspectives. To better understand these intriguing occurrences, consider the borders between perspectives not as separators but as connecting lines (Wilbur, 1979). Wilbur asserts that most problems are based upon the illusion that oppositions must be separated, whereas they can be seen as aspects of one underlying reality. Thus, we can posit that when organizational members implicitly adopt the 'one underlying reality' view by recognizing and accepting as legitimate the differences in perspectives among their peers, conjoint action can emerge. Such action is made more likely if the raw energy created by differences can be harnessed by the pull of a heliotropic image of future organizational possibilities (Cooperrider, 1990). That is, people (like Alex and Pam in the chemical spill case) may differ in their perspectives, due to differences in interpretive histories, yet agree on and work for a future social reality that they all construct as desirable (such as a safer work environment).

As noted earlier, the images that individuals use to describe the conflicts in which they are involved can themselves be an important research focus. Asking individuals to name a metaphor that represents their view of a particular conflict process could reveal much about how conflict is formulated. Since a generative metaphor such as the kaleidoscope seems to change the way in which individuals formulate a conflict, it should prove fruitful to investigate how the metaphors in use by various parties to the same conflict influence their processes of discourse and reality construction.

Researching multiple perspectives

The foregoing sections of this paper point to the inadequacy of research that classifies a specific conflict into a single, objective category. Reliance on such data, which are all that can be found in organizational records, has steered research away from the interpretive study of organizational conflict espoused here. The challenge is to record and use data in a way that is true to social construction of reality concepts. As Gould (1981) has argued, objectification of a phenomenon leads to treating the data as the phenomenon itself. A means must be found to capture in data enough of the complexity of the phenomenon that interpretive analysis is aided rather than impeded. In our case, we confronted over one hundred summaries of interviews with grievants. In order to analyze them in a way that respected their complexity, we created a classification scheme that reflects the figure-ground concept from the kaleidoscope metaphor. It does so by allowing the coding of several perspectives for a single individual, with those that are dominant for the individual (figure) indicated differently than those that are less strong (ground).

Applying this coding system, twenty cases were coded of three - party grievances in Belgian firms. As can be seen in Table 4.1, perspectives that are strong for a particular actor are recorded as upper case letters (S = Substantive perspective; R = Relational; P = Procedural; A = Action), those that are moderately strong as lower case, and those not present or weak are indicated by a dash. The viewpoint of the complainant, the superior, and a third party were distinguished. One advantage of the data coding process was that it revealed sub-perspectives for the relational (social environment, interpersonal relations, personal development) and expressive (expressed actions, expressed feelings, power) perspectives. After a short training period two coders reached agreement of approximately seventy per cent in coding unstructured reports of grievance conflicts, showing that reliable coding of multiple conflict perspectives from participants' open - ended interviews is feasible. Open-ended interviews avoid imposition of the researcher's constructs and language on the research subjects, an important requirement for interpretive study.

The reliable coding of perspectives in a complex form permits study of individuals' formulations of conflict and their influence on social negotiation processes. Each row of the table represents one grievance case, as seen by three parties to it, the complainant, the superior, and a third party. This table provides only those cases that closed (finished) with an integrative (win-win) outcome. Similar tables were constructed for conflict cases producing four other types of outcomes. Not represented in the table, but also coded, were the perspectives that were reflected in each case's outcome. Examining and comparing these tables led to a number of speculations that can guide further study. We touch on a few here.

Table 4.1
Perspective formulation and interaction outcomes

Outcome		Perspective Code		
	Case	Complainant	Superior	Third Party
Closed-	2	SR-a	S--a	S--A
integrative	5	Sr-A	S--A	Sr-a
	6	Sr-a	Sr-a	Sr--
	9	Sr-A	SR-A	Sr-a
	19	SR-a	Sr-a	Sr-a

Note that in Table 4.1 no-one expressed a procedural (P or p) perspective. Further, a multiplicity of perspectives within one person and differences across persons seem to be the general rules. Following the figure-ground distinction, the configuration of perspectives for one person can be conceived as forming a gestalt with one perspective in the foreground, usually the substantive one, and other perspectives fading into the background to varying degrees. Another general observation was that there is nearly always a content or substantive perspective involved. This focus, as it were on things, allows parties to attempt to manage their differences through reliance on a 'web of rules' (Dunlop, 1958) that defines the desired state of these things such as, for example, workers will test the safety equipment weekly. We found that even in cases where a relational issue is dominant, the substantive perspective still emerges in the outcome. A substantive formulation may serve as a public legitimization of a conflict issue.

It can be hypothesized that the substantive perspective offers a common ground to reach new shared meaning. The grievants in our cases seemed to be more skilful at reaching agreement in the substantive area.

Other analyses of our small sample of cases suggested such findings as: social interactions among parties with dominantly relational perspectives leads to distributive (win-lose) outcomes or escalation; and, a diminished focus on relational elements is associated with integrative outcomes. By adding to such analysis information on parties' interaction strategies, future research can focus on the nature and consequences of various social processes involving the interplay of particular patterns of perspectives, producing the kinds of process knowledge we called for above.

It is unlikely that the development and potential resolution of conflict is dependent only on the social negotiation processes used by the parties and independent of parties' formulation of the conflict itself. Hence, conflict research can benefit from having a method of capturing the nature of social constructions that are in interaction in a dispute, enabling it to relate those particular constructions to the social processes by which a conflict develops. The important requirement in any such analysis is that the coded data remain true to an interpretive approach by capturing the complexity of individual formulation and by examining the patterns of perspectives involved in the social interaction.

Implications and conclusions

This paper has proposed concepts based upon the premise that conflict is a core organizational process involving the interaction of multiple perspectives to renegotiate meaning. The paper's most general theme is a call for research on organizational conflict from a social construction viewpoint, in order to learn more not only about conflict but also about the fundamental nature and processes of organization.

While the authors' research has concentrated on grievance conflict, other forms of organizational conflict, such as interdepartmental, peer, and producer-supplier, can be examined to investigate the conceptualization of conflict, processes for negotiating meaning, and their consequences for organizational action. We have focused here much more on the existence and interaction of differing perspectives than on the social processes themselves, that is, on the what rather than the how of grievance formulation. Research is needed not only on the nature of perspectives themselves, but also on the social histories and discourses that give rise to diverse perspectives and influence their salience in different situations, the social processes by which perspectives interact among parties, and the consequences of meaning negotiating for individual commitment and action. By attending to the conceptualization of conflict and the social construction of reality, new issues are raised for research on conflict resolution. For example, when parties interact, what structuring or intervention leads to a questioning of one's own formulation? What metaphors lead to appreciation of others' perspectives? What types of discourse lead to reformulation and the social acceptance of a common meaning? What does resolution mean and how do we define desirable outcomes?

Research that takes models such as the four-perspective model presented above and examines the antecedents of individuals' perspectives represents a marriage of the social construction and systems paradigms. By moving beyond the confines of one paradigm, such research can lead to knowledge of how structural elements of the society and organization influence individuals' conceptualizations of their situation and how these conceptualizations, in turn, lead to new structures.

The concepts presented here point to the divergence of perspectives and interaction of multiple perspectives that constitute grievances as part of ongoing reality construction in organizations. They also point to the importance of parties in a conflict understanding the presence of multiple perspectives. A further step in conflict research, one that can be guided by social constructionism is to examine the discourse processes by which one party comes to value others perspectives, seeing them not as threatening one's own understanding but as enriching it. Each perspective used to interpret a conflict situation assesses actions in light of current norms and beliefs about what is possible and desirable (Vickers, 1968), valuing certain actions and solutions more than others. Conflict formulation is a process for appreciating or failing to appreciate another's values concerning how things should be.

The implication of our discussions here is not that grievances should be treated in ways that lead to their 'resolution' in a win-win fashion. Rather the most important practical implication of the multi-perspective view is that individuals and groups in organizations should engage in conflict with a full realization that they are negotiating meanings. These meanings will guide their future actions and interactions. The interplay of differing perspectives will be ongoing and will continue in future conflicts. Organizations that accept pluralism will have a tolerance for this interplay of divergent perspectives, for different values, that will make conflict processes and the renegotiating of meaning more open than in organizations where one party devalues another's perspective. In this regard, the 'turning the kaleidoscope' metaphor carries a normative implication: Acknowledging the value and legitimacy of multiple perspectives permits the examination of a broader set of interpretations and alternative actions, and eases individuals' acceptance of (and commitment to) actions that do not accord entirely with their own dominant perspectives. We suspect that such examination and acceptance would lead to more effective organizational functioning, but perhaps our thoughts are too strongly rooted in the cooperative model of organizations. As Pondy's portrayal of organizations as arenas for conflict is explored, conflict research based on the social construction paradigm may challenge the managerial view of organizations as cooperative systems and the academic emphasis on organizational effectiveness. Instead of conceiving of conflict primarily in terms of its deleterious or beneficial effects on organizational effectiveness, studies of grievances and other organizational conflict can focus upon the meaning of organizations to humans, including the dynamic interchange of perspectives that creates meaning for organizational members and underlies the social activity of organizing.

References

Allport, F.H. (1955), *Theories of Perception and the Concept of Structure*, Wiley, New York.

Aram, J. & Salipante, P. (1981), 'An evaluation of organizational due process in the resolution of employee/employer conflict', *Academy of Management Review*, 6, pp. 197-204.

Barrett, F.J. (1990), *'The development of the cognitive organization'*, Doctoral dissertation, Department of Organizational Behavior, Case Western Reserve University.

Berger, P. & Luckman, T. (1967), *The Social Construction of Reality*, Doubleday, New York.

Bouwen, R. & Salipante, P. (1990), 'The behavioral analysis of grievances: Episodes, actions and outcomes', *Employee Relations*, 12, 4, pp. 27-32.

Brown, L. David (1984), 'Managing conflicts among groups', in Kolb, D. *Organizational Psychology*, Prentice Hall, Englewood Cliffs, N.J.

Capra, F. (1982), *The Turning Point*, Simon & Schuster, New York.

Cohen, M.D., March, J.G. & Olsen, J.P. (1972), 'A garbage can model of organizational choice', *Administrative Science Quarterly*, 17, 1, pp. 1-25.

Cooperrider, D. (1990), 'Positive imagery, positive action: The affirmative basis of organizing', in Srivastva, S., Cooperrider, D. & Associates, *Appreciative Management and Leadership,* Jossey Bass, San Francisco. pp. 91-125.

Cyert, R. & March, J. (1963), *A Behavioral Theory of The Firm*, Prentice Hall, Englewood Cliffs, N.J.

Day, R. & Day, J. (1977), 'A review of the current state of negotiated order theory: An appreciation and a critique', *The Sociological Quarterly*, 18, pp.126-142.

Deutsch, M. (1973), *The Resolution of Conflict: Constructive and Destructive Processes,* Yale University Press, New Haven.
Dunlop, John T. (1958), *Industrial Relations Systems,* Holt, New York.
Durkheim, Emile (1915), *The Elementary Forms of Religious Life,* The Free Press, New York.
Eco, F. (1976), *The Theory of Semiotics,* Indiana University Press, Bloomington.
Evan, W. (1961), 'Organization man and due process of law, *American Sociological* Review, 26, pp. 540-547.
Filley, A. (1976), *Interpersonal Conflict Resolution,* Scott-Foresman, Glenview, Illinois.
Fisher, R. & Ury, W. (1981), *Getting to Yes,* Houghton Mifflin, Boston.
Freire, P. (1981), *Pedagogy of the Oppressed,* (transl: M.B. Ramos) Continuum, New York.
Gadamer, Hans-Georg, (1975), *Truth and Method,* Seabury, New York.
Geertz, C. (1983), *Local Knowledge: Further Essays in Interpretive Anthropology,* Basic Books, New York.
Gergen, K. (1978), 'Toward generative theory', *Journal of Personality and Social Psychology,* 36, pp. 1344-1360.
Gergen, K. (1985), 'The social constructionist movement in modern psychology'. *American Psychologist,* 40, pp. 266-275.
Gergen, K. (1986), 'Correspondence versus autonomy in the language of understanding human action', in Fiske, D.W. & Shweder, R.A. (eds), *Metatheory in Social Science: Pluralisms and Subjectivities,* University of Chicago Press, Chicago.
Gordon, M.E. & Miller, S.J. (1984), 'Grievances: A review of research and practice', *Personnel Psychology,* 34, pp. 117-147.
Gould, S.J. (1981), *The Mismeasure of Man,* W.W. Norton, New York.
Gray, B., Bougon, M.G. & Donnellon, A. (1985), 'Organizations as constructions and destructions of meaning', *Journal of Management,* 11, 1, pp. 77-92.
Gray, B. (1989), *Collaborating: Finding Common Ground for Multiparty Problems,* Jossey Bass, San Francisco.
Kelly, G.A. (1955), *The Psychology of Personal Constructs,* Norton, New York.
Kolb, D.M. (1983), *The Mediators,* MIT Press, Cambridge, Mass.
Kuhn, J. (1961), *Bargaining in Grievance Settlement,* Columbia University Press, New York.
Lewin, D. & Feuille, P. (1983), 'Behavioral research in industrial relations', *Industrial and Labor Relations Review,* 36, pp. 341-360.
Lewin, D. & Peterson, R. (1988), *The Modern Grievance Procedure in the United States,* Quorum Books, New York.
Morgan, G. (1986), *Images of Organizations,* Sage Publications, London.

Mulder, M. (1976), 'Power distance reduction in practice', in Hofstede, G. & Kassem, M.S., *European Contributions to Organization Theory*, Von Gorcum, Amsterdam.

Pinkley, R.L. & Northcraft, G.B. (1989), *'Cognitive interpretations of conflict: Implications for disputant motives and behaviors'*, Paper presented at the 49th Annual Meeting of the Academy of Management, Washington, D.C.

Pondy, L.R. (1992), 'Overview of organizational conflict:Concepts and models', *Journal of Organizational Behaviour,* 13, 3, pp.255-261.

Pondy, L., Frost, P., Morgan, G. & Dandridge, T. (1983), *Organizational Symbolism,* JAI Press, Greenwich, CT.

Prigogine, I. & Strengers, I. (1985), *Order Out of Chaos*, Bakker, Amsterdam.

Reis-Louis, M. (1977), 'How individuals conceptualize conflict: Identification of steps in the process and the role of personal/developmental factors'. *Human Relations*, 30, pp. 451-467.

Rogers, C. (1965), 'Dealing with psychological tensions', *Journal of Applied Behavioral Science*, 1, 1, pp. 6-24.

Rowe, M.P. & Baker, M. (1984), 'Are you hearing enough employee concerns?' *Harvard Business Review*, May-June, pp. 127-135.

Salipante, P. & Aram, J. (1984), 'The role of organizational procedures in the resolution of social conflict', *Human Organization,* 43, pp. 9-15.

Salipante, P. & Bouwen, R. (1990), 'The behavioral analysis of grievances: Conflict sources, complexity and transformation', *Employee Relations*, 12, 3, pp. 17-22.

Salipante, P. & Fortado, B. (1989), 'Employee rights: Required vs. desired', in Osigweh, C.A. (ed.), *Managing Employee Rights and Responsibilities*, Quorum Books, Westport, CT.

Sayles, L.R. (1958), *The Behavior of Industrial Work Groups*, Wiley, New York.

Schein, E. (1973), *Process Consultation*, Addison-Wesley, Reading, Mass.

Schmidt, S.M. & Kochan, T.A. (1972), 'Conflict: Toward conceptual clarity', *Administrative Science Quarterly*, 17, pp. 359-370.

Schon, D. (1980), 'Generative metaphor: A perspective on problem setting in policy', in Ortony, A. (ed.), *Metaphor and Thought*, Cambridge University Press, Cambridge.

Scott, W.G. (1965), *The Management of Conflict: Appeal Systems in Organizations*, Irwin, Homewood, Ill.

Searle, J. (1984), *Minds, Brains, and Science*, Cambridge University Press, Cambridge.

Shepard, B.H., Blumenfeld-Jones, K. & Roth, J. (1989), 'Informal third - partyship: A program of research on everyday conflict intervention', in Kressel, K., Pruitt, D. & Associates, *Mediation Research*, Jossey Bass, San Francisco.

Smircich, L. & Stubbart, C. (1985), 'Strategic management in an enacted world', *Academy of Management Review*, 10, 4, pp. 724-736.

Strauss, G. (1982), 'Bridging the gap between industrial relations and conflict management: An introduction', *Industrial Relations*, pp. 1-31.

Thomas, K. (1976), 'Conflict and conflict management', in Dunnette, M.D. (ed.), *Handbook of Industrial and Organizational Psychology*, Rand McNally, Chicago, pp. 889-935.

Tuchman, B. (1962), *The Guns of August*, MacMillan, New York.

Vickers, G. (1968), *Value Systems and Social Processes*, Tavistock, London.

Walton, R.E. (1969), *Interpersonal Peacemaking: Confrontations and Third - Party Consultation*, Addison-Wesley, Reading, Mass.

Walton, R.E. & McKersie, R.B. (1991), *A Behavioral Theory of Labor Negotiations*, 2nd ed, ILR Press, Ithaca, N.Y.

Weick, K.E. (1979), *The Social Psychology of Organizing*, Addison-Wesley, Reading, Mass.

Wilbur, K. (1979), *No Boundary: Eastern and Western Approaches to Personal Growth*, Shambhala, Boston.

Notes

1. Editors' note: the authors are here using the expression 'relational perspective' to mean something different from that which is meant by Dachler and Hosking (this volume).

5 The social construction of grievances: Constructive and constructionist approaches to a relational theory

Mary Gergen

This commentary is the last formal artifact of a long, interesting and congenial exchange with Salipante & Bouwen. Our discussions have revolved around the question of what constitutes a relational account of grievance research. As they so aptly pointed out in their paper, people can work together amicably on their mutual projects without always sharing the same perspectives. In our case, we have been able to produce this tandem piece while using varying definitions of the nature of social constructionist processes. Salipante put his finger on the divergence of our views early in our interchanges when he declared that the paper was probably 'too constructivist' for me, a social constructionist. As we communicated with each other on several occasions it seemed that this difference of viewpoints was lessening. In this respect the paper has a strong and successful relational history. Now, differences are smaller still. However, there are still questions that emerge from this separation of discourses. The central difference between us remains that of deciding what is social constructionism and its related practices, and what is not. In my commentary I wish to suggest: (i) ways in which the authors fruitfully used social constructionist frameworks; (ii) where the term is used as a synonym of social constructivism and; (iii) where there is a latent positivist drift away from the development of a relational understanding of grievance problems.

Distinguishing between a constructionist and a constructivist approach to grievance accounts research

The major distinction between a constructionist and a constructivist approach is made over the question of where and how reality is constructed. A strong social constructionist position holds that the material for analysis is to be found on the surfaces of inquiry. It is in the interstices of dialogue and action and in what people say to each other; in how their languages shift over time and in context; in what people do with one another with this language. The social construction of reality depends upon a community of speakers/actors, who share in repertoires of meaning provided by their culture. For constructionists the meaning of any event or statement depends on how it is negotiated within context. Whether an event is understood as serious or funny, worth a suspension of a warning, a walkout or a raise, is not fixed within a situation. Rather, it is achieved through elaborate processes of social negotiation over time. The meanings made are considered partial, tentative, historically finite and dependant upon their co-creators. They are continuously open to reinterpretation, never objective or clear-cut.

The authors often seem to agree with the account outlined above: 'social construction helps us analyse organizational conflict in a new way by implying a continuous striving for coincident meaning by parties having differing views'. They continue by emphasizing the cultural constraints of constructions. They observe: 'several forms of relationships are available in discourse, and each interchange between and among persons has at its disposal a certain range of scenarios from which it can draw'.

Alternatively, the constructivist hand behind the text is revealed with every attempt to explain the making of meaning via phenomenological experience, cognitive mechanisms, and other internal processes attributed to autonomous single individuals. Salipante & Bouwen suggest a constructivist position in their section on' new paradigm thinking'. For example, they speak of the 'crucial role played by the experiencing of subjective reality' in recognizing multiple perspectives. Constructivist positions mentioned after that include George Kelly's personal construct framework, Berger & Luckmann's phenomenologically based arguments, and Karl Weick's organizational behavioural theories. In each case the emphasis is on the individual perceptions, interpretations and judgments as central to meaning-making, rather than the interpersonal activities of groups creating meanings.

Within the paper the terms constructionism and constructivism are often used interchangeably; this seems to me to obscure significant differences. There are many similarities between the two approaches, especially in their emphasis on the interpretive function of theory and in their opposition to the objectivity claims of positivist approaches. However they differ considerably in their explanatory focus. The oscillation within the chapter may come from Salipante & Bouwen's transition from a more traditional positivist approach to a relational interpretive theory based on social constructivism/constructionism. They verify this claim by saying, 'our research program started from the former [positivist] orientation, but eventually found it wanting...The difficulty with the traditional approach was that it required researchers to look for the 'real', objective basis of conflict. With this orientation, only one construction of reality can be considered the truth at a given moment in time.' The willingness to admit to a change of heart in methodological practice is laudable. It suggests to others that they also can gain by considering the limits of positivism and the possibilities of constructionism. However, this transitory status produces at times a confusing amalgam of discourses.

Gains and losses in taking on a social constructionist approach

Salipante & Bowen also seem somewhat ambivalent about what they are gaining, and what they are giving up in their new venture. In one instance they point to a basic problem of using a constructivist approach; 'How can we deal scientifically with subjective realities and make an 'objective' analysis of the social environment?' This question is a good one. It is crucial for traditional empirical social scientists who adhere to 'objective' methodological standards. It also is important to social constructionists who wonder how to infer the subjective reality of another, and who prefer to study someone's language and actions directly. The social constructionist's position is better outlined by Allport, 'The way a man [sic] defines his situation constitutes for him its reality'. One notes Allport's emphasis on the use of a discourse term rather than a cognitive term: one *defines* rather than experiences or cognizes one's reality. Yet even Allport is insufficiently constructionist, for the emphasis remains on the individual definition. For a constructionist, individual definitions are ultimately linked to communal projects.

While critical of constructivists, Salipante & Bowen point out a potential problem for a social constructionist approach, as well: 'An individual may fail to accept the socially negotiated interpretation of a group, or prefer one group's interpretation over another'. Indeed, we have all heard of instances where ex-employees, fired for some reason or another, return to seek revenge against former employers in a variety of violent ways. Surely the former employee's construction of events does not jibe with the boss's. In this instance we are tempted with the notion that constructivism is a more useful mode of studying the construing reality. However, social constructionism offers an answer to this dilemma. It suggests each of us is embedded in multiple communities, so having the option to select a narrative that may be appropriate for one group, but not another.

Integrating constructivism and constructionism in grievance work

The authors' tendency to integrate these two forms (constructivist and constructionist) is illustrated by their use of Weick's arguments concerning the core processes of enactment, selection, and retention. To me, the general formulation is an amalgam of constructivist mind games and constructionist social play. Their framework has great intuitive appeal because it closely parallels common sense talk in everyday life, but its utility is limited, as I hope to show. It suggests that people first engage cognitively, selecting and interpreting events in the external world. They then are said to release public statements about these internal states as they interact and negotiate with others. This leads to further internalized processing, which later re-emerges as social activity. The general presentation suggests a strong interactive model of cognitive and social processes alternating over time. In an important sense the analysis tries to have the best of both worlds by joining these two separate, and indeed, incommensurate paradigms.

The major critique of this approach is that two levels of explanation, each of which can be seen as totalizing, are mixed temporally. The cognitive/ constructivist approach is designed to explain everything as a result of the internal mental process of a single individual. Speaking and other social interactions are results, caused by forms of internal processing. However, the social constructionist position, which talks of the interaction among people as they produce social rituals and forms of language games, also is a totalizing explanatory system. Interaction produces interaction; ongoing dialogue gives meaning to the ongoing dialogue. Within social constructionism, there is no necessity to appeal to internal processing to explain why, for example, 'you're welcome' follows the remark, 'thank you'. While not denying the existence of multiple bodily conditions including brain activity, the social constructionist analysis is dependent on social interaction as an explanatory device. When analysed closely, one can notice that mixing the two together involves a duplication of explanatory locus and a competition between the two theoretical orientations. Because both discourses are totalizing, they cannot be interactive, much as H20 and water cannot be interactive in a single analysis of the earth's composition. Each discourse is complete without the other.

The authors are eager to adopt a social constructionist approach in order to investigate the multiplicity of ways in which grievance disputes are framed. The authors state that in the study of grievance reports, 'investigating perspectives is an important task for research' because it is crucial in explaining how people behave in grievance situations and whether the problems are resolved. Using a social constructivist/ constructionist approach greatly facilitates the analysis of grievance disputes, in part, because it bypasses the notion that it is possible to obtain an objective account of the events that caused the trouble. Through inductive techniques, reflecting the positivist origins of this research, the authors suggest they have isolated four perspectives. These are said to be useful for describing the narrative of grievances given by three different parties, the complainant, superior and third party. The data are primarily illustrative. However analysis of these grievance accounts seemed to reveal that the perspective from which the story is told influences whether or not the grievance gets settled ('grievance outcome'). It seems that if these various perspectives are useful ways of understanding conflicting views and opinions, this could be of great use to organizational scientists and practitioners.

As Salipante & Bowen describe them, perspectives are internal cognitive states; this leads them in a constructivist direction. Instead, the authors might have taken a more social constructionist turn by defining their perspectives as possible elements in a feasible grievance story. Thus, one can tell a grievance story that includes the breaking of substantive rules, the breakdown of a relationship, a procedural violation and/or power/authority issues. In Table 4.1 it appears that the vast majority of the three subject types (complainant, superior and third party) used very similar story lines (i.e., SR-a). For example, all the grievance stories, except for that of one superior, contain some mention of the rules governing the situation(s). To a narratologist, this finding suggests that the current cultural repertoire of grievance stories requires that a rule element be mentioned as part of the story. If these perspectives are seen as elements of story forms, researchers could look at such variables as what ingredients in stories lead to high agreements between major contenders or to positive outcomes for the resolution of the problem, and which ingredients are disruptive. For example, it may be that a grievance story that is only about conflicts of power is doomed to unsatisfactory resolution.

Turning the kaleidoscope: generative metaphors in the grievance research process

The authors recognize that their categorization runs the risk of being too static a formulation, lacking a relational dimension. In consequence, they shift to an auxiliary strategy that emphasizes the dynamic relational aspects of grievance discussions. This step is effected by the introduction of the semiotic notion of metaphor. Salipante & Bowen suggest that by producing a generative metaphor, the turning of a kaleidoscope, to inform the process of grievance telling, involved parties come to accept that there are a variety of legitimate ways to tell a grievance story. In addition, the procedure of introducing metaphors enhances the self-reflexivity of an involved party: they are helped to reflect on why they choose to emphasize certain features of the situation over others. People involved in the grievance situation learn to accept that their stories are just one possible construction of the world, and that others also can be valid.

Formulating relational entities: a new research option

A relationally oriented organizational science would see more point in creating a different kind of research process, focusing on a different question. The process would focus on the manner in which the involved parties come together and negotiate a form of story among themselves that is satisfactory in resolving a grievance. The issue would no longer be formulated in constructivist terms: separate and autonomous individuals, trapped in their own heads, creating their own private stories. Instead, something more interactive and co-constructed would be considered. One possibility, yet underdeveloped, is to create units composed of relational entities instead of individuals. Such an approach would, for example, assess the grievance story of a complainant in the presence of the boss, or a co-worker or a union representative. Equally, the grievance stories could be traced over time from the mouths of each participant. One might expect some form of merger to occur over time, if the most felicitous perspectives or narratives are used by the participants.

Metaphors are indeed helpful for highlighting the multiple points from which a narrative can commence. Teaching participants about the relativity of any formulation has the possibility of engendering greater prospects for group survival. It also may facilitate the development of less friction and unproductive conflict in an organization. Languages for assessing and controlling conflicts of interest could also be developed within such groups. This move to a discourse level is very congenial to social constructionism and suggestive of future possibilities of creative work among organizational practitioners.

Concluding dilemmas for relational research

Of course if is easier to suggest new ways of organizing research programs than it is to carry them out. How can one create a relational, narrative-based social constructionism with high utility for organizational scientists interested in processes of conflict? How can one succeed in rejecting revered traditions belonging to highly recognized cognitive and empirical scientists and still gain their attention? Yet, the research of Salipante & Bowen shows a strong answer to this challenge. They have brought interpretive ideas into the heart of their research domain, experimented with forms of multiple reality constructions and applied them to a serious organizational problem. Their openness to new modes of study, and their efforts to move away from positivist lines, are exemplary. They have illustrated that exciting challenges are available to those who move beyond the limits of traditional social sciences.

6 The case of group sado-masochism: A dialogue on relational theory

Kenwyn K. Smith and Mary Gergen

Introduction

In this chapter we are exploring the creative possibilities that come from a dialogue between two people who talk about relationships in very different ways. We have structured the paper in two interwoven parts. Kenwyn Smith (called Smith from here on) presents an actual case in which his thinking and acting within a relationship are described. He addresses the overt behaviours he was observing and the hidden dynamics he was tuning into. He outlines the constructions he placed upon these actions as he thought about and observed them.

Between sections written by Smith, Mary Gergen interjects. This voice (called Gergen from here on) is italicized in the text. Within the flow of Smith's commentary she interrupts with queries, interpretations, and replies. Her words work to situate the ongoing descriptions - Smith's versions of events - within a frame she calls relational. Each author is enticed by the notions of relational theory, and by what such theory might mean for the analysis of group behaviour. Each is a stranger to the other's views. We hope to talk over the corpus of Smith's case, chewing on the bones of the other's text, so to speak. Gergen's endeavour is to pursue a construction of reality that depends upon the surface of things that is, upon what people say and do together. Smith prefers to pursue the unconscious processes of either groups or individual selves. But are we able to reach a point of mutual consent? As Shakespeare wrote and Hamlet declared, 'Aye, there's the rub'. Perhaps Smith does not consent to sacrifice the discourse of the deep for what may seem a becalmed sea. He may find it too dull to dismiss what he understands to be the dynamite of discord seeping from oceanic psyches; he may not accept the muddled discourses bandied about in thin and airy prose. At times Smith replies to Gergen. He is a part, and yet apart. The work revolves about our dialogue. What will be the nature of our co-mingling? Each brings to this scene our own special way of talking. Will new possibilities spring from our diverse positions? Or will traditional concerns for posture and prestige impede our cooperative designs? What can be achieved? A central concern of this chapter is to address these issues.

Readers also are included in a farther reaching of our exchange. You add to our relatedness as well - looking over our shoulders - lipsynching in mime our words as your own, and adding your reasons and rebuttals. The relational possibilities of the text are multiplied in ways that we cannot predict. We invite this dialogue to continue and expand.

The case: Sadist, meet the group's masochists!

The occasion: I was facilitating a self-analytic group dynamics course at the University of Pennsylvania. Participants were processing their own experiences to learn about aspects of group life that normally are out of members' awareness. The event: A participant, Brent, started to interact in a way that triggered a complex authority dynamic. This provoked me to feel very combative towards him. I did not express my feelings because I thought he was craving to be collaborative with me, and because it would have been inappropriate given my purposes as facilitator.

The experience recounted here taught me four things about the role of the group facilitator. I think these are relevant to all authority figures in groups, be it the classroom teacher, the business manager, the community developer, or parents. The lessons are as follows. First is the idea that expressions of abrasive affect towards group members, including the authority figure, may be a sincere attempt to construct meaningful relations with others in the group; they may not be intended to be negative. Second, there is the valuable recognition that group members may interact with each other in ways that, like a Laingian knot, have people 'saying the opposite of what they mean in order to mean the opposite of what they say' (Bateson, 1972, pp.179-182). Third, are the powerful consequences of recognizing that symbols have many facets. The meanings attached to surfaces not immediately visible might be more important than those that are apparent. Last, creative possibilities follow from seeing the relationship between two parties as a representative enactment of the larger dynamics of which they are a part. From the elaboration of these basic ideas throughout the episode with Brent our current collaboration is derived.

The basic details of this case fragment have been described elsewhere (Smith, 1990) so here they are merely summarized. My purpose is to explicate how I thought about these events while I was in the midst of them and to make available for scrutiny how I was interpreting my own experience and that of others. I do this using the frames of the clinical organizational behaviour tradition (Alderfer, 1980; Berg and Smith, 1988; Glaser and Strauss, 1967). I offer this as a basis for the dialogue that forms the essence of this paper, expecting that the major understanding will come from attempting to merge Gergen's insights with my own interpretations. My goal is to create a sense of what I consider I am doing when I think I am thinking relationally.

I should begin by saying what I mean by the term relational. First the behaviours of any individuals interacting can be seen from multiple vantage points. For example, they can be simultaneously looked at from intrapersonal, interpersonal, intragroup, and intergroup perspectives. Each frame provides quite different interpretations of what the exchanges could mean both to the participants and those affected by them. Second, behaviours that seem to be driven by forces internal to the individual may reflect an inner discourse or struggle between different parts of the self that are becoming realigned. Third, individuals' actions need to be understood as taking place within a context. Contexts contain an array of potential meanings that can be chosen and affixed to someone's behaviour as an explication for action. The potential meanings can be chosen in much the same way that the local library offers many books on its shelves from which one can make a choice.

Our differences are obvious to me from the beginning of Smith's outline of 'the case'. For example, his reference to a 'self-analytic group dynamics course' inscribes a certain type of activity. It is one that relies on peoples' abilities to recognize invisible, nonverbal, 'unconscious' happenings, processes and feelings and to clearly define and analyse them for themselves and others. The leader, Smith in this case, will undertake to train the students in these processes. The title also suggests that Smith's code for understanding has roots in psychoanalytic theory. An alternate view, and one that I advocate, resists the shaping of reality by hidden, but real, individual and group dynamics. According to my framework, people do not discover or sense dynamics. Rather, through their interaction they can generate a sense of their dynamics. People act together to create recognizable events. Without the participants making and naming processes and effects, dynamics do not exist.

Smith locates the group problem in a complex authority dynamic. He says he felt 'combative' and hostile towards one group member, despite knowing that this young man was trying to ally with him. Smith takes this interaction as the critical relational text from which to build the group's lesson. The latter is outlined in four pedagogical goals. In the main, the goals are to explain Batesonian notions of relational formation and reversals. These can be used to reveal hidden meanings in the interactions, and to release tensions that are not only between the two individuals, Smith and Brent, but stem from the entire group's interactions. Smith says that his version of relational thinking comes *from the tradition of clinical organizational behaviour. For Smith (in my reading) relational theorizing begins with how people behave together, in this case, in a group. Yet, he is not committed to finding the origins or causes of these behaviours in the interactions themselves; for these he will, as it were, dig deeper. Here is an important site for the difference in our views of relational theorizing; these differences will become more sharply drawn as the chapter progresses.*

However, I should first offer a caveat: the possibility that I am in a position within our group (Smith and Gergen) that is parallel to the one held by Brent in the group dynamics class. Brent has intervened in the proceedings, and, while wanting to be collaborative, has aroused some hostile feelings in Smith. I wonder if, trying to collaborate, Smith might not react with similar negative feelings. Will I set an interaction pattern in motion that has a long history in our culture? Can we avoid this option? My move is intended to encourage our collaboration not Smith's resistance.

It was the group's second session and Brent was provoking strong feelings. He was charming and many group members were attracted to him. However, he was also cruel. Members were frightened by him but often indicated that his cruelty seemed justified. I experienced Brent as very aggressive towards me while also convincing others that this was totally justified. I also thought Brent was behaving sadistically towards everyone in the group, and I found my own sadistic side engaged by him. I wondered if others in the group might have similarly felt their sadistic sides stirring.

I interrupted the proceedings after several group members said that they found Brent's behaviour disturbing. I asked Brent what he was up to in this group. He responded with all the good things he saw himself as doing, showing no awareness that others might have felt abused by him. I asked him if he could see any negative consequences of his behaviour. He could not. I tried to point out to Brent how his actions were hurting others. He could not or would not see it. He treated everything I said as an accusation, responding like a skilled defense lawyer. Group members seemed pulled into the jury role. Although some of them were also his victims acquittal, so to speak, seemed likely. While I was searching for a new way to connect with Brent he said something that prompted fresh thinking for me. He said 'What you are saying just does not fit my experience.'

The word 'fit' jumped out at me. At first I thought he might be saying that I was trying to map my interpretations onto his experiences and they just did not fit; such non-fitting clearly justifies rejection. Second, I thought of fitting in terms of demands to fit in; I speculated that Brent's comment might be a request to let him be what he is. And third, I thought of Von Glasserfeld's (1984) discussion of fitting in terms of the metaphor of a key fitting in a lock. Von

Glasserfeld noted that any key that opens a particular lock may be viewed as fitting. This image of the key and the lock led me to listen to Brent in a different way. I assumed that his statement about my comments 'not fitting' was a message to search for a different key - one that might help unlock what was imprisoning our interactions. This opened new possibilities for me, and I quietly waited for the right moment.

After one of his outbursts that I thought was sadistic but group members seemed to take quite passively, I asked 'Brent, what is it like for you being in a room full of masochists?' Of course, I was now speaking not only to Brent but to the relationship between him and the others, to the partnership of sadism and masochism as it was evolving in this group. The other group members seemed stunned by my question. Not Brent. A slight smile appeared on his face as he replied

>'I kind of like it'.
>'Does it seem familiar?' I asked.
>'Hardly! I am usually with other sadists.'
>'How does it go for you when you are in a room full of sadists?'
>'I often get really hurt.'
>'Why? Is your own sadism not up to the task'?
>'Usually not'!
>'So you must be feeling pretty good that you can get all this practice at your sadism here when there are no sadists to match your skill'!
>He gave a slight nod.
>'Where did you learn the art of sadism'?
>'In my family.'

These interventions began to move Brent and the group along at a fast clip. No longer was there a struggle about whether my interpretations did or did not fit; they were fitting in the 'key in the lock' sense. Every few sentences opened yet something else that had been closed. Also, I felt very much on Brent's side. After Brent had done some significant exploration, I turned the attention to those I was labelling as masochists, and invited them to explore the ways they acted like voluntary victims, looking for fights in which they could come out second best, and then blaming the world for its cruelty. This opened another path, which led all group members to recognize: that those who passively accepted Brent's abusive behaviour were actively responsible for the pain they were experiencing; and that the emergence of the sadistic side of the group was being fostered by those adopting the masochistic position. In addition, I ceased to feel I had to protect the group, for now the group as a whole seemed capable of self-monitoring and self-regulation.

In summary, this case highlights three issues. First, it took a while for me to learn that what I was experiencing as Brent's fighting behaviour was as much a request to connect as it was to alienate or dissociate. Second, new possibilities were created by taking the symbol 'fit', a term that Brent used somewhat casually, and expanding it beyond its most self-evident meaning to explore its special, indigenous content. Third, the character of the interactions in the group altered dramatically as explanations for what was happening shifted from individualistic terms to ones that were more socio-relational. Both Brent's and my thinking had been very individualistic: I saw him as behaving in a problematic way; he saw me as an incompetent facilitator. As we moved, our views of what we were doing became more socio-relational in the following ways. We began to talk in terms of sadism and masochism. We saw these as collective processes that co-define each other; like light and dark, you cannot have sadism without masochism and vice versa. By then we were seeing that our interpersonal exchanges had a cyclical character, each of us was prompting in the other the very things we were reacting to. In addition, we came to see that the text we were following was not just spontaneously emerging from the two of us. Rather we saw that the whole group was crafting collectively: by virtue of who was taking sides with whom, and through the constant encouragement to keep this interaction at the forefront of group life. Last, it can be argued that the wider organizational and cultural context in which the group was temporarily embedded was characterised by plenty of this type of sadism-masochism. A socio-relational perspective suggests that the interactions between Brent and me could be viewed as a microcosm of the larger macrocosm of which we were all a part.

In this portion of the paper Smith describes the crucial scene in which he wrestles with three interpretations of what is occurring between Brent and the rest of the group. The third formulation, implicating the entire group into a sado-masochistic ritual, seems to attract the greatest support from Brent and attention from the other group members. This interpretation contrasts strongly with the preceding two by virtue of its relational framing. In this move, Smith describes the Brent-group interactions as a mutuality, rather than as an individualistic event caused by Brent. This portion of the paper is very exciting in that change is taking place before our very eyes. Indeed the relational scripting of the group's activities clarifies the dynamic that has apparently been stifling group productivity. Simultaneously it seems to erase the notion of anyone being to blame for the disruptions. Smith describes how they are involved in a culturally embedded ritual crafted by the entire group, not just Brent, or Brent with Smith. The sado-masochistic scene can be viewed more as a dance among the group partners, with every person contributing the necessary steps, than as expressions of individual psychic dynamics. According to Smith once the group took the offered key to understanding, they moved at a fast clip. This framing of events suggests that a relational interpretation is useful in catalysing group activity.

To make sense of the group dynamics Smith also used Bateson's notion that people often convey the opposite of what they intend. In particular he refers to Brent's 'fighting behaviour' as a 'request to connect'. To me this statement slips away from a relational analysis back into a private realm of individual intentions, goals, motives, and perhaps unconscious processes. For a relational theorist interested in the social construction of reality, individualistic terms such as these are not particularly useful. They serve most often as substitutes for a group interpretation. If the group interaction is the basic unit of analysis, internal processes of individuals cease to be relevant. To remain in the realm of interaction, one might prefer to say that at times people in groups are unable to coordinate their meaning-making systems, or say that 'uncooperative' statements may cause interesting shifts in rhetorical strategies.

Smith's shows that symbols can acquire special relevance if fitted to the ongoing indigenous content. He also shows that relational terms open the way to examine larger systemic relationships. These moves are more in accord with a relational standpoint as I employ it. Using Smith's form of interpretation one could imagine new syntheses about how to analyse groups. However, a caveat may be in order here. The explication of the 'case' fits so smoothly the multiple goals and expectations that the group, facilitator, reader and I might hold. Perhaps therefore it is a relatively easy move to accept as the best, or even as converging on truth. This delicious possibility, however, must be declined, although Smith's version may be most preferred for now.

The earlier described events can be understood in many different ways. I will continue by discussing some of my relationship thinking, at both the personal and group level, as I engaged Brent.

Personal and interpersonal relationships

First, I want to comment on how I was thinking about what seemed to be Brent's relationship with himself. One way to think about his actions was that the level of uncertainty in this structureless group evoked such anxiety in him that he engaged in some rather basic splitting processes. The concept of splitting has been defined by Laing (1969, p.95) as 'the partitioning of a set into two subsets', here, a person or group into two parts. Brent could be seen as splitting in that he construed himself as doing positive things for the group and other members while being unaware of the negative side of how he was actually interacting. When presented with an image of himself as vindictive and malicious Brent saw this as perfectly justified because of how he experienced others as treating him, although they were being relatively kind in contrast to how he was treating them. It was as though he saw in others' actions the negative side of himself, which he had split and relocated in them. Then he dealt with these projected parts of himself as a manifestation of the characteristics of the other group members and not of himself.

In addition, some group members were beginning to act vindictively towards Brent, which is what he accused them of, without ever recognizing how he had actively, though unknowingly, created those feelings in them in the first place. Having introjected what Brent had attempted to displace of himself upon them, these members began to express the desire to exonerate Brent for how he was now treating them. This was one form my thinking about Brent's actions in the live moments of this group's interactions.

Smith's approach to relational theorizing has become more complex but, I think, ultimately self-refuting. What began as an account of a sado-masochistic ritual between Brent and the group gets subdued as Smith returns to an analysis of Brent as an individual actor. Smith first reifies Brent's interiority, positing psychological states, by using the phrase, 'basic splitting process'. Echoing Laing (1969), Smith analyses Brent as split into a good/bad self, with the bad self being projected onto the group. In addition, the group comes to accept the projection, and thus becomes masochistic in its response to 'good' Brent. The interactions that go on between the two public units, Brent and Group, are viewed as residuals or side effects of the unconscious psychological projections and introjections taking place. Smith seems to be creating an arena of fantasy war games, with Brent's split bad self being the catalyst for the engagement. Smith's approach is relational - Brent is relating to himself - but the action goes on out of sight, out of conscious mind; only Smith's ability to call these mysterious events to account is in the public sphere.

Given Smith's speculations about Brent and the group, my question is why not allow the theoretical investigation to focus on the patterns of discourse among group members instead of in psychodynamic depths? If we accept that meanings are made relationally, that is, in the social construction practices of the group, why do we not investigate them? Why must we slip away to the unconscious level where only indirect evidence can be obtained? The answer to this question may be that, at this stage in the development of relational approaches, our repertoire of discourse available to understand a group's interaction is inadequate. So we use the language of intentions, motivations, cognitions, or emotions, all of which refer to the psyches of individual group members. Although efforts have been made to talk relationally, the challenge of creating a richer language of interpretation remains (Bruffee, 1993; Butler, 1990; K. Gergen, 1994; M. Gergen, 1994; Harre, 1986; Shotter, 1993).

Group and intergroup relationships

I also found myself thinking about this same concept of splitting, referred to earlier as potentially useful for examining group and intergroup processes. In his early anthropological work Bateson (1936) conceptualized a social version of splitting where whole units that began in an undifferentiated state evolved into two partitioned subunits. He illustrated this with tribal dances where one subgroup took on the role of dancers while another became the spectators. With time, these partitions became intensified: dancers got increasingly specialized in their performance role and the audience more locked into the role of spectator. Bateson saw this as one subset taking on certain attributes on behalf of the whole, while the other adopted different traits, again for the whole. He viewed splitting as the basis of role differentiation. Once such partitioning begins, and both parties fully engage in their part of the process, the splitting intensifies until role delineation has occurred.

This Batesonian image of splitting kept occurring to me as I thought about the pattern of sadism and masochism at the group level. I wondered what we might come to see if we let go of the idea of sado-masochism at the level of the individual, and instead, saw it as an aspect of group life. Patterns that characterise a group as a whole have to be expressed through the behaviours of individuals. For this reason, it is very easy to gloss over the group dynamic and treat the person who expresses a behaviour as possessing an attribute. How then might the sadism in Brent's behaviour be understood at this collective level?

Taking a Batesonian view, it could be that the group is being partitioned into a tribal-like pattern of beaters and beaten or aggressors and aggressed upon. Each fuels the other; just as with tribal dancers, exhibitionism heightens spectatorship and vice versa. So what started in a somewhat muted form may have escalated over time into an intensified partitioning. However, this dynamic interchange is going on out of the field of awareness of the members. Each side of the split attracts different members into its camp, as it were. In this case many of the group seemed to carry a little bit of the masochistic side. But the cumulative effects of many bits of masochism meant there was a rather large piece of complementary and oppositional sadism to be manifest. Across time, as the masochism grew stronger, in this case because many members seemed to be invested in that side of the split, the sadistic side got augmented as well. So what may have begun as minimal group based sadism, expressed through the actions of Brent, grew stronger and stronger to counter the emerging force of the collective masochism. Since Brent alone was being pulled into the position of giving voice to this side of the split, his behaviour seemed so extreme that it was easy to view this as an attribute of him, as individual actor.

So the question I confronted as the facilitator, if this collective theorizing made any sense, was how to speak to the group dynamic as a whole while actually addressing Brent. The key was to keep giving voice to the 'other side', whatever that other side was, to constantly tip the symbols over and frame the dynamic in relationship terms, and to resist the pressure to attribute characteristics to any individual, particularly to Brent. By these means I would be working to counter the dynamic of role suction where individuals get 'filled up' with specific emotions on behalf of the group and then treated as actually having those attributes as persons (Gibbard, Hartman and Mann, 1974).

Another important question for me while all this was taking place was that if this sadism was a group dynamic why was it Brent who was moving into this position and not someone else? One possibility stems from the perspective that each person can be seen as a carrier of his or her group identities from elsewhere (Rice, 1969; Alderfer, 1986). So could it be that Brent was importing into this setting certain experiences from his own earlier group experiences, especially from his family? If so, could his behaviour in this group be treated as a mirroring of the particular sadistic-masochistic patterns enacted in his family? Brent might be treated as a conveyer of his own family group's particular mode for dealing with these dynamics. If so, why might he have regressed to the family group? The argument, suggests Sutherland (1985), is that the greater the anxiety, the deeper the regression. This increases the likelihood that the dynamics imported will be from the family, a person's first group experiences. Others in the group, who may have experienced less anxiety, may have been prompted to regress less and therefore to import experiences from more contemporary settings.

An entirely different vantage point is that what occurred in this group was an expression of the larger intergroup context in which this group was embedded. For example, could it be that the relationships in the school might have contained a great deal of sado-masochism? The students could be viewed as masochistic given the large tuition bill they paid. Their mid-term assessment in accounting often appears to enact a very sadistic side of the examiner, or the accounting department, or of the school as embodied in the actions of the accounting department. We do know from embedded intergroup theory (Alderfer and Smith, 1982) that what is going on in the larger setting profoundly shapes how relations among group members at the more microcosmic level get played out.

I have not been trying to say there is a right way to think about these relationships. My goal is to simply explicate some different relational frames, which can be activated when in the midst of such complex dynamics. I think, the 'rightness' of any interpretation rests on the outcome of the actions taken. At the time my experience was that I did manage, but clumsily, to learn a way to operate within these multi-faceted, multi-levelled relationships. This seemed to enable deeply problematic dynamics to be transformed in a way that augmented both the dignity of participants and the quality of their understanding of their interactions.

In this portion, Smith's remarks are made within a strong relational framework, interwoven with rich, suggestive materials from the intrapsychic world. Smith again uses the splitting metaphor, only this time he applies it to the group's transformation. In this account we see a more complex version of their interaction, the group being said to split into sadistic and masochistic camps. Smith enlarges our former understanding of the concept of splitting, adding a lamination to Batesonian discourse. We are now entreated to see group behaviours from a 'tribal' or primal group perspective, rather than as individual behaviour in the here and now. Smith suggests that each member is carrying into the group some prior relational form(s), or roles, from other groups. His work as leader then becomes one of shifting the dynamic balances of sadism and masochism within the group to open new possibilities of action. At the same time, Freudian theory is never far from hand. In predicting various individual performances, for example, Smith suggests that people regress in accord with their anxiety levels. Brent's high level of anxiety causes him to regress to his family unit. Group members with lesser anxiety do not regress so far. Again we turn away from relational forms of explanation to a form in which the patterns of overt discourse are merely shadowplays from which the real dynamics can be inferred.

Smith contends that his interpretations are social constructions rather than a right way to think about these relationships. He concludes that the utility of his relational theorising resides in producing desired outcomes - helping the dynamics of the group to be transformed. This emphasis on the pragmatic implications of an explanation fits well into the constructionist/relational realm. Since there are no foundational principles or given grounding values in the constructionist position, it is participants (and others) who create the basis for assessing the processes and outcomes of any interaction. There is also the understanding that any agreed upon interpretations are open to the possibility of continuing and deferred re-interpretation.

The social constructionist approach is also fruitful for questioning the use of the phrase 'to understand'. This appears throughout the paper, and consistently in everyday life. Frequently 'understanding' suggests that one has come upon the right interpretation through a thoughtful examination of the relevant facts. Earlier Smith described how he had attempted three different interpretations of Brent's actions, and had eventually moved in the direction that Brent's reactions suggested might be most acceptable to him. Smith said that he had found a key that worked to unlock the mysteries of Brent's behaviour, at least at that time. One might wonder what social processes produce the sense that a key *fits the lock, or more generally, why some explanations seem to contribute to understanding better than others. One might reframe the question and ask what social conditions prevail that certain understandings are preferred over others. To what extent is this fit between key and context legislated into an authoritative position by the social skills of Brent and Smith? More generally, the question of whether the most acceptably formed interpretation of reality is that which allows the most powerful person (s) in a group to have their goals met is at large.*

Last, I would like to underscore the power of the leader-therapist, consultant-author, which often escapes notice in case study writings. Along with Donald Spense (1982) and Roy Shafer (1981), among others, I would caution that all descriptions and interpretations serve as powerful resources to shape reality within groups (of members and of readers). Smith is clear that the interpretations he gave this group served his desired pedagogic goals. Although his efforts may be well intended, as the facilitator-author of this group, the rhetorical power is his, not theirs or ours, at least in terms of the final interpretive text. Smith's descriptions of his analytical strategies focus primarily on his efforts to create meaning for the group. Seemingly, only Brent's actions blocked him and served to redirect his framing in the early stages of this interaction. This text emphasizes the contested realities of two people. What of the points of view of the other group members? Where do their voices get a space? How can a writer of case studies make room for dissonant, overlapping or cordial versions of what (else) happened? To enlarge the sense-making aspects of relational approaches there needs to be more space for the co-constructing practices of all the group members. Yet, how far can one go in being inclusive? When other voices are added, the orderly aesthetic of one person's presence will become fragmented, even lost. Is that the price one must (un)willingly pay? Even then a suspicion arises that the inclusion of others' voices is a sleight-of-hand, a false inclusion. Ultimately, all these judgments are without foundation, but must be based on other shared codes of meaning, and these can always be contested.

Searching for more inclusive frames

Now both our voices have been expressed; our differences are clear. Gergen's critique is poignant, and I accept the validity of many of her points. Often however her comments prompted my muffled reaction of 'that is not what I meant'! When reflected back by you, Mary, my statements end up sounding different from what I thought I was saying. It is my responsibility to express what I mean. But this underscores how meaning is created in relationship, in the interaction, rather than in the statements.

For us to engage meaningfully, given our differences, we have to find or create a similar frame. It must be a frame that is readily accessible to readers since we are doing this in print. This is very complex for, as Gergen points out, we writers have the rhetorical power. The text is the product of our reality - shaping acts. How then can we enable readers to be authentic copartners in our meaning creation rather than consumers of our products? This question prompts me to explore the following three issues.

First, we come full circle to our initial question: 'what do we mean by relationship?' This kind of circularity may be frustrating and unacceptable when viewed as distance travelled and destination reached - the traditional external verification criteria of science. But for a relationship, meaning has a strong sense of the internal. For it to be rich, relevant parties must experience it as rich. Relationships are interactive and therefore the linear approach contributes little. We may say that the quality of the art form is central; returning to starting points, and charting paths that crisscross like a rich symphonic work, are at the heart of relational theory.

Second, Gergen and I are engaged in a parallel play through of the very content of this paper. We have to create a common frame, a shared meaning system. Coming from such markedly different starting points we have to find or create a way for our ideas to intersect. There are choices to be made. Like Brent and me, we could struggle over whose frame is more right (according to what values?), more elegant (by whose aesthetic?), more inclusive (by what criteria of inclusion/exclusion?) and so on. This is likely to prompt a pointless cycle of conflict as each postures for the inevitable arguments. Or we could choose one of our frames and work exclusively from that vantage point. Or we could attempt to create a meta-frame as an agreeable umbrella that simultaneously preserves our separate frames and helps us to transcend them.

Third, how the above choices are made shapes the relationship we, as authors, have with each other. Is one voice to dominate? Are we to fight or collaborate? Will one voice proclaim while the other simply critiques? Can one perspective accommodate the other to build, as it were, a bilingual perspective?

So, let me turn to my coauthor. Mary, your critique leaves me uncertain how to go on. I confess my hope was that I might learn some new ways to think about relationships from you, some new conceptual doors would open. You point clearly to what limits me. However, I feel I do not have an adequate language for thinking about relationships and I wonder how to get one. I know I am looking for a teacher. Is this a role you would choose with me? I am looking for a fuller set of relational concepts, a broader way of thinking. Do you have a conceptual language that I lack that would enable us all to think about relationships purely in relational terms? Your critique hints that you do, but I can tell neither what those concepts are nor how to use them. Can you help me?

Your lament about lacking a relational language strikes a common chord in me. We are in the early stages of trying to work out what the shape of such a relational language might be. So, if you see yourself as struggling you are in the company of others, including those writing in this book. What might be useful for you is to let go of any commentary about interior or psychic functioning and look instead as if watching a dance. What do you see in the choreography? How is one dancer reacting to the moves of the other(s)? What are the counter moves? Take for instance, the early stages of your interaction with Brent. What other patterns were there in how you interacted with each other that might in some ways have invited those that followed?

That is an interesting issue. I referred to Brent and myself getting caught up in a complex authority dynamic but I said little of what I mean by that. Nor did I present the encounters upon which this conceptualization is based. So I will use this as an example to see what emerges.

To begin, I will give some more contextual detail. How this course was structured stimulated many of the dynamics that unfolded. All potential participants were interviewed three months in advance and were briefed as follows.

> The course is designed to facilitate learning about those all-pervasive dynamics in a group that usually fall out of the field of vision of participants...The class is experiential. Each member belongs to one of two groups that have the task to explore its own dynamics while they are happening. A group usually exists to produce something and the dynamics that evolve support or hinder the achievement of specified goals. Here there is no production task. The central purpose is to explore dynamics usually treated as secondary. Each group rotates working in session with observing each other 'fish bowl' style. The joint experience of participating and observing heightens the learning about these group based patterns. I facilitate each group while it is in session. In this role I do not take the lead. The group as a whole decides its own paths. I merely provide commentary on what I see the group and its members to be both doing and not doing. This course can be intense and members should expect the normal emotional fluctuations of life to be heightened. Therefore it is important to explore whether you are emotionally ready for exchanges at a deep level.

The reader should know that I use these comments as an opener to discuss concerns and to identify those who lack the emotional stability required to handle the demands of such a course. This is important for American campuses where such a course attracts people seeking psychiatric help. Potential participants and I explore together whether they are emotionally equipped to take such a class. Usually if the course is inappropriate the potential participant simply chooses not to register, with no intervention from me.

This briefing removes certain preconceptions and leaves participants with such unfamiliar expectations that the result is considerable ambiguity. Therefore all enter the first experiential group session knowing that they do not know what to expect; understandably, they see me as the author of their confusion. The groups have no predefined activities and there is no one to tell them what to do. As facilitator I take no lead. Members begin with a sense of being lost; together they seek direction. During their early encounters it is usual for some member(s), directly or obliquely, to channel hostility towards me for failing to provide the guidance they feel they need. They talk about having been abandoned or set up.

There is reality to these feelings. This group dynamics tradition is based on the following four points. First, leaders get filled up, so to speak, with what group members knowingly and unknowingly expect of them. Second, the cumulative effect of these shared expectations (which is much larger than the sum of the individual parts) hinders group functioning. Third, it is only as members discover the character of these expectations that the group as a whole learn how to free itself of them and can create more reasonable expectations of itself and its leader(s). Last, the refusal of the facilitator to be the leader creates a vacuum that, as it were, flushes out these mutual, but mostly unacknowledged expectations.

At this point I recognize Mary is probably concerned that I am again talking about hidden stuff. I do not want to divert into that here, but feel that I must explore what I have called a 'complex authority dynamic'. Stated simply, that which I set up, as group organizer, contributed a great deal to what happened in this group. Brent's hostility has to be seen in the context of my actions that, from the outset, put demands on all members to alter certain of their realities. Brent's moves need to be seen as a response to my moves. In addition, how all group members dealt with my lack of leadership, and the attendant clashes over which of the possible paths to follow, influenced Brent profoundly. Early encounters among members become conflictual because there are no guidelines. Members attempt to position themselves with respect to which of the possible directions the group is to take and so create informal coalitions.

It seems risky for members to challenge the facilitator at the outset. When they have, as it were, sorted out the lay of the land, it is common for there to be a significant revolt. This is focused on ridding the group of the facilitator who is experienced as an incompetent leader. This frequently occurs as a critical step in working out if and how they will lead themselves. There is a large literature that refers to the revolt against the leader in groups. (For examples see Bion, 1961; Slater, 1966; and Gibbard, Hartman and Mann, 1974).

In the fish bowl design of this course, Brent was an observer for the first session. So, for the first hour he watched fourteen other class members struggle with each other over what to do in this unstructured setting. They talked circuitously for the whole session on how to deal with each other. The comments I made, all of which were pointing out what they as a group seemed to be doing or not doing, were seen as offering no help during this first session, All, Brent included, saw me as deliberately stirring up trouble, trying to make conflict. This was neither my purpose nor my experience, though I know why I was experienced this way.

As an observer, Brent was keenly examining my actions during this first session and, in his words, was concerned with what 'that group was letting me get away with.' He decided to stop me from doing this to his group. He entered the first session of his group with the posture of a warrior, primed to take on his and other's battles. If no one else would stand up to me, he would. He was not going to wait until his group formed so that they could work out together, whether to ignore me, treat me as a buffoon, revolt against me, or whatever. We have to stop him straight away or it will be too late was Brent's view, and he cast himself in the role of saving the group. However, other members were adopting a variety of ways of joining with their group and were not ready for a revolt; at least not outwardly.

Perhaps it is time to pause, and examine what can be understood here from a relational perspective. Brent is responding to what you have created, which you describe as a conflict filled context. So the conflict he is expressing has a large structural component; it is built into the very architecture of these group experiences. It might be enlightening to remain focused at this level rather than resort to internal dynamics formed early in life to explain what happened, as you were doing earlier.

Twin processes are at play in the early stages of group life. On the one hand, there is the struggle of members to preserve their individuality while becoming a part of the group. On the other there is the struggle of the group to become a whole entity while individuals withhold themselves until the group's character gets formed. For the individual, the issue is how much of oneself to give to the group, but they will not know until the group has formed. So holding back until it is clear what the group is like makes sense. But the crafting of the group's character relies on what the members give to the group. As a result, we have the following conundrum. Each person holds back until the group's character is formed, but that formation does not occur until members start contributing to the group. Thus, the withholding by members makes the group a place where it feels essential to hold back in the first place (Smith and Berg, 1987). Brent's contribution to our clash was presented as his gift to the group. His package was to give the group a chance to become something of their own creation by getting rid of the facilitator, and he was willing to do that for the sake of the group. However, members experienced this as Brent forcing his own agenda on the group. In support of this they noted that Brent never checked with other group members to see if they wanted to throw the facilitator out. They saw Brent as assuming that everyone wanted what he wanted.

In many ways, members voiced the opinion that if they let Brent go on they might all be at war and their shared life would have been totally decided by him. They felt they must not let that happen. To support him would effectively make him the leader and they had no evidence of what kind of leader he would be. He could be worse than the incompetent one (me) he wanted to reject. His warrior stance might result in a militarism that would overwhelm other possible ways of being the group could develop.

From the very beginning Brent's position was untenable, even though many other group members shared many of his views about being rid of me. As in all such situations, it serves many interests to leave the incompetent leadership in place for a period until the group can sort itself out. Then, when the time comes, the very incompetence of the leader will help to galvanize them in seeking an alternative. The actual incompetence of the leader will have served the important role of keeping the leader's seat occupied by a person who is obviously temporary. Although, as facilitator, I do not cast my role as a leader, others always insist on seeing it in this light, for that way it prevents some member prematurely grasping the reins.

The early experiences of such a group always contain a great deal of conflict much of which is masked. There is a violence to both the conflict and the ways it is avoided in these formative processes of collectives. It is this that I was earlier referring to when I used the word 'sadism'. And coming along with the sadism is masochism for these are two concepts that co-define each other. They are opposite sides of the same coin, as are light and dark and hope and hopelessness. As sadism (masochism) emerges in the collective, a countervailing component of masochism (sadism) will be taken up or expressed by others. In this regard, Brent's outbursts that I characterized as sadistic may be seen as simply giving voice to one side of the violence in the group's formative processes and he was the vehicle by which the collective was expressing this facet of its emergent life. Also, through the ways the others were encouraging Brent's aggression to them all, they were expressing the group's masochism, sadism's copartner.

In the above interpretation evidently context is essential in structuring how actors engage. Using the metaphor of dance, context shapes the actions as does the stage a ballet, the ballroom a prom, and the hay filled barn a square-dancing. Further, there are key social props that the context provides that are like the role music plays for dancers. The description offered here spoke of identifiable social patterns rather than invoking invisible intrapsychic explanations located in imagined historical processes that come from one's family of origin. My preference for the social explanation lies in its recognition of meaning as a joint endeavour and action as a product of meaningful interaction.

I am however, intrigued by one further question. Was there anything of a social and interactive nature that might have prompted Brent to be the one to express what you are calling the group's sadism?

Actually there was. For various reasons Brent's entry to the class was different from others. It so happened that he had been a reserve and, as a last minute addition, was never interviewed by me as were all the others. I happened to be out of the country for the weeks just preceding this course and I deputized a colleague to make last minute adjustments to the class membership. The same procedures were followed for Brent as for others, but I was not the person admitting him. Therefore, the beginning of Brent's and my relationship was different from his fellow members. He also felt (he said so later) lucky to get in the class. Feeling 'privileged to be included' (his words) may have created in him heightened expectations compared with the other students. Since Brent had never seen me in any other role than that of facilitator, as had all the others, I may also have been more of an enigma for him.

For my part, I knew much less about Brent than I did about the other participants. In the first session he and I were undoubtedly checking each other out in ways that differed from what was happening with others. We did have this extra dimension to our first encounter. I am also sure he only partially took in my colleague's pre-course briefing about what this class would be like. As a result, there was probably greater incongruence between my behaviour and his expectations than was the case for others. Such background experience, or its lack, might have heightened how we engaged for the first time.

It is useful, I think, to turn to explicit prior experiences for a first suggestion of explanation. These interacts contain the seeds of a different kind of insight, one that is social and interactive, in contrast to the deeper intrapsychic ones that focus on individuals' levels of anxiety. If relational theory remains focused on patterns of social interaction it will, in my view, be more fruitful in a variety of ways than the kind predicated on hidden dynamics.

Having struggled with discussing interactions in concert with Gergen's exhortations, for which I am grateful, I still find myself reluctant to let go of all explorations of inner landscapes, although these might be hard to get at. I know for myself that what happens in my internal life, connected though it is to the outside world of interactions, is the seat of so much of my personal meanings.

Those meanings, while being a product of social processes, are also a co-creator of the processes that come to life in my encounters. I accept that resorting exclusively, or even primarily, to this type of explanation has problems, but might we not lose a lot if we preclude it entirely?

I offer one last experience with Brent that tantalized me and, I suggest, becomes more understandable if inner landscapes are included as legitimate territory for exploration. The experience simply will be described with no further comment from me.

During this semester Brent's maternal grandfather died. This provoked great grief for him that at one point he talked about at length in the group. He highlighted how he felt he had lost his one male role model in life, and he felt devastated. Someone asked if he had a father. His answer was 'Yes! But he and I never got along'. On the last day of semester, Brent came up to me with a very old, tattered photo of his father. He said 'I wanted to show you this because it will help you understand why I reacted to you the way I did. Look at this picture. You and my father look exactly alike'. I was startled; I could see no ways in which Brent's dad and I resembled each other!

There is a spine-tingling quality to this final story. It is a powerful rhetorical appeal to intrapsychic explanations. From a relational standpoint one might look at this story for evidence of how this incident affected the Brent-Smith connection. Comparing Smith to his father might be seen as a move on Brent's part to connect teacher and student more fully, to suggest cause for Brent's misbehaviour or to open means for other responses of Smith towards Brent. The lack of similarity seen by Smith to Brent's father might also be regarded as evidence that he was continuing to evade Brent's efforts to establish further intimate connections, within the realm of relational interpretations. As this example illustrates, multiple explanations are available for any action. Choosing becomes dependent upon matters of preference and training.

Perhaps a way out of the author's dilemma, so aptly configured by Smith, is to take an ironic stance. Irony allows the theorist to take a step back from the interpretative task and recognize the element of selectivity and arbitrariness in any claim to interpretative validity. At this point in the history of psychology, intrapsychic theories have been preeminent in group dynamics work. Yet many see relational theories as a means to develop new forms of understanding. Two authors in search of a convenient paradigm might benefit from taking an ironic stance concerning theory construction. They have the option to respect the direction from which the other comes, rather than having to annihilate the other's position. If ironic reflexivity were to prevail among theorists, holding a position might become less a matter of commitment than a temporary convenience or comfort to be shared. Finding novel discourses that reshape the world can be welcomed without the need to renounce past histories or relationships. I hope our dialogue here has illustrated the potential of this approach.

References

Alderfer, C.P. (1980), 'The methodology of organizational diagnosis', Professional Psychology, ll, pp. 459-468.
Alderfer, C.P. (1986), 'An intergroup perspective on group dynamics', in Lorsch, J. (ed). *Handbook of Organizational Behavior*, Prentice-Hall, Englewood Cliffs.
Alderfer, C.P. & Smith, K.K. (1982), 'Studying intergroup relations embedded in organizations', *Administrative Science Quarterly*, 27 (1), pp. 35-65.
Bateson, G. (1936), *Naven: A Survey of the Problems Suggested by a Composite Picture of the Culture of a New Guinea Tribe Drawn from Three Points of View*, Cambridge University Press, Cambridge.
Bateson, G. (1972), *Steps To An Ecology of Mind*, Bantam, New York.
Berg, D. N. & Smith, K. K. (eds.), *The Self in Social Inquiry*, Sage, Beverly Hills.
Bion, W.R. (1961), *Experiences in Groups*, Tavistock, London.
Bruffee, K.A. (1993), *Collaborative Learning*, Johns Hopkins University Press, Baltimore.
Butler, J. (1990), *Gender Trouble. Feminism and the Subversion of Identity*. Routledge, London.
Gergen, K. J. (1994), *Realities and Relationships: Soundings in Social Constructionism*, Harvard University Press, Cambridge, MA.
Gergen, M. M. (1994), 'Free will and psychotherapy: Complaints of the draughtsmens daughters.' *Journal of Theoretical and Philosophical Psychology*, 14, pp.13-24.
Gibbard, G.S. Hartman, J.J. & Mann, R.D. (eds), (1974), *Analysis of Groups: Contributions to Theory, Research and Practice*, Jossey Bass, San Francisco.
Glaser, B.G. & Strauss, A.L. (1967), *The Discovery of Grounded Theory: Strategies for Qualitative Research*, Aldine, Chicago.
Harre, R. (1986), *The Social Construction of Emotions*, Blackwell, Oxford.
Laing, R.D. (1969), *The Politics of the Family*, Vintage, New York.
Rice, A.K. (1969), 'Individual, group and intergroup processes', *Human Relations*, 22, pp.565-584.
Schafer, R. (1981), 'Narration in the psychoanalytic dialogue,' In Mitchell, W.J. (ed.) *On Narrative*, University of Chicago Press, Chicago.

Shotter, J. (1993), *Cultural Politics of Everyday Life; Social Constructionism, Rhetoric and Knowing of the Third Kind*, University of Toronto Press, Toronto.

Slater, P.E. (1966), *Microcosm*, Wiley, New York.

Smith, K.K. (1990), 'On using the self as instrument: Lessons from a facilitator's experience'. In Gillett, J. and McCollom,M. (eds.) *Groups in Context*, Reading, Addison Wesley.

Smith, K.K. & Berg, D.N. (1987), *Paradoxes of Group Life: Understanding Conflict, Paralysis, and Movement in Group Dynamics*, Jossey Bass, San Francisco.

Spense, D.O. (1982), *Narrative Truth and Historical Truth: Meaning and Interpretation in Psychoanalysis*, Norton, New York.

Sutherland, J.D. (1985), 'Bion revisited: Group dynamics and group psychotherapy,' In Pines, M. (ed.) *Bion and Group Psychotherapy,* Routledge and Kegan Paul, London.

Von Glasserfeld, E. (1984), 'An introduction to radical constructivism', In Watzlawick,P. (ed.) *The Invented Reality,* Norton, New York.

7 The manager as a practical author: A rhetorical-responsive, social constructionist approach to social-organizational problems

John Shotter

Currently, it is said, there is a transition afoot, a movement from modern to postmodern science, a movement which, among its many other features, accepts both a much more chaotic view of reality (or realities), as well as their made nature, a movement with a large number of implications for management studies.

Among many others, the movement involves at least these two major moves: The first is a move away from study of specialized, theoretical or technical knowledge toward the study of a third, more everyday kind of knowledge, knowledge of nonsystematic, practical-moral kind, embedded or situated in the particular human contexts in which we must act. In line with this, the second move is toward warranting our claims to this kind of knowledge rhetorically rather than scientifically. Thus central, is an increased interest in people as knowledgeable, socially accountable agents, concerned to be the authors of their own (socially constructed) individuality or identities. This shift also involves a change in standpoint from the detached, theory-testing spectator, or reader of situations, to the interested, socially involved and responsible actor or author, as well as, a shift from a one-sided process of investigation (in which only investigators are active) to a two-way, negotiated, multisensory interaction or transaction (in which both the investigated and investigators take part), gives rise to an account of rationality quite different from its Enlightenment version.

Taken together, all these changes mean, I think, that in managements studies, we must model the effective manager not upon the scientist, but upon the maker of history, the practical author. And that in the social sciences in general (and management studies in particular), we must give up our search for any overall, grand theory, and think instead of a conceptual repertoire or toolbag of analytic resources. And such a toolbag is what will figure centrally in the critical, social constructionist approach to the management of problems in human organizations that I shall discuss below.

Our topic in this volume is social-organizational theory. And there is no doubt at the moment, that these are turbulent times (Gergen, 1992) both for and in organizational theory, many theories are offered, but few seem adequate or helpful. My comments below will not alter this state of affairs. Indeed, for theory or theories as such, they offer only bad news. For their implication, at least in management studies, is that we should demote theory right to the back room of our thought, leaving it on hand, perhaps, for just an occasional recall, but no more. This is because I want to argue (following Vico, see below) that instead of modelling itself on the natural sciences, with their emphasis upon knowledge of the external world, management studies will fare better if it functions as a humane study, drawing upon the special knowledge we have from within our own being of what it is like to be human. For, by still treating management studies as a science, and by placing our central focus upon theories (even though we have ceased to worry about whether they are true or false, and treat them only as tools of thought), we hide from ourselves our lack of knowledge in at least two spheres of activity, crucial to an understanding of what is involved in the management of organizations.

For instance, we still do not understand the nature of the essential core ability to do with what it is that makes a manager a good manager. Clearly, it is not to do with finding and applying a true or false theory, but something to do with a complex of issues centred on the provision of an intelligible formulation of what has become, for the others in the organization, a chaotic welter of impressions. In this sense, a manager can be seen as a repairer, as someone who is able to restore a routine flow of action that has broken down in some way, to give it an intelligible direction. Thus, rather than as if doing science, managers may best be seen as actually involved in the making history. For, although they must often function (as Marx said in general about people making history) 'under conditions not of their own choosing', good managers, when faced with such unchosen conditions, can, by producing an appropriate formulation of them, create a landscape of enabling/constraints (Giddens, 1980) relevant for a range of next possible actions, a network of moral positions or commitments (understood in terms of the rights and duties of the players on that landscape), and are able to argue persuasively and authoritatively for this landscape amongst those who must work within it. If this is the case, if managers can within their own sphere of influence be seen as making history, then more than just a reader of situations, more than just a repairer of them. perhaps a good manager must be seen as something of an author too.

But they cannot just innovate as they please, for the fact is, not just anything goes, they cannot be authors of fictions, which bear no relation to what the unchosen conditions they face will permit, or afford[1]. Their authoring must be justified or justifiable, and for that to be possible, it must be grounded or rooted in some way in circumstances others share. This leads us to a second crucial sphere of knowledge/activity in which the idea of the manager as a scientist fails us. For in its provision of an abundance of tools for thought and perception, it hides from us its lack of provision of tools relevant to that other important side to any investigatory practice: that of being able to act from within a circumstance, through an instrumental aid, thus to know how further to act within it, the process of feeling one's way forward, so to speak. Indeed, because a theory as such, strictly, is a 3rd-person, external observer, systematic version of events, and is oriented towards influencing those events not from within, but only externally from without, such a theory can often seem to exclude action: thus a sense of being disempowered by one's own analysis is still possible even with the most complex and sophisticated forms of theory. What we need to understand is the nature and functioning of those kind of adjuncts, or (prosthetic) extensions to our organs of sense and action, which, as Polanyi (1958, p.55) puts it, 'are not objects of our attention, but instruments of it', through which we both act and know.

In fact, if we are to understand authorship, what we need, I think, is an account of people's use of language in these terms, an account which emphasizes (above its merely representative function) what might be called its formative power: the ability of people in otherwise vague, or only partially specified, incomplete situations (arising in the joint action between 1st- and 2nd-persons), to give or to lend to such situations a more determinate linguistic formulation (with all the required properties listed above, according to what they sense or feel that the only vaguely specified tendencies in the situation will allow (Shotter, 1984). To refer to a systematic theory when facing a crises in human conduct, is to treat it as like a certain, already well-known state of affairs. While this may seem to help in enabling one to prepare one's reactions ahead of time, in ignoring the precise tendencies in the situation, it may lead to one being surprised by the unexpected. In short, to be justified in their authoring, the good manager must give a sharable linguistic formulation, to already shared feelings, arising out of shared circumstances. In what follows, I shall merely fill in some of the background to this view in order to amplify it further.

Social accountability and rhetoric

Someone who long ago studied these aspects of creative language use, of people coping linguistically with crises or breakdowns in socially coordinating their actions, through the justified authoring of new linguistically mediated coordinations, was C. Wright Mills (1940) in a paper he very aptly entitled 'situated actions and vocabularies of motive'. As he saw it, all human conduct took place in socially constructed, evaluative contexts, in which the others in one's social group have a right to judge whether one's conduct is fitting or not, whether it really is directed towards the shared aims (or motives) of the group or organization. Hence, if one's actions are thought puzzling or unintelligible, or perhaps illegitimate in any way, and the routine responsiveness between oneself and others breaks down, then the others have a right to intervene to question one's behaviour. One may then justify one's conduct, Mills, suggests, by telling them of its motive, or better, by the use of motive-talk. For, motives are, he says,

> imputed or avowed as answers to questions (mostly from others, but also perhaps from oneself) interrupting acts or programs. Motives are words. Generically, to what do they refer? They do not denote any elements in individuals. They stand for anticipated situational consequences of questioned conduct (Mills, 1940, p.904).

They indicate what, in the circumstances, one is trying to do in one's actions.

Why I think Mills's paper is so important, is that he emphasizes the need for an 'analysis of the integrating, controlling, and specifying functions a certain type of speech fulfils in socially situated actions' (Mills, 1940, p.904). Indeed, his approach leads to a quite new appreciation of the primary function of language. In his view, the primary function of various forms of communication is not the representation of things in the world, nor the giving of outer expression to already well-formed inner thoughts, but consists in the creation and maintenance of various patterns of social relations. For, to use a language is to relate oneself to others in some way, and in so doing to determine (in that context) the psychological character both of oneself and of those others. If, in our experience, it seems undeniable that at least some words do in fact stand in our reality for things, then in this view, they only do so from within a form of social life already constituted by the ways of talking in which such words are used. As he put it right at the beginning of his article (Mills, 1940, p.903):

> The postulate underlying modern study of language is the simple one that we must approach linguistic behaviour, not by referring it to private states in individuals, but by observing its social function in coordinating diverse action.

And, to repeat, at different times and in different places, the dominant groups in a society make sense of questioned conduct in terms of different particular vocabularies of motives, or official forms of talk.

An important implication of this view here, is that we cannot always just speak and act as we please, but that often we must act into a jointly constructed, organized, moral (or better, moralistic) setting, containing amongst others, certain powerful (and authoritative) groups and individuals, managers, for instance, must persuade not only their professional equals but also their bosses. Indeed, should managers do anything these others judge to be inappropriate in some way, they run the risk of being sanctioned by them - unless, that is, they can provide them with a justificatory account of their behaviour. Thus what is at issue here, is not a matter of whether what we say corresponds with the world in some way, but of whether we can, solely through the use of currently accepted ways of making sense, persuade the others around us (as well as ourselves) to coordinate their actions amongst themselves in a certain way, a way which assumes the world to have or to be capable of taking on a certain form, that it is as we say it is, in our talk. It is the persuasive rather than the logical nature of our thought and talk which is crucial in achieving this goal.

So, if we now turn to this persuasive aspect of thought, it is relevant to mention Billig's (1987) work. It is he more than anybody, who in his rhetorical approach to social psychology has shown why we must take the argumentative and responsive nature of thinking seriously. He has discussed the problem-solving approach to the nature of thought, and although he does not think that it is wrong, he does think that it offers a very narrow, unflattering, and especially, 'a one-sided image, in which thinking has become reduced to the unthinking operations of a filing-clerk' (Billig, 1987, p.129); it draws upon a bureaucratic model of thought. But, he points out, even bureaucrats, never mind ordinary people in everyday life, 'rather than being unimaginative rule-followers, ... are often rule-benders and even rule-creators as well. As they fight their inter-departmental battles, bureaucrats need to show all the skills of witchcraft' (Billig, 1987, p.129). It is to degrade even the intelligence of bureaucrats, to think that they need no appreciation of their circumstances in applying their skills aright.

It is this new emphasis upon the rhetorical, situated, two-sided, socially responsive, nature of processes of thought, and especially their conduct within an argumentative context of justification and criticism, introduced by Billig, which I want to explore further below. It will reveal why the idea of thinking as problem-solving fails to capture the nature of those circumstances in which we act, not with conviction (according to principles), but by being persuaded (by good reasons), where, to quote Perelman and Olbrechts-Tyteca (1969, p.28), we can 'apply the term persuasive to argumentation that only claims validity for a particular audience, and the term convincing to argumentation that presumes to gain the adherence of every rational being.' The nuance here may seem slight, but it is crucial; it is the difference between the claim that one's conclusions are valid irrespective of the context of their application, and the appreciation that, although not universally valid, they can still be justified, to persons of a particular kind, within their situation.

Difficulties with the image of the manager as scientist

The outline I have provided above, of some of the problems raised by training managers to orient themselves towards business problems as if they are scientific problems, is not new. These problems were all, for instance, outlined in Giambattista Vico's 1708 oration called 'On the study methods of our time', in which he attacked the introduction of the new geometric methods of the Cartesians into the universities. Vico was a professor of rhetoric, then understood as the art of arguing, in an essentially indeterminate situation, as to which course of action, amongst those it affords, it is best in the situation to follow, and he was concerned that 'the greatest disadvantage of our (new) method of study is that, in expending so much effort on the natural sciences, we neglect ethics, and in particular that part which deals with the nature of the human mind, its passions, and how they are related to civil life and eloquence' (Pompa, 1982, p.41). With this in mind, let me first examine some the difficulties raised by the image of the manager as a scientist using theories, as his or her main operational tool, making use of Gareth Morgan's account as a stalking horse, thus later to cite some of Vico's comments against the background of difficulties with Morgan's views.

Although theory is central in any scientific approach to problems, the crucial move outside of science, is the putting of theory into practice. This is, so to speak, where the gap lies; this is where the relation between an experimentally proved theory and reality is still not obvious. If we turn to one of the most successful books in this area at the moment, Gareth Morgan's (1986) 'Images of Organizations', we find two new trends in attitudes to theory evidenced: One is the offering of a whole range of possible theoretical structures as throwing light on the nature of organizations, organizations as machines; as 'organisms'; as 'brains'; as 'cultures'; as 'political systems'; as 'psychic prisons'; as 'unfolding, holographic, implicate orders'; as 'instruments of domination', with an explicit attempt to face the task of dealing with organizations as activities rather than as things, as developmental processes rather than as final products, with them as partiality and indeterminate tendencies rather than as exhibiting the operation of predetermined functions, and so on.

The other trend, is the offering of these possible structures, these images, not within the classical context for the presentation of scientific theories, in which evidence is presented for the truth of just one of these theories as corresponding with reality, but of them all as tools or aids to reading within the overarching metaphor of the organization as a text. Morgan takes this approach to the problem because, as he sees it, the problem of understanding organization is difficult in that 'we do not really know what organizations are, in the sense of having a single authoritative position from which they can be viewed ... the reality is that we are all like blind men and women groping to understand the nature of the beast' (p.341), hence the multiplicity of the aids he offers. For, 'effective managers and professionals in all walks of life, whether they be business executives, public administrators, organizational consultants, politicians, or trade unionists, have to become skilled in the art of reading the situations that they are attempting to organize or manage' (p.11).

Unlike his supposedly more pure social scientific colleagues, Morgan can take this more pragmatic stance towards theory as, after all, his task is not that of training of scientists, but of effective[2] managers and professionals. And there is no doubt that dissatisfaction with a science-based approach to professional and managerial training is rife. For instance, as is well-known, we have Schön (1983, p.vii) suggesting in his book on the reflective practitioner, that

> universities are not committed to the production and distribution of fundamental knowledge in general. They are institutions committed, for the most part, to a particular epistemology, a view of knowledge that fosters selective inattention to practical competence and professional artistry.

And as Schön sees it, that particular (inappropriate) epistemology, 'technical rationality' as he calls it, involves approaching socio-practical problems as requiring the application of a science, the putting of a theory into practice, the learning of a certain limited set of conceptual frameworks for the solving of problems. Whereas, as he sees it, the problems faced by practitioners are of quite a different kind from those faced by the solitary thinker, attempting to choose between complex alternatives for the solution of a problem; it requires a skill, not of problem-solving, but of 'problem-setting':

> the process by which (corporately) we define the decision to be made, the ends to be achieved, the means which may be chosen ... Problem-setting is a process in which, interactively (along with everyone who must solve it), we name the things to which we will attend and frame the context in which we will attend to them (p.40).

Thus the task not one of choosing but of generating, of generating a clear and adequate formulation of what the problem situation is, of creating from a set of incoherent and disorderly events a coherent structure within which both current actualities and further possibilities can be given an intelligible place, and of doing all this, not alone, but in continual conversation with all the others who are involved. As a character, the manager is clearly very different from that of the scientist, and clearly requires a very different kind of education.

Now, as I have already mentioned above, someone who foresaw the nature of these problems very clearly, and who spoke against the modelling all of a university's study methods upon those of science, was Giambattista Vico. Besides speaking out on the many dangers to do with failing to grasp the proper nature of the relation between our knowledge, our theories, and our actions, and the fact that we can only be said fully to know a thing, if we know how human beings came to make it as is, his verum-factum principle, to which I will return to in a moment, Vico also spoke out, in a way which might almost sound sacrilegious, against the single-minded search for truth in the following terms:

> Since the sole aim of study today is truth, we investigate the nature of things, because this seems certain, but not the nature of men, because free will makes this seem extremely uncertain. This method of study gives rise to the following disadvantages for young men: that later they neither engage in public life with enough wisdom, nor know sufficiently well how to imbue oratory with morality and inflame it with feeling. With regard to prudence in public life, we should remember that the mistresses of human affairs are opportunity and choice, which are extremely uncertain, being governed for the most part by simulation and dissimulation, which are both extremely deceptive. Thus those whose only concern is truth find it difficult to attains the means, and even more the ends, of public life. More often than not they give up, frustrated in their own plans, and deceived by those of others. We assess what to do life in accordance with those passing moments and details of things which we call circumstances (Pompa, 1982, pp.41-42).

For, in Vico's terms, the knowledge we need in dealing with those passing moments we call circumstances is not knowledge formulated in terms of systematic and fixed principles, but practical wisdom, where clearly, and I want to go into this in more detail in a moment, compared with the kinds of knowledge of which we are all familiar, this is a distinct kind of knowledge, *sui generis*.

It does not seem to be a decontextualized theoretical or factual knowledge (a 'knowing that' in Ryle's (1949) terminology), for it is unformulated knowledge and we are unaware of possessing except in a practical context; but it is not the knowledge of a technical skill or craft (a 'knowing how'), for we cannot acquire it when acting all alone, as individuals. It is a separate, special kind of knowledge which one acquires only from within a social group, an institution or society; rather than a knowing that, or knowing how, we might call it a 'knowing from'. A special contextualized form of knowing, a knowing of a third kind which takes into account (and is only accountable within) the social situation within which it is known. Thus, says Vico (in terms which might seem to anticipate Foucault), the difference between the imprudent academic and the wise man is this:

> The imprudent academic, who moves from a universal truth straight to particular truths, uses force to make his way through the maze of life. While the wise man, keeping his eyes on eternal truth amid the turnings and uncertainties of life, follows an indirect route because straight ones are impossible, and prepares plans which will be successful in the long term, as far as the nature of things allows (p.43).

Imprudent academics must use force because they act in accordance with how circumstances ought to be, according to their theories, rather than in accordance to what they actually are. But what is their nature, what are human circumstances, and in particular, the circumstances within organizations, like?

Images and contests: realism and constructionism

Given what has been said so far, it is now clear that there are two distinct ways in which we might attempt to answer this question: 1) We may still, like scientists, like uninvolved, third-person, external observers, attempt to produce a theory which fits or mirrors them [the circumstances] in order to manipulate them by manipulating their surrounding conditions. Or, we might approach the problem in a very different manner: 2) as like ordinary, everyday first or second-persons involved in them, not trying to mirror or to picture them, nor by trying to say in what ways they are like something already familiar to us, but by trying to make ourselves reflexively self-aware of the ordinary, everyday activities and practices by which we normally succeed in conducting our affairs successfully, in order to sustain such conduct in a knowledgeable manner. These two approaches are very different in many ways, and I shall run through a catalogue of differences in just a moment.

But let me straight away bring out one fundamental aspect in which they are markedly different: In everyday life, much of what we talk about has a contested nature, that is, our talk is not about something which already actually exists, but is about what might be, what could be the case, or what something should be like. To take some rather grand but obvious examples: In our arguments about the nature of democracy, society, the person, the individual, the citizen, and many other essentially political concepts, we cannot assume that we all already know perfectly well what the 'it' is that is represented by the concepts we are arguing about. Political objects such as these are not already out there in some primordial naturalistic sense before our talk about them; we make them make sense in the course of our arguments about them. They are, in W. B. Gallie's (1955) sense of the term, 'essentially contested concepts,' that is, they are concepts whose proper clarification gives rise to endless disputes, philosophically. In other words, by their very nature, they are not amenable to resolution simply in empirical or theoretical terms; all proposed clarifications of such concepts, to the extent that they can only be persuasive rather than proved, are themselves a part of the practical politics of everyday life. The same is the case, I suggest, about many less grand but much more common notions about which we argue; for instance, the concept of our situation here and now, or our concept of our organization. In other words, the fundamental aspect in which the two different approaches markedly differ is in whether one takes a realist or social constructionist stance towards the problem here in hand, and in my estimation, the realist stance although empowering in some ways (for individual managers) is disempowering in others (for organizations as a whole).

That is, if mangers still think of themselves as like scientists, and take a realist attitude, they will talk as Morgan (1986) does of the difficulties they face as arising out of 'the fact that the complexity and sophistication of our thinking does not match the complexity and sophistication of the realities with which we have to deal' (p.339). So, although they may accept that 'any realistic approach to organizational analysis must start from the premise that organizations can be many things at one and the same time' (p.321), in an attempt to increase the sophistication of their thinking, the fact must still be that 'we can see certain metaphors fitting certain situations better than others' (p.342). Thus, no matter how fluid and flexible this approach may become, by the adoption of images taken from Bohm's (1980) notions of an implicate order, or Maturana and Varela's (1980) of autopoiesis, or Taoist or Marxian logics of dialectical change, the fact is that the manager is still cast in the passive role of someone who, before he or she can do anything, must first find out something, i.e., as someone who must first think in order to do. As Morgan (1986, p.322) puts it: their first step is to produce a diagnostic reading (using different metaphors to identify aspects of the current situation), while their second step is to make a critical evaluation (of the usefulness of competing diagnoses), an evaluation which ultimately involves that mysterious ability of making, he says, a judgement of the situation at hand.

Now, it is not just that this, as I have already said, leaves the nature of the crucial core ability, of what it is that makes a manager a good manager, hidden, but among the abundance of tools for thought and perception it provides, it also hides the loss of the opportunity actively to enter into the shaping of one's own circumstances. Indeed, as Morgan realizes (p.266), a sense of being disempowered by one's own analysis is still possible. For, even if we understand our lives in a complex and sophisticated way, as determined by the logic of unfolding oppositions, for instance, the fact is, we can still experience our everyday lives as

> ... shaped by forces over which we have little control. (Thus) a manager may feel that he or she has no option but to follow the rules of the market and general environment in shaping corporate policy. (Or) a worker may feel that job opportunities and career prospects are predetermined by his or her eduction or social background. (Where) in each case, the logic of the system or the environment is seen as being in the driving seat.

That is, we will experience it in this way if we continue to adopt a passive attitude to social reality.

However, if we adopt a more active attitude, we can attempt to reframe the tensions and oppositions underlying the forces shaping the system, and thereby influence their direction. Thus,

> Dialectical analysis has major implications for the practice of social and organizational change. It invites us to think of ways in which oppositions ... can be reframed so that the energies generated by traditional tensions are expressed in a new way. Dialectical analysis thus shows us that the management of organization, of society, and of personal life ultimately involves the management of contradiction (p.266).

Well yes, I could not agree more. But Morgan having seen that this is a problem, what is the solution he offers? He merely offers improved reading skills. For, as he sees it, theory is still crucial because, even though he has already said that organizations can be many things at one and the same time, he feels that 'practice is never theory-free, for it is always guided by an image of what one is trying to do' (p.336), thus as he sees it, the 'people who learn to read situations from different (theoretical points of view) have an advantage over those committed to a fixed position. For they are better able to recognize the limitations of a given perspective' (p.337). And indeed they do have an advantage. But as mere readers, they do not have an advantage over those who know also how to function as authors. Those who do not feel themselves bound to live according to any particular, already existing, well-formed images, but are able, so to speak, to get in 'touch' with the vague 'feelings of tendency' (James, 1890) within themselves to which their circumstances give rise, are much more free to lend or to give such tendencies an intelligible expression of their own choosing, thus to become more the authors of their own lives.

Written texts

Our task, then, is to try to construct an account of what it is like to act, not like a Cartesian scientist who first observes, in order next to plan, who then acts according to the plan, thus next to observe, and so on, but like an ordinary person who is able, in the course of acting, to be aware of what is currently occurring, and the degree of their own responsibility for it, thus to use that awareness to inform their own further conduct in the situation. In other words, I want to explore further the nature of the third kind of knowledge I mentioned above - that special, contextualized form of knowing which only comes into being in the course of acting from within the social situation within which it is known.

Before undertaking this exploration, however, it is necessary to add that in discussing the nature of this form of knowledge philosophically, i.e., solely within a textual context, within a systematic written text, unrelated to any particular practical context of action, we must be aware (as in fact Morgan warns), of the already established images, hidden in our already, professionally established ways of writing about these problems. Indeed, central to the different perspective I want to formulate, is this claim of Rorty's (1980, p.12), similar to Morgan's, that: 'It is pictures rather than propositions, metaphors rather than statements, which determine most of our philosophical convictions.' Such hidden images occur, because theorists, in attempting to represent the open, vague, and temporally changing nature of the world as closed, well-defined, and orderly, make use of certain textual and rhetorical strategies to construct within their text a closed, systematic set of intralinguistic references. And in moving from an ordinary conversational use of language to the construction of a systematic texts, there is transition from a reliance on particular, practical, and unique meanings, negotiated on the spot with reference to the immediate context, to a reliance upon links with a certain body of already determined meanings, a body of special, interpretative resources into which the properly trained professional reader has been educated in making sense of such texts. Being able to make reference to already determined meanings, thus allows a decrease of reference to what is and a consequent increase of reference to what might be. One must then develop methods for warranting in the course of one's talk, one's claims about what might be as being what is. It is by the use of such methods, that those with competence in such procedures can construct their statements as factual statements, and claim authority for them as revealing a special true reality behind appearances, without any reference to the everyday context of their claims (see

Dreyfus & Rabinow, 1982, p.48).

This reliance in textual communication upon intertextuality, the drawing upon people's knowledge of a certain body of already formulated meanings in the making of its meanings, is not the case in ordinary conversation. Indeed, as Garfinkel (1967) points out, in ordinary conversation people refuse to permit each other to understand what they are talking about in this way. A meaning unique and appropriate to the situation and to the people in it is required. But that is not easy to negotiate. Thus, what precisely is being talked about in a conversation, as we all in fact know from our own experience, is often at many points in the conversation necessarily unclear; we must offer each other opportunities to contribute to the making of agreed meanings. Thus, only gradually do we come to an understanding (and even then it is often limited just to matters in hand, so to speak). As Garfinkel (1967, p.40) says about such understandings are developed, and developing, within the course of the action; indeed, to quote him, they are only known by both parties 'from within this development ...', making use of the third kind of knowledge I have already called above a knowing from. Ignoring it, leads us to ignore not only the unique nature of situations, but also, the unique nature of the people within them, we treat them, in Garfinkel's terms, as if they are 'cultural dopes'. We can thus begin to see why, when Garfinkel had his students try to talk as if words should have already determined clear meanings, it produced a morally motivated anger in the student's victims. People felt that in some way their rights had been transgressed, and as Garfinkel shows, they had!

What should we say then about the nature of words and their meanings, if we are not to see them as having already determined meanings? Perhaps, rather than already having a meaning, we should see the use of a word as a means (but only as one means among many others) in the social making of a meaning. Thus then, the making sense, the production of a meaning, would not be a simple one-pass matter of an individual saying a sentence, but would be a complex back-and-forth process of negotiation between speaker and hearer, involving tests and assumptions, the use of the present context, the waiting for something later to make clear what was meant before, and the use of many other seen but unnoticed background features of everyday scenes, all deployed according to agreed practices or methods. These are in fact the properties Garfinkel claims of ordinary conversational talk. And as he says (1967, pp.41-42):

> People require these properties of discourse as conditions under which they are themselves entitled and entitle others to claim that they know what they are talking about, and that what they are saying is understandable and ought to be understood. In short, their seen but unnoticed presence is used to entitle persons to conduct their common conversational affairs without

interference. Departures from such usages call forth immediate attempts to restore a right state of affairs.

Moral sanctions follow such transgressions. Thus, to insist words have predetermined meanings is to rob people of their rights to their own individuality. But even more than this is involved: it is to deprive one's culture of those conversational occasions in which people's individuality is constituted and reproduced. It is also to substitute the authority of professional texts in warranting claims to truth (on the basis as we now see of the unwarranted claim that they give us access to an independent, extralinguistic reality), for the good reasons we ordinarily give one another in our more informal conversations and debates.

Two changes in our image of the nature of knowledge

If we are to understand how to live, not according to the already existing, well-formed images in our texts, but, so to speak, according to the vague feelings of tendency we can sense within ourselves to which our circumstances give rise, then we must construct an account of what it is like to act as an ordinary person who is able, in the course of acting, to be aware of what is currently occurring, thus to use that awareness to inform their own further conduct in the situation. An understanding of its nature requires, I think, at least two changes in our current attitudes towards the nature of knowledge: one involves a movement from the form of knowledge acquired by observation to that acquired through feeling; the other, a movement from knowledge acquired by finding to that acquired by making.

Psychological instruments: prostheses and indicators

In exploring the relational nature of knowing-from, as I have called it, the first change of perspective that I would like to introduce is that, instead of the image of the mind as a (passive) mirror of nature; of knowledge as accuracy of representation; and thus of the knower as being like a scientist cast in the role of an external observer, I want to substitute another set of images: The image of the knower as being

a   as if one of a community of blind persons exploring their surroundings by the use of sticks or through other such instruments;
b   of the knowledge important to them as being to do with them knowing their way around in ways communicable between them; and

c   of the mind as actively making sense of the relatively invariant (Bohm, 1965; Gibson, 1979) features they discover in their instrument-assisted explorations of their surroundings, a shift from knowing by looking at to knowing by being in instrumentally-aided contact, or in touch with.

Indeed, I want to argue that it is only in terms of activities like these, that the kinds of knowledge we possess and make use of in conducting our everyday affairs are possible.

But such instruments or devices may have for us both a prosthetic and/or an indicative function: they may be like the blind person's stick, for use in actively investigating our situation in ways which would otherwise be inaccessible to us; or, they may be like the pointers on dials, indicating some remote state of the world.

Prosthetic devices, we might say, reside on the side of the agent, we may come to 'dwell in' them (Polanyi, 1958), and learn how to embody them as an instrumental means through which to achieve our ends. As such, they do not have any content in themselves, but become transparent, blind people do not feel their sticks vibrating in the palms of their hands, nor do they have to infer as if solving a problem that the terrain ahead of them is rough; they experience it directly as rough, as a result of their stick-assisted way of investigating it in their movement through it. Furthermore, the knowledge they obtain in that way can be complete and not fragmentary, for any gaps in it can be further investigated. In a similar way, by acting prosthetically through our words, e.g., in telling or asking things of other people, we can actively discover things about them. As Polanyi (1958, pp.55-57) describes it, we attend in such activities from ongoing and changing 'subsidiary awarenesses' to a 'focal awareness' of their organized result, there is a movement from a knowing how to a knowing what. It is only when the flow of activity mediated by such instruments breaks down or is otherwise interrupted in some way, a tool is damaged (to use Heidegger's example), or there is no connection between our activity and the state of the instrument, that we become aware of them as instruments as such. They become unsuitable for use as ready-to-hand equipment, and become conspicuous as 'present-to-hand' things or objects (Heidegger, 1967, pp.102-103), i.e., from being transparent they become opaque, but they may still function then in an indicatory mode.

In their indicative function such devices may be said to be on the side of world, and we confront them as having a meaning which we must interpret. In this mode, they do have a content: they indicate a state of the world. But it must be constructed from the fragmentary, incomplete data they provide, and, as the misinterpretation of the instruments in the Three-Mile Island nuclear power station disaster illustrates, if the hook up between the instrument and the world is not as it should be, that interpretation can be wrong. Again, we may say that a from-to structure of sense-making is involved, but now, in attending from the fragments of data provided to an overall organized resultant, it is not open to us to investigate the world by their use further to fill in any gaps - indicators are not prostheses; imagination is required to achieve coherency. With prostheses, we are in an embodiment relation to them, while with indicators our relationship to them is an hermeneutical one: and obviously, it is that relation to our language which is most salient to us. And it is from the fragmentary data provided to us in our surroundings, when we stop to reflect upon them, that we construct a new artificial or imaginary context for our activities.

The hermeneutical stance, however, hides from us the equally important prosthetic relation: for mostly, we see through the language we use and are unaware of its prosthetic functioning. Only when the flow of activity between ourselves and or interlocutors breaks down, do we find ourselves confronted, so to speak, by just our utterances: to restart the flow, to clarify their meaning, they then seem to require interpretation - hence the apparent primacy of an hermeneutical account of language. But interpretation in that sense is not required as long as the flow is maintained. One's words are a transparent means through which one can achieve a sensible contact with those around one. Thus clearly, language possesses what one might call a tool/text ambiguity: for as each utterance is used prosthetically in its saying to move another person and thus to reveal in those movements something of their character, so what one has said remains on hand (to use another Heideggerian term) as a text, constituting an aspect of the situation between oneself and one's interlocutor.

Finding and making

In the hermeneutical account of knowing described above, the development of one's knowledge, from the vague feelings of tendency we can sense within ourselves (to which our circumstances give rise) to the formulation of an intelligible account of them, is quite unlike any so far discussed in the empirical tradition: It is not a process of induction (for it does not depend upon the discovery of any regularities), nor is it one of inference (for the unique and particular nature of circumstances cannot be understood by assimilating their details to any already established theoretical categories and premises). As each part of the description is supplied, a conceptual whole has to be fashioned to accommodate it. Mentally, we have to construct a context (a world) into which it can fit and play its part, where each new fact points to or indicates a reality in which they all have their place or function. And the hermeneutical process continues as each new fact is added to the account: the whole must be progressively transformed and articulated, metamorphosed in fact, in a two-way, back-and-forth process, in such a way as to afford all the parts of the whole an undistorted accommodation. In this form of knowing, then, a process of making or construction is at work.

But it is not a completely unrestricted process of construction, for a two-way, interactive mode of construction, constrained by an investigation of the possibilities already available in the situation, is involved. Thus it is not a wholly predetermined form of making (preformationism), nor is it merely the finding of a predetermined order (causal necessity), but a making constrained by an order of possibilities; a process which must oscillate between making and finding. Thus, instead of thinking of our task as that of finding an order in things, ready-made, we must consider activities which begin with vague, but not wholly unspecified tendencies which are then open to, or which permit a degree of actual further specification. Further: instead of thinking it possible for special individuals trained in special methods simply to make discoveries, any further specifications of states of affairs, if they are to be considered intelligible and legitimate to those around us, must be negotiated in a back-and-forth process with them. In other words, we must now think in terms of processes of investigation involving both finding and making.

Indeed, with respect to our powers of making, Vico came to believe that they gave us a special access into the nature of human beings. For what ever the instrumental powers the natural sciences provided, there is a sense, Vico thought, in which we can know more about our own and other people's experiences and actions, in which we acted as participants, indeed as authors, and not as mere observers, than we can ever know about non-human nature which we only observe from the outside. This is his verum-factum principle. Thus he reversed the degree of certainty that one could expect from humane studies compared with the natural sciences, claiming that certainty was more possible in the science of history (as he conceived it) than in physics, because while we may have made its mathematical theories, we have not made its substance, and thus cannot know the physical world *per causas*, i.e., not merely that it is, but what it is, and how it came to be such. 'For to know is to grasp the genus or form by which a thing is made, whereas consciousness is of those things whose genus or form we cannot demonstrate' (Vico in Pompa, 1982, p.58).

> (Thus) history cannot be more certain than when he who creates the things also narrates them. Now, as geometry, when it constructs the world of quantity out of its elements, or contemplates that world, is creating it for itself, just so does our Science (create for itself the world of nations), but

with a reality greater by just so much as the institutions having to do with human affairs are more real than points, lines, surfaces, and figures are. (Vico, 1948, para. 349)

Vico's claim here, that in essence logical necessity only because logic is a free creation of the mind, is reminiscent of Einstein's well known statement: 'Insofar as the propositions of mathematics give an account of reality they are not certain; and insofar as they are certain they do not describe reality'.

I have tried to include the main aspects of the two-way process of making and finding involved in formulating and fitting an account to circumstances in Figure 7.1 below:

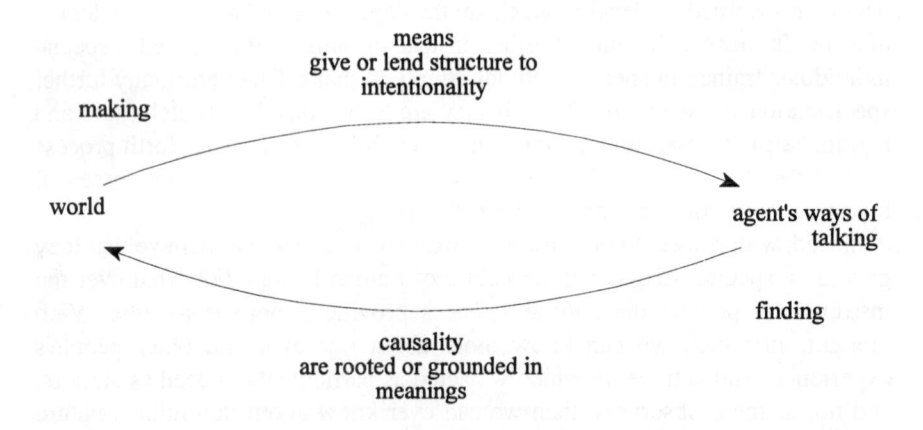

```
                    means
              give or lend structure to
                 intentionality
    making
                                              ─────────▶
    world                                         agent's ways of
                                                       talking
              ◀─────────
                                                     finding
                    causality
              are rooted or grounded in
                    meanings
```

Figure 7.1 Processes of making and finding

To adapt the useful direction of fit terminology introduced by Searle (1983), what this shows (bottom limb) is that in the world-to-agent direction of fit, as in classical empiricist approaches, we could say (i.e., the facts will afford us saying) that our ways of talking depend upon the world; they are rooted or grounded in its nature: To that extent our talk is about what we find to be there. But on the other hand (top limb), in line with hermeneutical or interpretive views, in the agent-to-world direction of fit, it is equally true to say that what we take the nature of the world to be depends upon our ways of talking about it: To the extent that they give or lend its otherwise open nature a determinate (and legitimate) structure and significance, its significance for us is as we make it to be.

Thus the fact is, not only can one make both of these claims, but one must assert that both are true. Indeed, as Derrida (1976) would point out, they owe their distinct existences to their interdependency; one claim is an absent-presence in lending intelligibility to the other. Thus although one should say only what the facts will permit, the nature of the facts here are such that, although they draw upon different systematic discourses for their representation, two equal and opposite truths can, and must, be asserted. And this, of course, is precisely what Billig (1987) is now arguing in relating the importance of rhetoric and the two-sidedness of human thinking generally.

Bakhtin's theory of the utterance

Within the confines of this single chapter, there is insufficient space to take these investigations much further. But it is relevant to mention that no fully adequate account of conversation should ignore Bakhtin's (1986) account of the nature of utterances (as opposed to sentences). In opposition to such linguists as Chomsky and his followers (who in turn followed de Saussure), Bakhtin claims that the utterance not the syntactical sentence should be treated as the real unit of conversation, in the sense that it marks out the boundaries in the speech flow between different voices. This is not the case with sentences: '... the boundaries of the sentence as a unit of language are never determined by a change of speaking subjects' (Bakhtin, 1986, p.72). 'The first and foremost criterion for the finalization of an utterance is the possibility of responding to it or, more precisely and broadly, of assuming a responsive attitude to it (for example, executing an order)' (Bakhtin, 1986, p.76). The trouble with the sentence is that it has no capacity to determine directly the responsive position of the other speaker. The sentence as a language unit is only grammatical, not ethical in nature' (Bakhtin, 1986, p.74).

An actual utterance must take into account the (already linguistically shaped) context into which it is directed. Thus for Bakhtin:

> Any concrete utterance is a link in the chain of speech communication of a particular sphere. The very boundaries of the utterance are determined by a change of speech subjects. Utterances are not indifferent to one another, and are not self-sufficient; they are aware of and mutually reflect one another ... Every utterance must be regarded as primarily a response to preceding utterances of the given sphere (we understand the word response here in the broadest sense). Each utterance refutes, affirms, supplements, and relies upon the others, presupposes them to be known, and somehow takes them into account ... Therefore, each kind of utterance is filled with various kinds of responsive reactions to other utterances of the given sphere of speech communication (Bakhtin, 1986, p.91).

Listening too must be responsive, in that listeners must be preparing themselves to respond to what they are hearing. Indeed,

> the speaker does not expect passive understanding that, so to speak, only duplicates his or her own idea in someone else's mind (as in Saussure's model of linguistic communication mentioned above). Rather, the speaker talks with an expectation of a response, agreement, sympathy, objection, execution, and so forth (with various speech genres presupposing various integral orientations and speech plans on the part of speakers or writers) (Bakhtin, 1986, p.69).

Where what is constituted in the use of a particular speech genre is, among many other aspects of an ongoing social world, a particular set of interdependently related, but continually changing speech positions. They allow on the one hand the use of various voices, in which we are answerable for our position, and on the other, permit speakers certain forms of addressivity, aimed at certain addressees. It is in their allowing and permitting of some speech forms and their sanctioning of others, that organizations and institutions constituted by particular speech genres are repaired and maintained. For example, as a manager, I may speak with the voice of the company, my section, as myself, as a customer, a government inspector, an administrator, and so on, each voice answering for a position within a particular speech genre. Where the point to emphasize is how, in the never ending flow of communication in which this form of life is sustained, every utterance is a rejoinder in some way to previous utterances.

Concluding comments

I began this article by claiming that the essential core ability to do with what it is that makes a manager a good manager, was not to do with finding and applying true or false theories, i.e., being able to read the situation they must manage for the images which are hidden in them somewhere, but was to do with a complex of issues centred on the provision of intelligible formulations of what, for the others in the organization, had broken down into a chaotic welter of impressions. Their task in such situations is to give a shared or sharable significance to the already shared, but vague feelings of tendency, arising out of the circumstances in question shared amongst those in the organization, thus to restore a flow of action that had become unintelligible in some way. Thus essentially, the good manager, I wanted to suggest, should be seen doubly, not as if involved in doing science, but as actually involved in the practical making history, thus besides being a reader, or a repairer, a good manager should also be something of an author too. But not as an author of texts, but a practical-ethical author, a conversational author, able to argue persuasively for a landscape of next possible actions, upon which the positions of all those who must take part are clear.

This claim essentially implies another: that an important aspect of management studies should not been seen as a science, but should be seen as an aspect of what traditionally is known as humane studies. Elsewhere, I have argued for the discipline of psychology to be seen in these terms (Shotter, 1984). Thus, rather than an empirical-explanatory science working in terms of theories, I have talked of it as a practical-descriptive, one working in terms of instructive accounts, i.e., as providing prosthetic (as well as indicative) aids to thought, perception, and action in this sphere: in which making (or practical authoring) is at least if not more important than finding. In attempting to give an instructive account of the nature of the knowledge involved in this skill, the third kind of knowledge from within (or embedded within) circumstances of which Vico talked was emphasized, thus I have not introduced a new and systematic theory, but just a list (more or less) of possibly useful analytic devices or resources: the formative power of language; the importance of feelings of tendency; the nature of knowing-from; practical authoring; responsivity = answerability + addressivity; breakdown and its restitution; conversation vs. written texts; psychological instruments: prostheses and indicators; rhetoric: justification and criticism; realism vs. constructionism; making and finding.

In the past, in assuming our procedures of inquiry to be secure, and our problems to be located (mainly) in the nature of our subject matter, we have indulged in a great deal of metatheoretical and epistemological discussion, we discussed theories because we felt accurate theories were the goal of our investigations. In the approach being canvassed here, our supposed objects of study are of less concern to us than the general nature of our investigatory practices. In other words, instead of metatheory, we become concerned with metamethodology. Primarily, we become interested in the procedures and devices we use in both socially constructing the subject matter of our investigations, as well as, how we establish and maintain a contact with it (this is the critical aspect of the constructionism discussed). For the hook up, so to speak, between such devices and our surroundings, determines the nature of the data we can gather through their use. We thus move away from the individual, 3rd-person, external, contemplative observer stance, the investigator who collects fragmented data from a position socially outside of the activity observed, and who bridges the gaps between the fragments by the imaginative invention of theoretical entities, towards a more relational, interpretative approach, in which outcomes occur as a result of joint action (Shotter, 1984) between all the participants involved.

Another consequence of the social constructionist position taken here should be emphasized, a point usually hidden by the implicit realism induced in the scientific approach to these issues: the assumption that when we talk about such entities as the company, the market, the customer, the product, the current situation, the office directive, etc., we all know perfectly well what the 'it' is that we are all talking about. We find it difficult to accept that objects such as these are not there in some primordial naturalistic sense; that they only make sense as they are given significance within a discourse. But to claim this: that discourses work to produce rather than simply to reflect the objects to which the words uttered within them seem to refer, is still to make an unfamiliar claim within the social sciences. We still unconsciously assume (like Humpty-Dumpty) that when we use a word, it means what we (think it means) and want it to mean, nothing more, nothing less. Nowhere is this more apparent than in our talk about talk, in which we assume that words are surrogates (Harris, 1980) which stand in for the things in our world, and communication is a process of telementation (Harris, 1981) in which we put our ideas into words in order to send them to the minds of others. It is these unrecognized image-schematisms, implicit in almost all our talk about talk which makes us blind to the fact that much of our talk is either conducted in a context of misunderstanding and mutual bewilderment, or, requires much greater openness to the argumentative negotiation of meanings, if it is to be better understood, in other words, our forms of communication at the moment lack management.

References

Bakhtin, M.M. (1986), *Speech Genres & Other Late Essays*. Trans. by Vern W. McGee. University of Texas Press, Austin, Tx.

Billig, M. (1987), *Arguing and Thinking: A Rhetorical Approach to Social Psychology*, Cambridge University Press, Cambridge.

Bohm, D. (1965), *The Special Theory of Relativity*, Benjamin, New York.

Bohm, D. (1980), *Wholeness and the Implicate Order*, Routledge & Kegan Paul, London.

Derrida, J. (1976), *Of Grammatology*. Trans. Gayatri Spivak, Johns Hopkins University Press, Baltimore.

Dreyfus, H.L. & Ribbon, P. (1982), *Michel Foucault, Beyond Structuralism and Hermeneutics*, Harvester Press, Sussex.

Gallie, W.B. (1955-56), 'Essentially contested concepts', *Proc. of the Aristotelian Soc.*, 56, pp.167-198.

Garfinkel, H. (1967), *Studies in Ethnomethodology,* Prentice-Hall, Englewood Cliffs.

Gergen, K.J. (1992), 'Organizational Theory in the Postmodern Era', in M. Reed & M. Hughes (eds.), *Rethinking Organization,* Sage, London, pp.207-226.

Gibson, J.J. (1979), *The Ecological Approach to Visual Perception*, Houghton Mifflin, London.

Giddens, A. (1980), *The Constitution of Society,* Polity Press, Cambridge.

Harris, R. (1980), *Language-Makers*, Duckworth, London.

Harris, R. (1981), *The Language Myth,* Duckworth, London.

Heidegger, M. (1967), *Being and Time*, Blackwell, London.

Maturana, H. & Varela, F. (1980), *Autopoesis and Cognition: The Realization of the Living,* Reidel, London.

Mills, C.W. (1940), 'Situated actions and vocabularies of motive', *American Sociological Review,* 5, pp.904-913.

Morgan, G. (1986), *Images of Organization*, Sage, London.

Perelman, C. & Olbrechts-Tyteca, L. (1969), *The New Rhetori: A Treatise on Argumentation*, Trans. by J. Wilkinson & P. Weaver, University of Notre Dame Press (1958), Notre Dame.

Polanyi, M. (1958), *Personal Knowledge, Towards a Post-Critical Philosophy.* Routledge & Kegan Paul, London.

Pompa, L. (1982), *Vico: Selected Writings*, edited and trans. by Leon Pompa. Cambridge University Press, London.

Rorty, R. (1980), *Philosophy and the Mirror of Nature*, Blackwell, Oxford.

Ryle, G. (1949), *The Concept of Mind*, Methuen, London.

Schön, D. (1983), *The Reflective Practitioner: How Professionals Think in Action*, Maurice Temple Smith, London.

Searle, J. (1983), *Intentionality: An Essay in the Philosophy of Mind*, Cambridge University Press, Cambridge.

Shotter, J. (1984), *Social Accountability and Selfhood*, Blackwell, Oxford.

Vico, G. (1948), *The New Science of Giambattista Vico.* ed. and trans. T.G. Bergin & M.H. Fisch, Cornell University Press, Ithaca, N.Y.

Notes

1. I am influenced in my use of the word afford here by Gibson's (1979) ecological approach to perception in psychology. As he sees it, we do not perceive our visual surroundings like a camera, taking pictures, for perceive it 'for action', in terms of what actions it affords.

2. 'Effective' here remains, of course, problematic.

8 Social constructionism and the postmodern turn of management theory

Emil Walter-Busch

It may be said that modernization reaches its postmodern stage, when the industrial system penetrates the whole world, and at the same time is losing faith in the grand myths of reason, which formerly legitimized its expansion. J.-F. Lyotard defines postmodernity simply as 'disbelief in meta-narratives' (*l'incrédulité à l'égard des métarécits*; Lyotard, 1979, p.7). Under postmodern conditions, scepticism toward all kinds of dogmatism and monolithic worldviews, those of reason as well as those of unreason or irrationalism, becomes unavoidable. Voices of demystification are now everywhere (Gergen, 1991, p.96), including those voices that demystify demystification itself. Disbelief and cynicism toward science, technology and business, the still predominating forces of change, proliferate. Multiperspectivism, radical pluralism and (de)constructionism on the one hand, fundamentalistic movements on the other hand try to make sense of the new situation. Its essential ambiguity, however, still withstands many of these sense-making endeavours.

Among other things, management practices and theories, too, have to adapt themselves to the new postmodern conditions. John Shotter criticizes conventional ways of seeing managers (or people in general) as scientists (Shotter, in this volume, and 1990, p.452). He favours a metamethodological, social constructionist approach to management. According to Shotter, realist theories defining management as the objective reading and rational changing of situations must be abandoned. In order to empower managers as well as whole organizations, managers should not any longer be conceived as mere readers, but as people knowing how to function as authors. Acting as authors, they would be able to get in touch with the vague feelings of tendency ... within themselves to which their circumstances give rise. They would therefore be much more free to lend or to give such tendencies an intelligible expression of their own choosing, and would thus become more the authors of their own lives (Shotter, in this volume). As to authorities supporting this increased interest in people as knowledgeable, socially accountable agents, concerned to be the authors of their own (socially constructed) individuality, Shotter refers mainly to the pioneering study of C.W. Mills on situated actions and vocabularies of motive, and to the classical defense of rhetoric and practical wisdom (*prudentia*), which G. Vico has written against the misleading claims of Cartesian scientism.

According to Martin Parker, it is useful to differentiate clearly between post-modernity as a historical period and postmodernism as a philosophical perspective (with Derrida, Foucault, Lyotard, Rorty and others as its spokesmen; cf. Parker, 1992, and Cooper & Burrell, 1988). Making use of Parker's suggestion, one may say that Shotter combines an emancipatory plea for managers as authors knowing how to respond to the challenge of post-modernity with a constructionist, postmodern philosophy of management. As Kenneth Gergen in several of his recent publications, Shotter too tends to move seamlessly between applying postmodernism to suggesting that organizations need to find new ways of working in the postmodern age (Parker, 1992, p.12). Parker thinks that the two kinds of arguments are incommensurable language games in the Wittgensteinian sense (ibid. p.10). It may be doubted, of course, whether thoughts about post-modernity on the one hand, about philosophical perspectives of postmodernism on the other hand are really incommensurable language games. (What does it mean, besides, and is it possible at all to say that something is incommensurable with another thing?) Accepting the useful distinction between post-modernity and postmodernism, however, I do think that detaching Shotter's predominately normative ideas about management practices in the age of post-modernity from his constructionist metamethodology may help to clarify some of the problems he is addressing. In the following section, I want first to discuss Shotter's critique of conventional models of management. In the following sections I suggest some general reasons against founding organizational or management theories too immediately on philosophical considerations.

Pitfalls of the alternatives of managers as scientists vs. managers as practical authors

Chester Barnard, accomplished both as a top manager and as a management theorist, used to say that whereas actors live in a cloud of events, abstractors live in a cloud of abstractions (Barnard, 1937, I p.11f.; cf. Walter-Busch, 1989, p.135). Barnard thought that to these different kinds of practices, different levels of discourse are appropriate: the level of practical discourse on the one hand, and that of scientific discourse on the other hand (Barnard, 1939/40, p.303f.). Concerning the difficult relationship between the two kinds of discourses,

Barnard favoured the tolerant principle of using both of them, depending on given circumstances: 'I use several levels of discourse about the same subject for different situations' (ibid. p.304). Barnard however would never have modelled acting managers as scientists. It was self-evident for him that in management practice, intuition, practical wisdom, exploratory decision making, or, as he preferred to say, non-logical processes are much more important than logical processes, which he even found to be often deleterious (Barnard, 1936, p.320).

With or without Barnard, I think probably only a very small minority of management scientists take actually the model of managers as scientists for an adequate description of what managers do in practice. So, if Shotter's model of managers as scientists has really to be understood as a descriptive, not as a normative model, it does not agree with how managers see themselves, nor with how they are seen by most management theorists. If on the other hand this model should only have to prepare the ground for Shotter's explicitly normative ideas about managers as authors, it should be mainly assessed by the pros and cons of this positive alternative to the unpleasant image of managers as scientists. I cannot find the alternative model of managers as authors much more attractive, however.

Shotter's conception of managers as authors uses elements of Karl Weick's model of sense-making processes in organizations. But unlike Weick's ideas, it is spiced with a pinch of Marxian theory. Shotter thinks that we must model the effective manager not upon the scientist, but, in Marx's sense, upon the maker of history, the practical author. The essential core ability of good management has nothing to do with finding and applying a true or false theory. It has, Shotter says, much more to do with providing an intelligible formulation of what has become, for the others in the organization, a chaotic welter of impressions. In this sense, a manager can be seen as a repairer, as someone who is able to restore a routine flow of action that has broken down in some way, to give it an intelligible direction. Thus, rather than as if doing science, managers may best be seen as actually involved in the making (of) history.

I think the connection that Shotter fosters between Weick and Marx is a rather uneasy alliance. From a Marxist standpoint, the main problem of at least the working class-minded others in the organization is definitely neither a collapse of their sense-making competence, nor an urgent need to let management repair their disorientation problems. Managers may be called makers of history but as followers of Marx are used to see it, management makes history in the wrong sense of exploiting workers, and its practice is urgently in need to be reoriented by the suppressed classes and their avantgarde. These are therefore the only forces in modern history who really know the true sense of history-making.

Examined from a political perspective, then, Shotter's picture of managers repairing the disorientation problems other members of organizations may have, is amazingly conservative. Conversely, the politically active role of authors', which Shotter would like to confer to managers, clashes with the postmodern philosophy on which his main arguments rely. According to ideas that are pivotal to the philosophies of Foucault, Derrida and many of their followers, both the individual subject of modernity and the author are dead (cf. Ingold & Wunderlich, 1991). And if, against all expectations of postmodernists, these dead corpses could ever be revitalized somehow, it would hardly be done by management.

Postmodern oversophistications of management theory

In Shotter's approach, not only the alliance between Weickian theory of sense-making processes and some Marxian motives, but also that between management theory and philosophical reflections appear to me to be rather debatable.

Changes of management theories often reflect changes of the general mood of the time, the so-called *Zeitgeist*. This seems to be the case with the following three recent movements, the culturalist-symbolic, the autopoietic, and the pluralistic turn of management theory and practice. First, management's symbolic and sense-giving functions were stressed from a sociological point of view (Pfeffer, 1981) as well as from that of the tremendously successful organizational culture movement. Secondly, the self-organizing, autopoietic capacities of the self-referential systems to be cultivated by managers were emphasized especially by promoters of a new, constructionist generation of system models (see e.g., Kasper, 1991). Finally, and most significantly for the postmodern mood of the last decade, the chances for formulating provocative antitheses to established knowledge (cf. Cohen, March & Olson, 1972, and Weick, 1979, for example) and for the acceptance of a plurality of different, often contradictory perspectives have grown dramatically. Almost anything goes now, if not in management practice, then at least in management theory. Today, the multiperspectivist principle that organizational realities are many things at one and the same time, and that theory's first obligation is therefore to sensitize its students or clients to these multiple realities, is well established (Morgan, 1986).

These theoretical innovations have also been noted by some management practitioners, as for example Peters' and Waterman's best-selling book 'In Search of Excellence' shows. Peters and Waterman explicitly linked talk of organizational cultures, the family feeling, small is beautiful, simplicity rather than complexity, heard during their investigation of America's best-run companies, to the new school of theoretical thinking of leading academics as for example Karl Weick and James March (Peters & Waterman, 1982, pp.8, 93). Similarly, one of the most innovative and successful German authors of popular management literature, Gerd Gerken, sees the theoretical foundations of the intriguingly postmodern ideas for management he is advancing in newer developments of autopoetic systems theory, chaos theory, synergetics, new age philosophy, etc. (Gerken. 1989).

Observing the different levels of contemporary discourse about management, one may get the impression that the distance between the implicit or explicit common sense-theories of experienced actors and the theoretical models of abstractors has become considerable. Compared to the situation at the beginning of this century, when management just began to be professionalized, the axis of increasing sophistication of argumentation has been expanded substantially. Consequently, there are now more levels of discourse between the extremes of simple proverbs of administration on the one hand, and of highly elaborated theories of management on the other hand.

The moving forces behind this growing distance between the everyday constructs of actors and the more or less elaborated theories of abstractors are once again the ever expanding economy, science and technology of modern societies. When the founders of modern management theory and practice - Frederick Taylor, Henri Fayol, Henry Dennison and others - wrote their pioneering works, they would never have thought of relating them to contemporary developments in philosophy, to the phenomenological movement of Husserl and Heidegger for example, or to Wittgenstein's 'Tractatus'. Today, only a few years after the publication of a key contribution to contemporary philosophy, bright management theorists try to show how significant, say, Habermas' communication theory, Foucault's post-structuralism or Derrida's deconstructionism are for the proper development of management theory and perhaps of management practice. This has been made possible mainly by the rapid professionalization of management. Its very densely populated field of knowledge can afford today to have many different kinds of contributors, the large majority of those who refine or invent concrete instruments and models as well as the small minority of pure abstractors who deal with the delicate interface between management theory and contemporary philosophy. Today, systems of management knowledge are even including import filters for philosophical texts, for texts saved in the difficult phd-format, so to say.

Management has become such an intensively cultivated field of knowledge that it obviously can afford now to entertain an astonishing diversity of different discourses. Consequently, the simple question of whether management theory really needs to import philosophical texts, and how adequate its import filters are, is seldom asked. If postmodern conditions of living are socially saturated (Gergen, 1991), those of today's management theorists may justly be called cognitively saturated. At its present stage of maturity, philosophically deduced management knowledge, as it is advanced by Burrell, Cooper, Kasper, Shotter, and others, tends to become oversophisticated. Many, if not most of the consequences contemporary philosophy might be supposed to have for management can be as well obtained by philosophically unassisted common sense. In the next section, I illustrate this contention by trying to show how everyday thinking is able to suspend problematic assumptions about the managerial world out there at least as effectively as constructionist approaches to epistemological problems do.

Common sense and the postmodern crisis of representational modes of thinking

Let us imagine a society in which everybody, instead of saying this is thing X, or this is true, or this is bad, prefers to say the thing we choose to call X, I have reasons to find this true, and I have reasons to find this bad. Such ways of speaking would be cumbersome but they could probably reduce some well-known disadvantages of the representational mode of arguing, which assumes that the meaning M_X of a concept or proposition is the factual thing X which it represents (that apple there, for example, or a certain event[1]). By using such a non-representational mode of argumentation, the author(s) A constructing the objects of a concept or proposition could not, as in the usual representational mode of asserting X by saying M_X, disappear behind the real world objects X out there, but would always be explicitly acknowledged as the subject(s) authoring $_A M_X$.

Everyday's common sense allows for both representational and non-representational modes of thinking. In everyday situations, we always have the possibility to put the claims of a realist assertion M_X into question by saying that $_{A!}M_{(X)}$ says more about its author A than about its object X. It may even be argued in such cases that X is real only insofar as A defines it as real.

Changing the focus of attention from the object of a proposition ($_{(A)}M_{X!}$) to its author ($_{A!}M_{(X)}$) does not necessarily presuppose a change from realism, which distinguishes between models of reality and the real world itself, to a constructionist epistemology, with its systematic criticism of this distinction. For the realist presumption that $_A M_X$ may more or less fit reality makes sense as well for the assertion $_{(A)}M_{X!}$ says something (more or less fitting) about X as for the assertion $_{A!}M_{(X)}$ says at least something (more or less fitting) about its author A.

Whatever the epistemological implications of a non-representational mode of thinking may be, it seems to be particularly well suitable for a skeptical, pluralistic perspective on human affairs. The things we choose to call X could also mean, for participants of other language games, Y, and the fact that I find this (X) to be true does not exclude, but on the contrary invites discussions with alternative standpoints and their reasons of finding X untrue.

How, then, should we assess the recent changes of discourse about managers and management mentioned above in section 2? John Shotter, in his contribution to this volume, thinks that a philosophical approach confronting the traditional with a theoretically advanced, social-constructionist view on management theory and practice helps to answer this question. He identifies established management perspectives with those of objectivist, tough-minded problem solvers and scientists, and contrasts this with the social-constructionist view of the manager as a highly context-sensitive sense-maker, reader, repairer, and, above all, author.

These latter attributes belong clearly to the class of idealized traits characterizing managers who know how to respond to the challenges of post-modernity. It is one thing however to justify such attributes by means of an epistemology whose main consequences for management theory and practice are already (or may be even are always already) known by ordinary common sense. Another, at least as interesting aim would be simply to describe as comprehensively and realistically as possible the awfully complex processes of management's postmodernization.

As I tried to show elsewhere, the interdependencies between different kinds of management words and deeds, theories and practices are extremely complicated. Abstract academic or applied theories, the theories-in-use and the practices of management are at best loosely coupled. Consequently, even presumably revolutionary paradigm switches in academic theory, which may often be much better understood as a continuous evolution of discursive practices, never have in practice the vast consequences attributed to them. Furthermore, theoretical innovations do not only anticipate, but often come after or at best together with corresponding developments in the wide field of practice, they comment, enhance and/or justify ongoing processes of social and cultural change (cf. Walter-Busch, 1989, 1991).

It would be a fascinating venture just to produce (in Geertz's sense) thick descriptions of evolving management discourses, their different levels and fields of application. Instead of contributing to a deeper understanding of the world as it is, however, many social scientists usually try only to change it.

References

Barnard, Ch. (1936), 'Mind in Everyday Affairs' in Barnard, Ch., *The Functions of the Executive*, Cambridge MA., Harvard University Press, pp.301-3.

Barnard, Ch. (1937), *Notes on Some Obscure Aspects of Human Relations. Address to Professor Cabot's Business Executive Group*, mim. Man., Baker Library Archives, Harvard University, Boston.
Barnard, Ch. (1938), *The Functions of the Executive*. Harvard University Press, Cambridge MA., (27th printing, 1976).
Barnard, Ch. (1939/40), 'Comments on the job of the executive', *Harvard Business Review,* 18, pp.295-308.
Benhabib, S. (1986), 'Kritik des "Postmodernen Wissens", eine Auseinandersetzung mit Jean-François Lyotard' in Huyssen, A. & Scherpe, K. (eds.), *Postmoderne. Zeichen eines Kulturellen Wandels,* Rowohlt, Reinbek, pp.103-27.
Clegg, S. (1990), *Modern Organizations. Organization Studies in the Postmodern World.* Sage, London.
Cohen, M., March, J., & Olsen, J. (1972), 'A garbage can model of organizational choice', *Administrative Science Quarterly,* 17, pp.1-25.
Cooper, R., & Burrell, G. (1988), 'Modernism, postmodernism and organizational analysis: An introduction', *Organization Studies,* 9, pp.91-12.
Gergen, K. (1991), *The Saturated Self: Dilemmas of Identity in Contemporary Life,* Basic Books, New York.
Gergen, K. (1992), 'Organization Theory in the Postmodern Era' in Reed, M. & Hughes, M. (eds.), *Rethinking Organization. New Directions in Organization Theory and Analysis,* Sage, London, pp.207-226.
Gerken, G. (1989), *Neue Wege für Manager: Erfolg zwischen High-Tech und Ethik,* Econ Tb., Düsseldorf.
Harvey, D. (1989), *The Condition of Postmodernity.* Basil Blackwell, Oxford.
Ingold, F.P., & Wunderlich, W. (eds.) (1992), *Fragen nach dem Autor: Positionen und Perspektiven,* Universitätsverlag, Konstanz.
Kasper, H. (1991), 'Neuerungen durch Selbstorganisierende Prozesse' in Staehle, W. & Sydow, J. (eds.), *Managementforschung 1,* Walter de Gruyter, Berlin, pp.1-74.
Lyotard, J.-F. (1979), *La Condition Postmoderne,* Editions de Minuit, Paris.
Morgan, G. (1986), *Images of Organization,* Sage, London.
Parker, M. (1992), 'Post-modern organizations or postmodern organization theory?', *Organization Studies,* 13, pp.1-17.
Peters, Th., & Waterman, R. (1982), *In Search of Excellence: Lessons from America's Best-Run Companies,* Warner, New York.
Pfeffer, J. (1981), 'Management as Symbolic Action. The Creation and Maintenance of Organizational Paradigms', *Research in Organizational Behavior,* 3, pp.1-52.
Shotter, J. (1990), 'Underlabourers for science, or toolmakers for society?', *History of the Human Sciences* , 3, pp.443-457.

Walter-Busch, E. (1989), *Das Auge der Firma. Mayos Hawthorne-Experimente und die Harvard Business School, 1900-1960*, Enke, Stuttgart.

Walter-Busch, E. (1991), 'Entwicklung von Leitmotiven Verhaltensorientierten Managementwissens', in Staehle, W. & Sydow, J. (eds.), *Managementforschung 1*, Walter de Gruyter, Berlin, pp.347-399.

Weick, K. (1979), *The Social Psychology of Organizing*, Second Edition. Addison-Wesley, Reading.

Whitley, R. (1988), 'The management sciences and managerial skills', *Organization Studies,* 9, pp.47-68.

Notes

1. Representational models of knowledge proceed from the assumption that giving meaning to a concept is fundamentally the same as naming a certain thing (giving the name of apple to that red round thing out there, for example), and that our concepts represent the world more or less adequately. Theories of knowledge which, like those of Nietzsche or Wittgenstein, criticize this view of language as picturing the essentials of reality (Gergen, 1992, p.213) could consequently be called non-representational approaches (see e.g., Benhabib, 1986 about the recent crisis of the classical episteme of representation). It should be mentioned, however, that Gergen describes precisely these non-representational ways of thinking as approaches trying to replace the real by the representational (Gergen, 1992, p.213).

9 Social construction and appreciative inquiry: A journey in organizational theory

David Cooperrider, Frank Barrett and Suresh Srivastva

Modern management thought was born proclaiming that organizations are the triumph of the imagination. As made and imagined, organizations are products of human interaction and social construction rather than some anonymous expression of an underlying natural order (McGregor, 1960; Schein, 1985; Morgan, 1986; Unger, 1987; Gergen, 1990). Deceptively simple yet so entirely radical in implication, this insight is still shattering many conventions, one of which is the long-standing conviction that bureaucracy, oligarchy and other forms of hierarchical domination are inevitable. Today we know this simply is not true.

Recognizing the symbolic and relationally constructed nature of the organizational universe, we now find a mounting wave of sociocultural and constructionist research, all of which is converging around one essential and empowering thesis: that there is little about collective action or organization development that is preprogrammed, unilaterally determined, or stimulus bound in any direct physical, economic, material or deep-structured sociological way. Everywhere we look, seemingly immutable ideas about people and organizations are being directly challenged and transformed on an unprecedented scale. The world, quite simply seems to change as we talk in it. Indeed, as we move into a postmodern global society, we are breaking loose of myopic parochialism and are recognizing that organizations in all societies exist in a wide array of types and species and function without a dynamic spectrum of beliefs and lifestyles.

Meanwhile, organizational theory has reached an impasse. For some, the issue is a crisis of relevance (Sussman & Evered, 1978; Friedlander, 1984; Beyer & Trice, 1982). For others, the discipline is in a state of bewildering disarray: 'The domain of organizational theory is coming to resemble more of a weedpatch than a well-tended garden' (Pfeffer, 1982). More than that, retorts Astley (1985), that, 'the management theory jungle is symbolic of deep fragmentation of the discipline marked by intense competition and rival paradigms' and which is daily becoming more dense and impenetrable'. The whole thing, especially in the international arena, seems recently to have reached the point of sterling crescendo as 'a violent babble of competing voices ... leading nowhere loudly' (George, 1988, p.269).

To this we must add that organizational theory is scarcely alone. Skinner (1985) spoke for many across the sociobehavioural sciences, when he talked about the postmodernist spectre that has infiltrated the troops, encouraging scholars everywhere to re-examine the ontological, epistemological and axiological foundations of their endeavours. It has, of course, been a heated search that has:

> ... been nothing less than a disposition to question the place of philosophy as well as the sciences within our culture. If our access to reality is inevitably conditioned by local beliefs about what is to count as knowledge, then traditional claim of the sciences to be finding out more and more about the 'as it really is', begins to look questionable or at least unduly simplified. Moreover, if there is no canonical grid of concepts in terms of which the world is best divided up and classified, then the traditional place of philosophy as the discipline that analyzes such concepts is also thrown into doubt. Epistemology, conceived in Kantian terms as the study of what can be known with certainty, begins to seem an impossibility; instead we appear to be threatened with the spectre of epistemological relativism (Skinner, 1985, p.11).

Threatened, indeed, responds Hazelrigg (1989): 'The spectre of a thoroughly radical relativism, a paralysis of thought and thus of thoughtful deed is well upon us' (Hazelrigg, 1989, p.2). The postmodern voices suggest that the Western conception of knowledge, including its romance with permanence, belief in progress, the search for reliable patterns beyond contingencies toward the service of predicting and controlling future events, has not fulfilled its promise.

Challenging virtually every assumption of a modernist science, including foundationalist verities such as an objectivity, value freedom, the picture theory of language, and the possibility of universal progressive knowledge, the critical turn has resulted in a cacophony of voices and styles which compels everyone to agree that something postmodern has happened. But nobody knows exactly what 'it' is. Part of the 'it', concludes Bernstein (1983) is an emerging consensus that seems to reverberate throughout an otherwise dissident set of encampments: that the scientific naturalism-materialism which has so confidently dominated the rest of the modernist-industrial era and so thoroughly implicated itself into every aspect of institutional life is now dying orthodoxy. For those who would continue to model the social sciences on the natural sciences, there is an all too conspicuous fact that is increasingly troublesome and impossible to hide: in spite of a century's worth of well-intentioned effort, there are still no universal laws (cf. Hempel) in the social sciences, not one single candidate (see Giddins, 1976). The promise for a cumulative sociobehavioural science has been an El Dorado. And it has been deconstruction of El Dorado, using words like debunking, demystification, break and rupture, that has led many, like Skinner into despair or even retreat. The quicksand of reflexivity, warns Wollheim (1980), may lead to complete immobilization of scholarship. Echoes Booth (1984), 'What could be more ironic than the making of statements about a world in which the making of statements is meaningless' (Booth, 1984, p.244).

Yet, none of this, we suggest, begins to appreciate the possibilities that can emerge in the free space for thinking. And none of this responds to the vital and empowering thesis that societies and organizations are made and imagined which means, of course, that they can be remade and reimagined (which is happening in stunning ways all around the world).

What we hope to show is that the postmodern implication that organizations are made and imagined can serve as an invitation to re-vitalize the practice of social science. The suggestion that knowledge is not a matter of accurately reflecting that world but is a relationally embedded activity, that the world we come to know and inhabit is a product of linguistic convention, is an empowering insight that can alter the way that social scientists construe their task. The postmodern move suggests that just as organizational arrangements are always and already an expression of social negotiation, so too is scientific activity relationally embedded and implicated in the universe it seeks to study (see Steier, 1991).

If organizations are indeed ours to reinvent, does not that mean, as Unger (1987) has written, that we can now cut the link between the possibility of social-organizational explanation and the denial or down-playing of our freedom to remake the organizational words we construct and cohabit? More to the crux of the matter, Gergen (1988, p.18) has written, 'the constructionist orientation invites experimentation with new forms of scientific discourse. For we as scientists are also engaged in forms of social construction - fashioning frames of discourse for living lives'. If this is our task rather than fashioning verbal mirrors, 'then isn't it true that we as theorizing scholars contribute to the forms of cultural intelligibility, to the symbolic resources available to people to carry out their lives together' (Gergen, 1988, p.10)? If it is true that as social scientists we help to create the categories and symbolic resources by which people carry on their lives, why would we want to hide our personal engagement, our own passions and interest in our research activity? Of course, none of this up to this point is so unusual (i.e., to actually attempt to take the constructionist viewpoint seriously). But in one way it is extraordinary in what it can do for the discipline, and it is this that feeds directly into the singular point of the present effort: That the understanding of organizations and their/our practical transformation is a single undifferentiated act. The productive act of organizational inquiry is at one stroke the production of self-and-world or subject-and-object as well as the historical context in which all living organizational theory: We must now recognize ourselves in it.

In this paper we shall attempt to bring to life this notion and explore exactly what it means for organizational behaviour to take on its own constructive project, that is, to fashion for itself a practice of social theory which simultaneously includes an explanatory approach to organizations and a program for organizational reconstruction and development. We shall begin with a brief examination of postmodernist thought and show that what is often castigated as a spectre of relativism can be read as an invitation to a relational understanding of knowledge. The relational vocabulary of knowledge, we contend, provides an opening for the constructive project at precisely that moment when things appear most nihilistic. There is a special charity in relativism, especially for a field like organizational behaviour that wishes to be of vital significance in arenas where human relatedness is by definition the focus of concern. With this conceptual prelude in mind, we shall be prepared to look closely at a firsthand experience in the field. The study contributes an illustration to an otherwise sterile abstraction or an even (mistakenly) superficial notion (i.e., that the understanding of organizations and their/our practical transformation is a single, undifferentiated act). Finally, we conclude by raising a number of key questions about the constructive project and what it means for our own discipline. We suggest that it is possible through our assumptions and choice of methods that we largely create the world we later discover, including ourselves in it.

The special charity of relativism

Briefly, the foundationalist project that came into ascendancy in the 18th century, is based on a Cartesian, dualistic epistemology: the individual mind and the external world are separate and distinct entities. The real world exists out there, independent of any attempts to perceive it or converse about it. The mind is depicted as a mirror (Rorty, 1979) that reflects the features of the world, registering sense impressions. Thus meaning making is an activity that occurs within the internal recesses of the individual mind. Within this paradigm, language is seen as a system of words that stand for something in the world and is capable of conveying meaning between subjective minds. Since knowledge is depicted as the accurate registering of sense impressions, precautions must be taken to insure that this perception is not misguided and not due to the influence of bias or some self-serving interest. Therefore, an attitude of scepticism and personal detachment is necessary. These are the pillars upon which positivist science has built the belief that bias and contaminating influences must be eliminated so that the facts about the world emerge independent of any particular vested voice or any particular locale. What is deemed knowledge is based on objective explanations that causally connect verifiable patterns that can become translated into transhistorical formulas. Thus, under the discipline of empirical rigor, objective knowledge can be accumulated and this will lead to the discovery of immutable laws among the contingencies of human affairs.

All of these assumptions, the separation of subject and object, observer and observed, words as representation devices, the elimination of bias, the rigorous discovery of a-contextual patterns and immutable laws, are being challenged by constructionists within a number of different fields. Today we can mention the names of Feyerabend, Rorty, Derrida, Wittgenstein, Kuhn, Habermas, Gadamer, Foucault and others without fear of scurrilous laughter or attack, or at least, as Becker (1980) would put it, with confidence that the scoffers are uniformed. In the last few years a new understanding has been taking place across the disciplines leading to a profound range of intellectual and cultural transformations, in what many now call the postmodern turn in social theory. What is most notable, as Hazelrigg (1989) is quick to point out, is that the work of someone like Derrida, though still widely criticized for its obscure and almost inaccessible approach, has not yet been contradicted or neutralized in quite the same way as Nietzsche, for example, whose work was dismissed for so many years as the jabberings of a madman. For some, the loosening of the naturalist claims that advocate a search for reliable patterns and predictable laws based on unbiased perception of objective fact, represents a threat to the very act of scholarship/knowing.

In this section we shall consider what some of these developments mean in relation to our discipline. Postmodernism, we argue, is more than a movement of endless negation. The five broad themes which we shall outline hold intriguing implications for the project of building a constructive organizational theory.

The truth of human freedom must count

It has been argued that postmodern thought has begun to forge new understanding of knowledge with which to carry to extremes the idea that originally inspired it - the view of society as an artifact. At the heart of the new discourse is, therefore, an uncompromising presumption of impermanence. The idea, as mentioned in our introduction, is that no matter what the durability to date, virtually any pattern or structure of socio-organizational action is open to revision. There are no iron clad laws. The only non-contingent fact of collective existence is its ultimate plasticity. While all human activity is contextual and thus affected by constraints of every conceivable kind, all contexts can be broken, that is, 'at any moment, people may think or associate with one another in ways that overstep the boundaries of the conditional worlds in which they had moved 'til then' (Unger, 1987, p.20).

While we may never overcome context dependence, we may alter it, re-shape it, and continuously find reminders that patterns of social-organizational action are not fixed by nature in any direct environmental, technological, psychological or deep-sociological way. While we create the contexts that constrain our practices (see Giddins, 1976), humans as agents are not rule-bound to obey the patterns of history or the procedures of familiar structures upheld by repeated practices. Indeed, to the extent to which human actions are vitally linked to the manner in which people and groups understand or construe the world of experience, and to the extent that people are capable of reconstructing the meaning of life events in an indeterminate number of ways, then any existing regularities discovered in the social world 'must be considered historically contingent' (see Gergen, 1982, p.16). No mistake about it, if there is anything uniting the postmodernism chorus of voices, it is this: 'The truth of human freedom, or strange freedom from any given structure must count, count affirmatively, for the way we understand ourselves and our history' (Unger, 1987, p.23).

Why has so little attention been paid to the possible ramifications of impermanence and plasticity for a theory of social science? More important than a quick answer is the challenge to unravel the assumptions that would depict humans as passive objects rather than active agents. Again, a Unger (1987) summarizes:

> The aim is not to show that we are free in any ultimate sense and somehow unconstrained by causal influence upon our conduct. It is to break loose from a style of social understanding that allows us to explain ourselves and our societies only to the extent we imagine ourselves as helpless puppets of the social worlds we built and inhabit or of the law-like forces that have supposedly brought these worlds into being. History really is surprising; it does not just seem that way (p.5).

Postmodernism is perhaps best known as a protest (whose own style unfortunately receives the vast share of public attention and thereby serves to deflect conversation from its explanatory and programmatic potential) if not outright rejection of the naturalist premise and any of its disguises in neo-naturalist compromise or equivocation. The naturalist premise has, of course, been an entrenched, if not pervasive, element at the epicentre of social thought throughout history. Its character has been expressed in a myriad of ways: the search for foundations (Rorty, 1979); constant appeals to laws or iron constraints removed from the understanding of creative agents (see Giddins, 1976); belief in an enduring or transcendent reality independent of the observer as a 'that-which-is-already' (see Hazelrigg's 1989 analysis of the historical roots of the spectator theory of knowledge); and the belief in some privileged authority with special access to the truth and thus able to pass out judgments about the natural state of affairs and the inevitable status and rankings within that natural order (see Gould, 1981). In whatever version, one of the greatest contributions of the new discourse is that it has brought to light, time and again, the recognition that the naturalist premise inevitably downplays our constructive freedom; it thereby produces and reproduces a vocabulary of society and organizations as established beyond the perspective of human interaction and will:

> Such is our quest for assurance of safety that we construct an assuring agent, clothe it in dim mists of forgotten Origin, and name it this or that intelligence to be accorded our everlasting homage. The name may be Providence, Divine Wisdom, Nature's Laws, Natural Right, Reason in History, Historical Laws, Unmoved Mover - it is all the same. And it is the same when we ask the authority of as *theoros* to tell us the ready path to all that we wish the world to be but is not, the ready path to our Utopia: asking the *theoros* to tell us that, just that, requires as our earnest the presumption that there are as yet 'laws' that stand behind us, or can stand behind us, as a universal intelligence - some sort of certification, scientific or otherwise, about an outward march of history - and to which we have only to put ourselves in harness for its direction, like ingredients in a recipe for cosmic stew (Hazelrigg, 1989, p.69).

But is there anything left after the postmodern protest (see Rorty 1989, p.319: 'hope that the cultural space left by the demise of epistemology will not be filled'). Is there anything more than the rejection of the major explanatory scandal of social theory? The challenge, we will now elaborate, is to recognize that the truth of human freedom is merely the beginning of insight, not the abandonment of explanatory ambitions (Unger, 1987).

Words enable worlds

One of the cornerstones of modernist, foundationalist discourse is what Rorty called the 'picture theory of words' (Rorty, 1979), the theory that the mind is a mirror that reflects features of the world and captures them in words. In this vein, referred to the conduit metaphor language, the belief that words actually contain information and are conduits by which people transfer meaning back and forth.

In its onomastic function, language is the vehicle that makes knowing possible by describing or picturing the objectivities of a 'that-which-is'. The illocutionary point (as speech-act theorists would say) is the neutral discovery and factual declaration of what one finds. The perlocutionary force of an utterance, the reverberating effect of the spoken word 'upon feelings, thoughts, or actions of the audience, or the speaker, or of other persons' (see Austin, 1975, p.101), if admitted at all, is viewed as a contaminant which must be cleansed or neutralized through greater operational precision. For Hazelrigg (1989) who traced the whole matter historically, the picture theory of language is the single most powerful tradition that has guided the development of dozens of conventional dualisms: littera and figera, theoros and poiesis, denotative and connotative, fact and fiction; and others.

In our own field, for example, Warriner, Hall & McKelvey (1981, p.173) ambitiously invited all organizational scholars to monitor the accuracy of their terms and to participate if formulating 'a standard list of operationalized observable variable for describing organizations' (Astley, 1985, p.497). Francis Bacon's early admonition retains salience: 'Words are but images of matter' and 'the truth of being and the truth of knowing are one, differing no more than direct beam and the beam reflected' (Hazelrigg, 1989, p.78).

It is here, in the linguistic turn that postmodernism presents us with ideas that could reshape the way we think and do organizational theory. Today the presumption that language operates in a Baconian sense as a picture of the world has, of course, been brought into sharp question by Wittgenstein (1963), Saussure (1983), Austin (1975), White (1978) and many others. As it relates to our effort, Barrett (1990) and Gergen (1985) provide the best overall synthesis of areas of conclusion and wide agreement.

First, what we take to be the world does not in itself dictate the terms by which such out there is understood. Words operate and derive meaning, not from their degree of correspondence to the world, but from their context and position within a language game. Within a given cultural context (or language game), one learns to read gestures and utterances in ways that facilitate interaction. For example, if we were to see two men striking one another and uttering loud sounds, how do we construe this situation? We might label these actions as aggression. Or perhaps we would say that the men are celebrating or dancing or performing a renewal ritual. If we see them laughing we might revise our account because such a response is inconsistent with our understanding of aggression. Or if we see one of them crying and holding his arm, we might eliminate the possibility of dance or play. We continue to make interpretive moves and revise our accounts depending on the network of words and concepts that are available. Would it be possible to perceive them practising karate with one another if no such word was in our vocabulary?

Not only does external reality not dictate the terms of which the world is understood, it may be the other way around. That is, we confront the world with languages already in place, terms which are given to us by the social conventions of our time: rules of grammar, structures for storytelling, conditions for writing, and common terms of understanding. In this sense, the function and purpose of words is not to picture an out there, but to help us navigate and coordinate our living relations with one another. Ordinary language philosophy (Bloor, 1976; Winch, 1946) proposes that it is no longer useful to think of words as pictures, but instead to think of words as tools that do something, as navigation devices that allow members of a culture to move about and coordinate ongoing relations with one another. Consider the word achievement motivation is useful if I want to explain a subordinate's poor performance. It is a useful word to talk about behaviour within a culture that values individual performance, the accumulation of capital, hierarchy (hence the word subordinate), etc. The concept may not make sense within a commune or religious organization. Words emerge in order to facilitate and support patterns of relevant activity.

What this suggests is that people have at their disposal a range of vocabulary that expands and contracts the repertoire of possible actions that are likely to follow. Each relational scenario is an ongoing negotiation process and the available expressions are like steering devices that lay out a possible pattern of interaction.

Since every word has meaning due to its position within a language game, a single word is never a single word. One word may carry a whole perspective that reverberates with a myriad of possible meanings. From this perspective, language is dialogical (Bakhtin, 1986) in that every utterance carries traces of meaning from other utterances spoken in other social contexts. 'Every utterance must be regarded as primarily a response to preceding utterances of the given sphere .... Each utterance refutes affirms, supplements, and relies upon the others, presupposes them to be known, and somehow takes them into account' (Bakhtin, 1986, p.91). So, for example, to refer to an organizational member as a subordinate triggers traces of other utterances that cite words like manager, chain of command, performance measures, etc. Fish (1980) refers to such groups as 'discourse communities', contexts in which members develop an agreed upon way of talking. Common presuppositions are triggered that allows people to communicate without explicitly articulating every warranting assumption. So, for example, when a medical student learns terms, diagnoses, treatments, she is joining a community of professional who employ similar interpretive repertoires that guide what they notice and talk about in relation to the human body. The discourse rules of the community dictate what is deemed reliable knowledge. Most physicians would not consider an intuitive sense of the patient's health problem as warranting a particular treatment. Rather, the physician lives in a community that regards hard scientific data backed by statistically sound studies as legitimate claims that warrant one particular treatment over another. An apprentice in homeopathic medicine adopts different linguistic practices with different implications for action that join her to quite a different interpretive community. Discourse communities involve membership in a linguistic practice in which certain convictions, beliefs, and perceptions are arguable and others are not (see Fish, 1980).

One central theme in constructionist thought is the indeterminacy of meaning. The culturally accepted meaning of a word does not determine how it will be applied in the future. Words develop new meanings through novel applications and alter the fabric of interpretive assumptions. Words are continuously extended beyond the boundaries of their existing applications. Wittgenstein addressed this directly: usage determines meaning, it is not meaning that determines usage (see Bloor, 1976). Wittgenstein likened the situation to the growth of an expanding town: like the creation of new roads and new houses, language is constructed as we go along. Consider, for example, the recent Quality revolution in American companies. It can in one sense be depicted as a rhetorical revolution, an altering of familiar words that reconstitutes peoples' experiences. What does it mean for example to shift the application of the word customer to include coworkers and other internal departments? The dislocation of this one word (that usually refers to external customers) and its family resemblances create a repertoire of potential actions that were once not under consideration. (A leading manufacturer recently issued a policy statement that reads: The job is not finished until the customer is delighted, and that includes the internal customers too.) It would be hard to imagine an assembly line foreman in a General Motors plant in the 1960's being chastised for not satisfying the internal customer. There was no network of commonly accepted words and no behavioral repertoires would allow the foreman to glean any sense from such an utterance. It does not mean that the conversation would have been false, or further away from the real nature of things. It simply means people did not talk that way and organizational patterns of activity would not render such an utterance intelligible.

No perception without perspective

While the traditional view holds that knowledge is the result of pure observation, the constructionist perspective holds that is not possible to perceive an object or event without some pre-understanding that guides what is noticed and how it is talked about. There is no such thing as immaculate perception. Whether one is talking about paradigms, schemas, disciplinary matrices or 'foreconceptions' in Heidegger's terms, all observation is laced with historically embedded conventions which anticipate and condition what is taken to be true or valid, and to a large extent govern what we as theorists and lay persons are able to see. Consider this example: an employee hears the CEO making references to winning and beating the competition. She probably does not read these gestures as referring to conflicts he is having with his son or ideological differences between his rabbi and a neighbouring priest. The cultural horizon within which she interacts consists of a network of words and family resemblances consistent with capitalistic organizational norms. Also, she knows that he is not suggesting that the competition should be physically beaten. Within her organizational culture, she has become familiar with these patterns of linguistic expression that depict other organizations in the industry as competitors to be conquered. However, if she were to hear references to beating the competition on an evening sports newscast, she would likely construe a different meaning. Even though these are the exact same words, she might construe a version of two football teams that do engage in physical struggle. As a competent discourse user, she is able to place utterances within varying contexts and networks of meaning and thus she is able to continue to carry on intelligibly with others. What allows her to successfully construe a meaning is her ability to place these words in different contexts and sets of social practices.

Indeed, as Unger (1987) not too deliberately put the matter, 'The contextual quality of all thought is a brute fact', but it is not necessarily a cruel one. Gadamer (1975) argued the interpreter's prejudgments do not so much get in the way but provide the necessary anticipation of meaning that draws us into constructive relationship where we are, our prejudices, and the object of understanding are all situated. Every access to the world, every way of reading the world is made possible because we are part of it and 'what exists ... is related to a particular way of knowing and willing' (Gadamer, 1975, p.408). All understanding, in this sense, is relational, like being part of a conversation or perceiving a piece of art (Barrett, 1990); and all knowing, as an anticipation of meaning, involves some kind of a priori basis on which to proceed: 'Never, in fact, does an interpreter get near to what his text says unless he lives in the aura of the meaning he is inquiring after' (Ricoeur, 1976, p.351). This is why the prejudices far more than judgments of fact 'constitute the historical reality of our being' (Gadamer, 1975, p.245). And this is why every generation will read a given situation or text in a different way with no means of determining which, if any is the more accurate interpretation: 'Gadamer's view has yet to succumb to criticism' (see Gergen, 1988, p.5). Thus we can begin to see that the locus of meaning begins to shift from the individual perceiver to the interaction between object and perceiver. The role of the perceiver is no longer seen as the passive recipient of sense data. Rather, the perceiver's projection of meaning is what makes knowing possible.

As it relates to the enterprise of knowledge, what this means is that from an observational point of view, all socio-organizational action is open to multiple interpretations, no one of which is or can ever be superior in a strict objectivist sense. Every theorist, as Kuhn (1970) and others have vivified, dwells within a unique historical context whereby particularized practices of knowing prevail. 'There are no bare facts', said Feyerabend (1976). While it would take us into too much complexity to try to trace the intricate and subtle variations in this argument, we must listen to the overall conclusion: 'If there is one single theme that runs the gamut of postmodernism, it is multiplicity of perspective' (Gergen, 1990, p.2). Yet, as reasonable as these views seem, we somehow forget, as Heidegger (1927) argued, that there must be some primary unity of subject and object prior to any effort at knowing. We continue to speak from the mother tongue of a dualist conception of knowledge using words like independent observation or subject and object (see Sampson's 1989 critique of the continuing bias of self-contained individualism in Western conceptions of modernist science). These words are important and have a perlocutionary force that directly affects, even if blindly, the way we do knowledge.

Every theory celebrates

The linguistic argument applies no less potently to our constructions and utterances we call theory To the extent that the primary product of science is systematically refined word systems - or theory - science, too, must be recognized as a powerful agent in the relational exchange governing the creation or obliteration of social existence. Social theorists are, argue Foucault (1972), authorities of delimitation; in our society they have been granted an extensive authority and privilege. Furthermore, terms such as learned helplessness, revolutionary praxis, and Theory X/Theory Y are not the result of an unclouded mirroring of the world. The observational terms and categories through which our understandings of the world are sought are themselves social artifacts, that is, real products of social relationships historically situated. As a powerful linguistic tool created by practising experts, theory may enter the meaning systems of a group or even a whole society and in doing so alter the patterns of social action. In this sense, all social theory is normative. This is precisely what Alvin Gouldner (1970) meant in what has become most often quoted sentences in today's conversation: Every social theory facilitates the pursuit of some, but not all, courses of action and thus, encourages us to change or accept the world as it is, to say yes or nay to it. In a way every theory is a discreet obituary or celebration of some social systems.

In what Giddins (1976) calls the double hermeneutic, theoretical knowledge spirals in and out of the universe of social life, reconstructing both itself and the social world. Social relations are ordered and re-ordered as linguistic constructs of theorists alter social conventions. By creating linguistic categories and distinctions that guide how people talk about life, how they report their own and others' experience, indeed how people actually have experience, social scientists are publicly defining reality (see Brown, 1978). It would be unlikely for a 19th century housewife to describe herself as codependent, for example. The constructionist contention is that it is not human nature that has changed but the language we use to talk about experiences and social theory helps to create what is regarded as normal and legitimate. Would it be possible, for example, to talk about someone's behaviour as unconsciously motivated or to depict one's athletic activity as sublimated energy if the terms of Freudian theory were not available? Further these linguistic repertoires expand the range of imaginable action. For example, once a word like codependency and its family resemblances becomes part of the linguistic repertoire of a discourse community, a set of inferences and actions become possible (such as the formation of support groups, seeking therapy, departing unhealthy relationship, etc.).

Often, as Hazelrigg (1989) comments, we adopt a foundationalist language, that denies the unity of making/thinking/doing:

> This abstracted thinking, whether addressed in the claims of language-as-science or those of language-as-poetry, reproduces itself in a division of labour that not only tries to separate head from hand, or 'intellectual ' from 'manual' labour, but also then struggles to relieve itself (i.e., its authorization of by/as 'the intellectual') of any odious identification as labour. It is self-alienated thinking because it denies its concrete historical integrity in/as poiesis, production (Hazelrigg, 1989, p.113).

So, again, we encounter the stubborn and coercive power of words. We 'discover' knowledge. We don't make it or invent it or see it as a poiesis (a making). When we do research, we are not creating but finding. We are searching to discover some truth regarding some mythical that-which-is-already. As we have argued throughout, something critical is involved here in the choice of such words, especially those words that arbitrarily separate theory from practice and downplay the idea that societies are made and imagined. The difference, for example, of continuing on with our utterances of a found world as opposed to a constructed world is enormously consequential for us. The difference is implicated into the way we do knowledge. Hazelrigg (1989) continues on this point:

> If a 'found world' is nothing more than a 'made world' travelling under disguise, if the (social organizational world is made and imagined) from beginning to end, then to continue 'telling our stories' in the traditional language of 'found world' is to reproduce passivity in regard to responsibility. Stories so told, practices so enacted, are stories/practices of a 'world' the most elemental basis of which (e.g., 'small bits of matter') and the most regular features of which (e.g., 'unchanging forces of nature') are placed outside the domain of human responsibility because they are placed outside the domain of human will. That is an enormously dangerous consequence of any retention of the 'found world' language storytelling (p.165).

In our view, the constructive potential of postmodern thought centres around the acknowledgment of our role in creating the world we pretend to find in our research. Our world changes as we talk, and the more rapidly it changes, the more the language of discovered world becomes irrelevant to contemporary concerns. If this reading is correct, our present task is to develop a new theory of theory with its own vocabulary that links knowledge with poiesis and, indeed, makes every act of inquiry an explicit celebration. Gergen (1978) has taken the single most important step in this direction with the proposal that the primary task of science is no longer the detached discovery and verification of social laws allowing for transhistorical prediction and control. Argued instead is an understanding that defines good theory in terms of its generative capacity, that is, its capacity to challenge guiding assumptions of a culture, to raise fundamental questions regarding contemporary social life, to bring about reconsideration of that which is taken for granted and most important, to furnish new constructions (theories) and alternatives for social action. Instead of attempting to present oneself as an impartial bystander or dispassionate spectator (as if one were not part of the world) of the inevitable, the social theorist would conceive of him or herself as an active participant, an invested participant whose work might well become a powerful source of generative conversation, affecting the way people see and enact their worlds. The constructive chorus discernible in postmodernism is that it invites, encourages, and requires that students of social-organizational life exercise their theoretical imagination in the service of their dynamically constituted vision of the good.

The democratization of mind

The final theme is largely a summarizing one. Throughout this sketch, one factor stands out among all others: Somewhere toward the defining centre of the postmodern dialogue is the emergence of a social as opposed to a dualist epistemology, or what more simply can be called a relational understanding of knowledge. Gergen (1988) has concluded in his synthesis of the postmodern challenge and aim: 'The concept of knowledge as a state of individual minds should be brought into sharp question. Much needed at this point is a view of knowledge that places it not in the hands of individuals, but within communities of discourse users'. Because of the multiperspective nature of knowing, the relational embeddedness of language, the impossibility of immaculate independent observation, the perlocutionary force of theory, the contextual quality of all thought, the idea that words are not autonomous pictures or maps of an independent out there or that-which-is-already, that historical conventions govern what is taken to be true or valid, it is for all these reasons and others that one can safely conclude that there is one more thing that unites many voices in the new era: the truth of human relatedness, our primary mode of connectedness must count, count affirmatively, for the way we understand ourselves and our history.

By the democratization of mind, we mean to suggest that one of the exciting agendas that must be placed high on the list in the creation of a constructive social-organizational theory is to actually place the practice of constructive inquiry into the hands of people in living relation, including ourselves in it. Programmatically, postmodern thought can be read as an invitation, as a call, to bring what we shall term secondary mode activity (the practice of knowing/making/developing) into congruence with life's primary mode (i.e., the preeminence of social relatedness) for the purpose of our constructive making and imagining of our common future. We have inherited it seems, a bad habit of treating the relational entities we call researcher and researched as if they were isolates. More than that, charges Hazelrigg (1989), we have fallen heir to the great conceit of intellectual labour, setting itself apart, simultaneously denying its presence in/as labour (i.e., making, producing, doing) and valorizing itself (without seeming to) as being superior to that which has been defined as doing and making.

> For where it is written that only an elite 'intellectual' can be a theory-maker? The historical condition of a 'division of labour' that gives distinctive space to 'intellectuals': or 'scientists' and 'philosophers' no doubt assigns them to the peculiar 'function' ... But does that mean that an assembly-line worker never theorizes? That a janitor or a nurse or a short

order cook never makes theories? What a terrible conceit that is. But it is, of course, a conceit that infects - no, that is integral to - the historical condition of intellectuals - though not only them, for it is also integral to the historical condition of janitor, nurse and other, insofar as they themselves are quite convinced that they never theorize at all (Hazelrigg, 1989, p.115.)

Thus, while postmodernist thought goes to extremes and is careful not to valorize one methodology over another, it does have a special interest in bringing primary and secondary modalities into congruence and hence, a democratization of knowing which advocates an engaged pluralism.

So, now in conclusion to this sketch we must return to the original question: What kind of domestication is afoot? What about Skinner's spectre of relativism and Wollheim's prophecy of an immobilization of scholarship? Does abandonment of the naturalist premise of any quest for foundations mean that inquiry is, therefore, meaningless cut loose, devoid of purpose? Does multiplicity in perspective and the so-called hermeneutic circle of thought sealed inside itself or the brute fact that all thought is contextual (scheme dependent, historical, language dependent) imply that our hands should be thrown up in despair? Surely we can no longer say that words operate as neutral pictures merely reflecting the contours of a world out there and surely we cannot say that words do no work? So does this mean we should do the next best thing and cleanse them as much as possible and then continue to talk as if unclean words were clean (whatever that means)? And what about the claim that theories are just another form of language, and that all theory is a value-saturated celebration or obituary for some social form. Furthermore, if theory really is labour and there is no way to judge the ultimate validity of various claims to good social theory, then why do we continue habitually to treat relational entities we call researcher and researched as if they were isolates? Would the democratization of theory intensify and ensure the spectre of relativism as a babble of competing voices, and topping it all off leading nowhere loudly?

It is our sympathetic belief that all of the fears concerning the vaunted paralysis of relativism are valid, so long as we cling to the conviction that social-organizational theory is (should be) a science based on any remaining trace of the naturalist premise. The problem of relativism exists as such 'only in dependence on a half-clothed wish for, or assumption of, an absolute standard for true or valid or even verisimilitudinous knowledge' (Hazelrigg, 1989, p.153). The reluctance to push to extremes the idea that society and organizations are made and imagined is habitually justified by the fear that its outcome will be nihilism. 'What precludes a Hitler from the building of a future?' or 'What firm ground, (i.e., what subject-independent and self-identical ground) is there to prevent the unleashing of all sorts of irresponsible claims, deeds, etc.?'

> Questions such as these are calculated to stop all talk of 'making rather than finding' ... As if we might actually awaken one morning to a world, even to an imagination, devoid of constraint, order control! Of course, we may build a Hitlerite future, or worse. Of course, we may end history a month or a year from today. However, an unquestioned belief in a found world as opposed to a world of our own making, will preclude neither possibility ... An argument of making, (i.e., of poiesis of subject-object relations, persistently argues against abdication of responsibility - our responsibility in/or/for the making of world, people, each other (Hazelrigg, 1989, p.261).

In its relational understanding of knowledge, postmodernism opens the door for a constructive co-creation of the future in the here-and-now of inquiry which is simultaneously the joint production of subject and object. The special charity of relativism begins the moment we see ourselves in it. It is to concrete illustration of this whole notion that we shall now turn.

A construction from the field: the emergence of the egalitarian organization

Kurt Lewin has said that there is nothing so practical as good theory. Karl Marx has observed that the point is no longer to interpret the world, but to change it.

In the study that follows we hope to advance the constructive project. In this case, which takes place in a large medical centre, we explore what will be discussed as the inevitable enlightenment effect of inquiry. As a side note, it can be recalled that according to modernist science, all potential enlightenment effects must be reduced or limited through experimental controls. In social psychology, for example, deception still plays a crucial role in doing research; enlightenment effects are viewed as contaminants to good scientific work. Sampson (1978) argues that all of this is tied to a paradigm committed to a bias of self-contained individualism and belief in the possibility of a contextual approach to the discovery of universal facts. Incredulously the force of the paradigm showed its grip on the human sciences when Rosenthal's (1966) discovery of experimenter effects was received with such stirring response. Today we would argue that it is precisely this, the reactive nature of social inquiry that provides organizational theory with its unique purpose, its potential impact and, ultimately, its *raison d' être*. Even if it could be controlled, we would not.

Early in 1980 we were presented with an opportunity to do an organization wide analysis of the Cleveland Clinic (CC), a private, non-profit, tertiary care centre located in Northeastern Ohio. In contrast to the typical image associated with the word clinic, the CC is one of the largest medical centres in the world. At the time we began, the CC had over 7,000 personnel and a physician group practice of more than 400 members (the second largest in existence). With over 100 specialties and subspecialties, the CC provided care annually to some 500,000 patients. The organization had a public reputation as a cutting edge professional partnership capable of providing high quality care in treatment of the most complicated of diseases. Recognized nationally, the United States Congress had awarded the CC the title of National Health Resource because of its pioneering advancement in clinical research, the development of new technology for patient care, and the education of future generations of physicians.

Beyond its medical contribution, however, the physician group practice of the CC was of theoretical interest as a social invention (Whyte, 1982) for the study of participation potential. Excitement for the exploration was ignited during an earlier study begun in 1979 concerned with the question of how professionals, when trained exclusively in their own medical discipline, would apply their professional instincts to the management of organizational activities (see Jensen, 1982). During that particular study it became readily apparent that the general spirit and guiding logic behind the organization's growth was markedly different than the predominate bureaucratic rationality of efficiency and effectiveness (Thompson, 1966). Somehow the professional mentality brought something different to the task of management. At the CC, an emerging consensus about the primary logic of organizing went beyond the economizing functional one (to make profits or fulfill a market demand) and centred around a broader, open-ended psychological one. The efficiency logic of instrumental rationality was by no means inoperable or rejected; it was simply circumscribed by the professionals' practical concern for the ongoing development of an interactive, responsive and cooperative relational process (later we refer to this as an interhuman rationality) in an organization committed to a democratic/participatory form of management.

It was no accident, for example, that the title of a book depicting the organization's 60 year history was 'To Act as a Unit' (Hartwell, 1985). Preeminent concern for the health of the relational side of organizing was focal, early on, in the awareness of each member in the group practice. Yet the full implications of this for a coherent theory of administration was admittedly fraught with ambiguity, myth and mystery:

> It is like Ezekiel's vision of the wheel, in which the big wheel moved by faith and the little wheel moved by the grace of God. The keys to success are the participants' desire to do what is best for the Clinic and their

confidence in one another's integrity. Businessmen looking at this 'unhierarchical' organization feel as mystified as Ezekiel did about what made the wheels work. But they do, and the reason can best be summarized in the expression of 'esprit de corps' (Hartwell, 1985).

Our effort began, therefore, as an attempt to understand this 'spirit' in terms of participation potential and soon progressed into a broader exploration seeking to generate grounded theory (Glaser & Strauss, 1967) into the defining dimensions, categories, and dynamic representatives of the emerging egalitarian or post-bureaucratic organization.

At the time we were beginning our study, we were advised by the Director of Human Resources at the CC of a recent article in Administrative Science Quarterly outlining a provocative research agenda for the field on the very topic of participation potential (see Dachler & Wilpert, 1978). Among other things, the authors raised a whole series of critical concerns about the field's allegiance to cannons of normal science. In particular, one question stood out as central: Why was participation potential such a conspicuously neglected area of study? There were numerous explanations offered, but four in particular, captured our attention and influenced virtually every step in our subsequent work. First, it was pointed out that research in this area, while obviously dealing with a social phenomenon, has, in its own biased way, emphasized individualistic and psychological qualities and has not grappled with the question of integrating the social-phenomenological and structural-functional considerations that integrate participation potential into a coherent systems of psychosocial and contextual factors. The second was even more disturbing: The continuing romance with the belief in value-free research. Here the authors were short and to the point. The traditional scientific view which maintains that value judgments and scientific inquiry are basically incompatible 'makes it difficult, if not impossible, to adequately research the potential of participatory systems' (Dachler & Wilpert, 1978) because the very word potential is normative and requires the research to enter into the realm of non-science and take on a moral burden of discussing what is meant by potential or improvement. Thirdly, as was sharply discussed, much of the organizational research (particularly in America) is politically conservative and frequently has a focus on pathology rooted in an economically utilitarian cultural matrix. The deficiency orientation is inherently conservative, argued the authors, because: the pathology (or management problem) is usually defined by those who hire the researchers; the statement of deficiency implies an a-priori set of assumptions about what is normal which generally typifies the status quo; and by being married to a view of what constitutes the ideal, the problem oriented approach tends to exclude the impulse toward novelty which, of course, is antithetical to the enterprise of generative theorizing (e.g., not many organizational theories in this area were found returning from their explorations refreshed and revitalized, like pioneers returning home, with news of lands unknown but most certainly there).

However, once one realizes that traditional science is not the only game in town, each of these concerns is not only defused but vitally transformed from sources of embarrassment into beacons of insight. As we have argued, the postmodernist turn has done more, much more, than criticize the received traditions of social theory. By beginning to take the ideas of society as made and imagined to the hilt, it has inaugurated a constructive view of the task of social-organizational theory which includes both an explanatory approach to theory and a program for social-organizational reconstruction. As discussed previously good theory, like any new idea unleashed in the world, is agential or formative in character and simply cannot be separated from the ongoing negotiation of everyday social reality. The question is not so much if theory is valid or good but what 'good' does the theory do? Because of this, all social-organizational research is a value concern, a concern of social construction and direction. The choice of what to study, how and what, if offered in public discourse, each imply some degree of responsibility. It also confronts us with exciting opportunity: the very choice of research topic, positive or negative, may be the single most critical determinant of the kind of world the scientific construction of reality helps bring to focus, and perhaps to fruition.

We were approached by the CC to continue our study on the professional mentality but to add to it an organizational diagnosis. Obviously in medical terminology the word diagnosis has a long tradition and is very much linked with a disease orientation as well as the idea of treatment and cure. So we made a counterproposal which essentially argued that health was not merely the absence of disease and that what we were interested in was the former. Following this logic we proposed a process of co-inquiry into the factors and catalytic forces of organizing that served to create, save, and transform the institution in the direction of its highest potential for a participatory system, a condition we later called the ideal membership situation. Data would be collected, a theory would be constructed, and a written article would be published and distributed to the entire organization.

With full agreement of the Board of Governors we began to refine the topic of participation potential with a group of co-researchers from inside the CC. While full details of the methodology have carefully been described elsewhere (Cooperrider, 1986; Srivastva & Cooperrider, 1986), it is important to point out that extensive data were collected, mostly through ethnographic methods, and that the data collection lasted for over a year resulting in more than a thousand pages of notes from the field. We conducted surveys that looked at the group's values and practices at various periods throughout our six year relationship. We facilitated dialogues and discussions about the survey results as well as plans and actions that emerged from these discussions. Equally important was our constructive interest and appreciative focus. We wanted the inquiry to be applicable and provocative, helping to stretch the organization's imagination and expand its sense of the possible. In this regard, our approach must be differentiated from other more ethnographic or cultural mappings. Especially during the data analysis, our approach was highly selective, looking specifically at those factors of organizing (social arrangements and unique cultural meanings) that appeared in association with the intensity, breadth, and duration of what became a dynamically defined notion of the ideal membership situation. The approach was like looking through a microscope seeking to understand even the tiniest markings of the ideal embedded in both reported and observed practices.

Stripped to bare essentials, the approach was based on:

a   an uncompromising presumption of the presence of the topic under scrutiny (since then we have come to the conclusion that virtually any topic related to human or social existence can be studied in virtually any organization anywhere);
b   a belief that grounded theorizing based on examples and discourse from the field, would have greater generative potential than more deductive or purely speculative methods;
c   that the generative potential of our work would be heightened to the extent we could selectively utilize positive deviations in the data to help ignite the theoretical imagination and mind; and
d   our constructive intent was to create a theoretical discourse with perlocutionary force, to help foster dialogue into that which was taken-for-granted and to generate compelling options and possibilities for continued organizational transformation.

In the rest of this section we shall quickly review the theory and then trace what happened.

In keeping with the constructionist principles we outlined earlier, to the extent that inquiry is the beginning of a conceptual order upon an otherwise 'booming, bustling confusion that is the realm of experience' (Dubin, 1978) then the first order of business of the theorist/inquirer is to specify what is there to see, to provide an ontological education (Gergen, 1982). The very act of asking questions highlights not only the parameters of the topic or subject matter but becomes an active agent as a cueing device, a tool which subtly focuses attention on particular possibilities while obscuring others. In some sense, the questions we ask in social science interviews guides what will be talked about and so can determine what we discover. This, of course, can be an occasion for the construction, renewal, or transformation of the interpretive repertoires of a discourse community - like any conversation.

As we mentioned earlier, in this study we were interested in taking an appreciative view into the participatory potential of the organization and focused our interview questions very deliberately so as to shape the contours of the conversation. For example, this was one of the interview questions: Please describe a moment in your career at CCF when you felt most alive, most effective, or most engaged? As a response to this question, one would scarcely envision a respondent recalling experiences of personal failure or illustrations of mechanical bureaucratic dysfunction. Typical in our interviews instead were passion-filled discussions of creativity, courage, achievement, and teamwork. Here is an example of a quote from one of the physicians interviewed:

> Without a doubt, one of the highpoints for me was one of the meetings when we were deciding whether to expand one of our facilities. I had only been here a few years, but I was learning quickly that this was unlike any other hospital I'd ever experienced. The doctors meet and meet and meet and discuss and debate issues that doctors at other hospitals have no voice at all in. Here we were sitting in this long meeting with docs from all different disciplines - it was like a town meeting - and we had been debating the issue very vigorously. And I mean vigorously. There were strong emotions on all sides. At one point I remember thinking that this was deadlocked. This is going nowhere. But then it started shifting. People started changing their views. And I got in it too. It was emotional. People were persuasive. Here's this famous brainy, unemotional, detached neuro-surgeon standing up there holding this fiscal study his committee had done, shaking it in the air and arguing very passionately that this idea would work. I remember thinking to myself, wow this is a dynamic place. People really care about what happens. Not only that. No one here is going to railroad a proposal through without letting all of us get in on it.

Clearly the direction of our question was an occasion for this physician to reinforce, if not create an interpretive repertoire that depicts competent physicians as passionate debaters, engaged in persuading one another to adopt various strategies for the future of the clinic.

Perhaps most interesting, even more than the framing of the discourse, was how news of the inquiry spread quickly to others. As the first series of interviews were completed it was not unusual for people to anticipate our questions and be thoroughly prepared for us. Here is an example of how one interview began:

Interviewer: 'We are here to ....'
Respondent/physician (interrupting):

> I know what it is about. My colleagues in surgery have warned me you are good interviewers. Actually 'warned' isn't the right word. They said they felt inspired by their talk with you. I'll tell you what makes this group vital and alive when it is working well. Let me tell you something about this group. When dealing with major issues we have to resolve it through consensus ....

This physician had begun to answer a question that the interviewer had not yet asked. His anticipation of the interviewer's intent and formulation of an appropriate discourse is testimony to Bakhtin's (1986) notion that every utterance is coauthored. The presence of the listener (interviewer) shapes the response of the speaker. Later in the same interview, we probed this physician in order to understand how she had been so prepared for our entry, what conversations she had engaged in with her colleagues in regard to the on-going interviews.

Respondent/physician:

> You know you set off quite a stir with this organizational study. People are talking about how precious our group practice democracy, our shared governance model really is. I think you called this the 'egalitarian organization'. The great opportunity here is to be involved in the information flow, the dialogue, and the negotiation of decisions.

What we want to emphasize here is how the inquiry we initiated created conversations and versions of events.

Consider the following response by one of the physician's we interviewed:

> Let's see, a time I felt good about being here. Well one time I guess was when I was on the committee overseeing the move to the new clinic building. It could have been a disaster, but it went very smoothly. We worked very closely together and we kept everyone informed - at time I thought we were overdoing it - but it was the right thing to do. The other docs just needed to be kept up on things so there were no surprises. But you want to know what made it rewarding for me?

Interviewer: 'Yes. What happened that made you feel effective?'
Respondent/physician:

Well I guess it was because no one really knew how much I was behind the scenes making all of this happen. I didn't want to be too bossy. I didn't want to be in control - at least not in terms of flashy power. I just made sure that everybody was included and everybody had input to the decisions about allocations and everything. It could have been a real battle. But it went very smoothly. I guess I was being pretty effective because there were no turf battles or anything. I just worked behind the scenes, got everyone's input and consent and coordinated this major move.

This is testimony to the relational formulation of knowledge. Who is doing the recalling here? Is it the physician whose simply triggers a ready-made schema from his long-term memory? Or is it the interaction of the physician and the interviewer as the interviewer provides a context and a cue that triggers a response? Relational basis of knowledge argues that all understanding is dialogical. The first physician's response, his description of the organization as vital and alive are categories and attributions that emerge in the space between him and the interviewer. This is testimony to the contagion effect of the inquiry and the dynamic, evolving nature of discourse communities. Would the doctors be reflecting and having conversations about their shared values if we were not there asking them these questions? And further, as we reflect back to them our construal of their experiences in our language - using words like egalitarian - do these utterances then become part of their interpretive repertoire, giving them another way to constitute their organizational lives? It is to this point that we address next as we constructed surveys that looked at their ideals and values.

Based on the real-life stories from the interviews, we constructed a survey in which inquiry into the egalitarian organization was extended by asking: To what extent do you feel the egalitarian theory is important as an ideal to be pursued by its organization? Which parts of theory (values) are most important to you and why? and To what extent is the theory reflected as an actuality in practice? The survey was created in correspondence to such questions and was used in a two-fold manner. The first would be to use the survey itself as a means for bringing the egalitarian theory directly into the culture of the CC and to the widest number of people for dialogue, debate and further development. Because of this, the survey was constructed a bit differently than most surveys intended supposedly for statistical analysis and independent measurement. The major difference was that the survey items often contained numerous concepts linked together, in contrast to the simple, concise one-concept items used in scientifically designed survey items. For example, the following statement has at least three different concepts in it, linked together showing the causal relations among concepts, as if it were a theory:

In this group practice there are minimal bureaucratic constraints because members are able to initiate changes when formal rules, procedures or structures are no longer useful or relevant. There is nothing sacred about any organizational arrangement that shouldn't be questioned or changed once it has lost its usefulness.

The second function of the survey was to collect quantitative data concerning members' agreement or disagreement with the ideals as it related to their own experience. These data would then serve not as proof or disproof but would serve as yet one more form of theoretical language which again would enter the common culture of discourse through processes of feedback. In this sense, then, numbers would play an important generative function because they are a concise rhetorical device which (in our Western culture) carry a great deal of authority and hence, have the power to stimulate dialogue and consideration of constructive alternatives.[1]

Feedback meetings were held with the various divisions in which members reflected on the results of the survey and continued their conversations about the values as they applied to division's culture. The divisions began holding half-day and full-day retreats at which members discussed and debated their strategic direction in light of these values. We found increasingly that the language of the surveys was permeating their discussions. Further, new action possibilities were proposed.

In its pragmatic form, the inquiry was designed around the idea that organizations are made and imagined and can, be remade and reimagined. Our hope was to contribute to what we now refer to as an organization's constructive integrity, that is, to contribute to its context-revising freedom on a collective organization-wide basis and to help increase the system's capacity to translate shared ideals into both experienced practices and responsive structures. Did this occur? Tables 9.1 and 9.2 present t-values for reported changes in organizational practices in two separate divisions of the CC over a two year period. Also, in the administrative division, a task force was assembled to discuss what changes had been initiated since the inquiry began. Table 9.3 presents a summary of their report. Most notable was the structural creation of a division-wide 'governing board' which would be made up of elected participants from every level in the organization. All in all there were more than 50 structural, behavioral, and relational-attitudinal changes reported by the group and each of these were supported by survey data that showed significant increases in such things as face-to-face interaction, consensus decision making, unity of purpose, opportunity for involvement, and others. Of important interest as well, data suggested that not only were people able to make their values known and used them as a guiding force for practice, they were also becoming increasingly idealistic as a group. Table 9.3 shows, for example, that virtually every rating in response to the question, 'How important is this statement as an ideal for the organization?' went up from time one to time two and seven moved significantly. What was most remarkable about the apparent shifts is that they happened in relation to values that were high to begin with. For example, tolerance for uncertainty, viewed as essential to an emerging egalitarian organization went from a mean importance of 5.79 to 6.37. There is just not much higher to go on a seven-point idealism scale.

The contagion effect of this theoretical inquiry on the discourse community did not end here, however. Analysis of data resulted in a set of theoretical propositions published shortly thereafter (Srivastva & Cooperrider, 1986). The primary ideas set forth in that paper argued quite forcefully that any organization, if it so chooses, could become an egalitarian system and that the iron law of oligarchy was, in fact, not a law but a construction, one which has served notoriously to undermine our sense of the possible. Our intent was not to downplay or deny real world constraints. Nor was our approach utopian. But what we were doing, as has been said, was searching for an explanatory practice that, by providing a credible account of emergent social novelty or innovation in a more egalitarian direction, would inspire rather than subvert the constructive project. In brief, the theory proposed:

a   that participation potential is activated by simple choice and commitment to three overarching values - inclusion, consent, and excellence;
b   that once publicly agreed, these egalitarian values give rise to an interhuman organizational rationality and discourse that will supersede the techno-rational mode as the basis for decision making about the organization itself;
c   that an interhuman logic serves to focus attention on possibilities for eliminating arbitrary barriers to active participation which seem inevitably to arise in organizations; and
d   that an interhuman logic seeks to create structures of interaction that empower human relationships in the work and political spheres (e.g., shared governance structures whereby there is no such thing as a formal hierarchy of authority in which subordinates are expected to surrender their own judgments to the commands of a superior) and serve as a democratizing and group building force.

Again, most important at this point, was not the content of the emerging theory, but the process of dialogue, debate, and organization/theory/self-development that took place over the next five years (see Cooperrider, 1986; Hopper, 1991). At this point we need to make something perfectly clear. At no point during the last six years did the authors make a contract with the organization that a long term project would be taking place in order to help the system improve its functioning. The only thing that was agreed to was that research would take place and that results would be shared and used by the organization, 'if' it so desired. We put the word 'if' in quotations because it is part of our common vocabulary which still thinks of research as though there is a difference between basic and applied research. In this case, at least, the phrase 'if it so desired' was false. There was no choice.

This is mentioned because we had literally no expectation of working on the study for the next five years. But as events unfolded, the process of inquiry took on a life of its own. After the Board of Governors reviewed the emerging theory, numerous departments and advisors came forward asking for copies of the article for discussion throughout their sections. For weeks we were contacted and asked to give presentations to managers, employees, and other professional specialists. Likewise, on the basis of the paper, we were invited to participate in literally dozens of departmental planning retreats. In one Division alone, which we will discuss in more depth, the authors attended more than 100 meetings from 1981-1983, all revolving around discourse and experimentation with the egalitarian ideas. Since that time plans were launched to make the emerging theory part of: socialization programs for new incoming members, and the newly created physician-in-management annual one-week management training program. We were even invited to speak to visitors of CC from overseas, all of whom came ostensibly to learn about the CC's unique approach to management.

We were continually struck by how the publication of the journal article became the springboard for many discussions. At one meeting with Medical Division council, members spoke about the impact of the article, illustrating that theoretical discourse has the potential to create the very phenomena that it proposes to find. One physician remarked:

> When I read this article I felt excited. Someone finally put words to what I think gets at the heart and soul of this organization. As I said in my interview, a person trained in management is just an administrator. That type of person hasn't a feel for this kind of organization or our field. They don't know how I think or what motivates a person like me. They only know what motivates them. They want to get to the top of the pyramid and jockey people around.

Another physician remarked at the meeting:

> Lately we have heard complaints that the consensus culture we've developed here is too slow, too many committees, too cumbersome. But I

think the study is right. It is not whether or not to operate democratically, it is a question of how to mobilize consensus faster. Without the consensus mode we will again experience a hardening of the lines of authority.

Note how, following Derrida (1978), the discussion of the article becomes an occasion to utter sets of differences that create and maintain the traces of what is taken as normal in this community. The definition of conventional managers/administrators as those who seek efficiency, keep memos, climb pyramids, create a sterile environment becomes an occasion to depict physicians as different: they have a feel for the organization, should not be invested only in efficiency, climbing the hierarchy, or creating sterile environments.

Karl Weick (1983) contends that managerial theories gain their generative power by helping people overlook disorder and presume orderliness. Theory energizes action by providing a presumption of logic which enables people to act with certainty, attention, care, and control. Even if the theory is inadequate as a conceptual description of current reality, if it is forceful it may provoke action that brings into the world a new social construction of reality which then confirms the original theory. Weick explains:

> The underlying theory need not be objectively 'correct'. In a crude sense, any old explanation will do. This is so because explanation serves mostly to organize and focus the action. Thus the adequacy of organizational explanation is determined by the intensity and structure it adds to potentially self-validating actions.

As linguistic phrases, such as egalitarian organization achieve acceptance as explanatory devices, further actions become justified which leads to more forceful explanations. Since situations can support a variety of meanings, their action-stirring potential are dependent on the way in which the theory enters into the domain of a given discourse community. By providing a language, a presumption of logic, and a basis for forceful action, theory goes a long way in forming a common set of self-fulfilling expectations for the future. Obviously in a single-case field study, it is impossible to isolate the transformative role that theory played in producing such change. Nor is that our intent. To say that the egalitarian theory caused the developments would be to fail to see that the transformations were also causing the theory and in this would serve only to contradict the point we hope to vivify. And what is that point?

It is here that we need a marriage between the two epigrams that opened this discussion. As Lewin put it, 'there is nothing so practical as a good theory'. But Marx apparently began to feel otherwise: 'The point is no longer to interpret the world but to change it'. Castoriadis (1987) makes an important observation when he says that the blinding light of Marx's statement does nothing to clarify the relationship between knowing and changing. Nor does Lewin's, for that matter. Each in their own way seems to imply that there may be a choice between the two. But a constructive view of knowledge cannot agree and posits that the enlightenment effect of all inquiry is a brute fact; all theory is at one stroke a doing that always involves an undergoing. By establishing perceptual cues and frames, by providing presumptions of logic, by transmitting subtle values, by creating new language, and by extending compelling images and constraints, perhaps in all these ways, organizational theory becomes a constructive means whereby norms, beliefs, and actual cultural practices may be altered.

There is one closing note on the CC experience. Looking back over the whole series of years, one episode stands as most memorable.

Shortly after the end of the first year, the Medical Division asked one of the authors to provide training at a staff retreat. The training was to centre around the very well known model of decision making by Victor Vroom. In brief, the model provides a decision-chart structure for helping a superior determine when it is appropriate to include subordinates in group decision making (GII) and when it is more effective for the superior to make the decision him or herself (AII). Articles on the model were handed out prior to the meeting so the lecture was brief, just enough to get people started analysing a few cases. Things went well. The author began thinking that the training was a perfectly good idea. Certainly it would be useful in exploring the ideas in the egalitarian theory because, as he recalled, most of the cases showed the reason and need for GII decision making. The author was taken back then when during a break one of the young physicians came up to him and said: 'You know this is all bullshit don't you!' He said then: 'I bet if you counted in both the article and your lecture the number of times the word subordinate was used, it would be close to fifty times.' The author responded: 'I hadn't realized that, but I guess it certainly is interesting.' The young physician then continued: 'The problem is that these ideas may be all right for the business world, but they won't do here. As you said yourself the other day in your survey, we are a partnership of physicians. I'm not a subordinate. I'm not just an employee here. I resent what your training is trying to do to us.'

The experience was powerful. It made the author think back to his use for years of this particular training program and how he had used the term subordinate unthinkingly thousands of times in his work with managers. But when he got home that night he mapped out what must have been going on for this young physician (see Figure 9.1).

As is obvious now, the word subordinates was not just some neutral descriptive term. There is no such thing as a subordinate out there somewhere in reality that can be pointed to and objectively described. The word subordinate is virtually nothing, meaningless as a descriptive term, until it is seen as a key link in a broader theory of bureaucracy, a theory that says that organizations work and work best when there is a hierarchy of offices and a clear chain-of-command. In such a system, orders are to be issued by those above and those below have the duty to carry them out. In fact, what makes the whole thing work is that the orders are impersonal, they are issued from offices or roles at a necessary higher level of command. The beauty of the whole thing is that, ideally, everyone just does his or her own job according to the prescribed scheme. As Weber (1947) himself put it, 'bureaucracy advances the more it is dehumanized'. There is no such thing - or need - for an emotion filled sense of partnership, responsibility and ownership for the whole. What is so memorable, then, was the author's virtual lack of awareness that he, himself, had time and time again helped to support and reproduce, in interaction with others, a powerful bureaucratic theory and ideology.

The language of bureaucracy, like all theoretical language, helps cue our attention on what is there to see. It helps to set expectations about what the world is or should be; and it subtly constrains our attention and our ability to recognize other possibilities. It was not until the young physician rejected the training that the author really began to recognize and ponder the role of theory in the scientific construction of reality. As it was, the egalitarian theory seems also to have had some impact: 'I'm not a subordinate', he said, 'I'm a partner'.

Conclusion: the constructive task of organizational theory

No discipline has ever taken the idea of society as made and imagined to the hilt. But once done, it can be surely anticipated that there will be no return to the old, not only because new vistas of study and construction will continue to appear, but because the theorist him or herself will come to experience what it is like to have their lives count, and count affirmatively, as it relates to the creative and crucial questions of the time. For our own field, to say that organizations are made and imagined does not go far enough. To pause at this juncture will only lead to further equivocation and aimless babble. To take the essential modern management insight to its logical conclusion, immediately brings the not-so-innocent question: If organizations are made and imagined, how can we excuse the organizational theorist from the same argument? Clearly the study discussed here is only a beginning. It was offered as illustration and as an open invitation to further exploration into the intimate unity of theory/practice/development.

We believe there will be an immense harvest of creative theoretical contribution when the constructed/constructuring nature of our work becomes the common and explicit property of all. The opportunity posed by this issue is so fundamentally important to the vital reconstruction of organizational theory that it would truly be impossible to overstress it. To say that the truth of human freedom must count; to acknowledge the primacy of multiperspective in social knowing; to affirm that words enable worlds; to state that every theory celebrates; or to grapple with the democratization of mind; no matter how the basic point is made, to place this at the epicentre of social-organizational thought is to take the crucial step in fashioning a theoretical enterprise of creative significance to society.

The 'how' or programmatic basis of a constructive approach to organizational theory is beyond the scope of this discussion. But a number of possibilities can be quickly put forward. All are based on the bedrock idea that the constructive co-enlightenment effect of all organizational theory is a brute fact. That is, the understanding of organizations and their/own practical transformation is a single undifferentiated act that consists of two moments: the moment of enlightenment whereby theorizing on organizational processes continuously enters into, reconstructs, and becomes part of the reality being considered, and the moment of reverse enlightenment, (i.e., by constructing ways of knowing in one or another manner the doer of this activity becomes their preconceived vision and concomitant construction). The following possibilities for constructive organizational theory are based on this understanding and stem from our experiences with organizations that have actually experimented with the idea on a collective and organization-wide basis.

A role for human cosmogony

Inquiry into organizations, if it appreciates human cosmogony (Barrett & Srivastva, 1991), can serve to cleanse our perceptions and de-reify our basic assumptions, liberating us to act in a world that appears more malleable. We need to study organizations as evolving and transforming, social constructions, malleable to human freedom. We need to appreciate history and the continuities in collective life, not in the sense of history as unfolding and predetermined as Comte, Hegel, or Marx would have it, for this kind of historicism would further the sense of inevitability and necessity for human action. Rather we need to appreciate the human cosmogony, the creative birth of diverse social arrangements. We need to direct our efforts not so much toward explaining why something functions but rather understanding how and under what conditions something was created, the choices considered and not taken, as well as the paths chosen, the conjectures, the possibilities, the accidental and unintended.

A focus on social innovation

The constructionist project requires that we actively cut the link between the possibility of social-organizational explanation and the denial or downplaying of our freedom to remake the social organizational worlds we construct or cohabit. It is partly because of our failure to notice alternative possibilities that we continue to be seduced into the frozen reality surrounding the naturalist premise. High on the agenda of the constructive project is to develop those explanatory practices that by providing us with credible accounts of discontinuous change and social novelty, inspires rather than subverts the constructionist's transformational aim: the effort to open the world, through our understandings and knowledge to our ever evolving values and constructions of the widest possible good. In our own work for example (Cooperrider & Pasmore, 1991; Srivastva & Cooperrider, 1990), we have inaugurated a ten year program of research into social innovations in global management. Here we are trying to create a new discourse into what we feel is the most important social intervention of our time, the people-centred global social change organization (GSCO). These transnational organizations which have emerged since World War II to deal with world issues of all kinds have a great deal to teach about the prospects for collective action at a global level (e.g., eradication of smallpox). Yet, in spite of its rapid proliferation and number (est. 20,000 GSCOs in the past 40 years), this social invention has been conspicuously overlooked in the leading organizational and administrative science journals in the field (not one article has been written about them in ten years). Many of the materials for generative theorizing are close at hand. To carry to extremes the idea that organizations are made and imagined requires that we capitalize on all these positive deviations instead of staying locked in the confining and belittling worlds of encrusted habit. History is really surprising, but only if we take time to notice.

No need to apologize for appreciation

Much of our work in recent years has been proposed as an approach to knowledge that complements the critical theory which somehow never goes far enough with its own constructionist arguments (Cooperrider & Srivastva, 1987; Srivastva & Cooperrider, 1990). For all its negativism, much of the field fails to tap into the inspiring potential of human cosmogony or social innovation and leads incessantly to a narrow conception of transformative possibility. In a world in which most everything is under assault, it has been our feeling that there is a need for a new vocabulary and grammar of understanding that is no longer imprisoned by the cynical, intimidated by the positive, or pulled into empty-headedness by the blatantly wishful. Appreciative ways of knowing are constructively powerful, we have argued, precisely because organizations are, to a large extent, affirmative projections. They are guided in their actions by anticipatory forestructures of knowledge which like a movie projector on a screen, projects a horizon of confident construction which energizes, intensifies, coordinates, and provokes action in the present. Our own work with appreciative forms of inquiry has left us with the ever present question: Is it possible that through our assumptions and choice of method, we largely create the worlds we later discover?

For much too long we have painted the picture of organizational life by leaving out a whole series of colours. One of those colours has been us.

Table 9.1
Means, standard deviations and T-values for administrative division practices across time

| | Time One | | Time Two | | |
| | N = 49 | | N = 40 | | |
Item	x	s.d.	x	s.d.	T-Value
Unity of Purpose	3.65	1.42	4.05	1.17	-1.44*
Shared Ownership	3.83	1.53	3.97	1.29	-0.47
Collective Authority	3.40	1.59	3.32	1.40	0.26
Face-to-Face Int.	4.10	1.63	4.97	1.42	-2.69**
Consensus D-Making	4.04	1.28	4.55	1.76	-1.93*
Communal Pol. Phil.	3.51	1.31	--	--	--
Free Choice	3.38	1.51	3.45	1.41	-0.21
Ongoing Learning	4.91	1.59	4.47	1.05	1.54
Candid Debate	4.00	1.53	4.00	1.67	0.00
Coll. Work Rel.	3.93	1.43	4.10	1.46	0.52
Tol. Uncertainty	4.12	1.31	4.02	1.47	0.33
Reward Diversity	4.20	1.64	4.65	1.83	-1.18
Ideas on Merit	4.20	1.67	3.82	1.39	1.17
Spirit of Inquiry	4.58	1.44	--	--	--
Opps-Involvement	3.12	1.64	3.72	1.89	-1.58*
Coll. Reward System	3.27	1.40	--	--	--
Trust & Confidence	3.76	1.50	3.67	1.43	0.29
Innovative Org.	4.75	1.45	4.45	1.56	0.92
Devotion to Excellence	4.65	1.45	4.72	1.20	-0.25

Inspirational System	4.28	1.51	3.77	1.87	0.78*
Colleague Control	14.15	1.38	--	--	--
Dev. Leadership	3.77	1.60	3.90	1.37	-0.41
Min. Bureaucracy	4.31	1.81	4.25	1.69	0.17
Dem. Partnership	3.59	1.51	3.87	1.57	-0.84
Permanent Dialogue	4.28	1.29	4.58	1.61	-0.95
Significant Work	4.63	1.66	4.35	1.51	0.84
Self-Authority	3.97	1.73	--	--	--
Dev. Colleagueship	4.27	1.63	4.55	1.37	-0.87
Shared Information	3.87	1.55	3.97	1.52	-0.30
Dem. Leadership	4.20	1.58	3.95	1.39	0.80

* p=. 05 one-tailed test of significance
**p= .01 one-tailed test of significance

These items were taken off the second survey by the Division's newly founded representative council.

Table 9.2
Means, standard deviations and T-values for the medical department's practices across time

	Time One $N = 49$		Time Two $N = 40$		
Item	x	s.d.	x	s.d.	T-Value
Unity of Purpose	3.50	1.46	4.60	1.24	-2.26**
Shared Ownership	2.81	1.32	4.26	1.32	-3.04**
Collective Authority	2.18	1.22	0.33	1.44	-2.37**
Face-to-Face Int.	2.93	1.53	4.40	1.50	-2.65**
Consensus D-Making	2.62	1.20	4.40	1.40	-3.77***
Communal Pol. Phil.	2.64	1.39	4.33	1.34	-3.32***
Free Choice	2.50	1.41	3.93	1.33	-2.90**
Ongoing Learning	5.00	0.89	5.33	1.59	-0.28
Candid Debate	3.37	1.58	4.33	1.49	-1.73*
Coll. Work Rel.	4.12	1.40	5.00	1.30	-1.79*
Tol. Uncertainty	3.50	1.46	4.13	1.18	-1.33*
Reward Diversity	4.00	1.78	4.13	1.72	-0.21
Ideas on Merit	3.75	1.52	4.26	1.43	-0.97
Spirit of Inquiry	3.75	1.48	4.13	1.30	-0.77
Opps-Involvement	2.62	1.40	4.33	1.75	-2.87**
Coll. Reward System	3.62	1.20	4.00	1.60	-0.73
Trust & Confidence	4.50	1.46	5.26	0.79	-1.83*
Innovative Org.	5.00	1.15	4.93	1.28	0.15
Devotion to Excellence	5.50	1.15	5.46	0.99	0.09

Inspirational System	4.12	1.40	4.66	1.29	-1.12*
Colleague Control	3.31	1.49	4.73	0.79	-3.33**
Dev. Leadership	2.81	1.37	4.00	1.64	-2.17**
Min. Bureaucracy	3.19	1.51	3.66	1.67	-0.83
Dem. Partnership	2.50	1.50	3.40	1.50	-1.67*
Permanent Dialogue	4.00	1.55	3.86	1.55	0.23
Significant Work	4.43	1.41	5.00	1.04	-1.25
Self-Authority	3.53	1.50	4.33	1.39	-1.51*
Dev. Colleagueship	4.56	1.36	5.26	1.20	-1.48*
Shared Information	2.68	1.44	4.26	2.05	-2.46**
Dem. Leadership	2.75	1.57	4.26	1.48	-2.76**

*   p= .05 one-tailed test o significance
** p= .01 one-tailed test o significance
***p= .001 one-tailed test o significance

Table 9.3
Positive changes attributed to appreciative intervention ('E.T.') by members of the administrative division

Structural/Procedural Changes
a   Formation of shared governance (Representative Council)
b   Increased use and effectiveness of cross-departmental temporary project teams
c   Formation of career ladders (i.e., interim positions)
d   Regular division-wide discussion versus informal meetings
e   Division-wide 'brown-bag' lunches
f   Interdepartmental meetings
g   Division representative at directors meetings
h   Formalized team-building program for each department
i   Implementation of flex-time
j   Development workshops for non-exempts
k   More/new responsibilities given to non-exempts
l   Introduction of new performance review system
m   Division-wide job audit
n   More frequent updates on strategic plans
o   Clarified tasks and interrelationships between individuals and departments
p   Monthly 'press meeting' luncheons
q   Participative agenda setting procedures
r   Career development program, cross-training, increased educational support
s   Establishment of move coordinators and participative planning process
t   Participation in the planning for new technology (i.e., computerization for the division)
u   New orientation program for division

Relational/Behavioral Changes
a   More members taking responsibility for self and their concerns
b   Improved divisional communication and less misunderstanding
c   Improved individual and departmental cooperation
d   Improved divisional work effectiveness through elimination of 'cracks' between departments
e   Increased dialogue in all departments and between departments
f   Increased opportunity for exempts and non-exempts to present and represent their ideas to the division

g   More recognition given to non-exempt employees (e.g., speeches at division-wide meetings)
h   Has allowed for more participation and contribution by people not otherwise involved
i   More sharing of information before decisions are made
j   Directors are listening more
k   More mentioning between specialists
l   Everyone behaves more as if they have power
m   Less unhealthy competition
n   Stronger, more open leadership
o   Learning group leadership skills among all levels

Relational/Attitudinal Changes

a   Heightened awareness of group and individual feelings throughout the division
b   Heightened awareness of the extent to which our practice is short of our ideals
c   Non-exempts are viewed more accurately and positively versus stereotypically
d   Increased readiness to deal with important issues and concerns
e   Non-exempts feel more included, more important
f   Less of a gap between the three levels, more equality
g   Feel like a whole division
h   Increased desire and drive for consistency around values
i   Increased mutual respect
j   More commitment and follow-through on projects
k   More integration of values into our day-to-day work with the organization and trying to help others understand and embody the values
l   Increased shared awareness of divisions/issues
m   Reduction of the caste system
n   Greater sense of professionalism
o   Feelings of optimism concerning the future

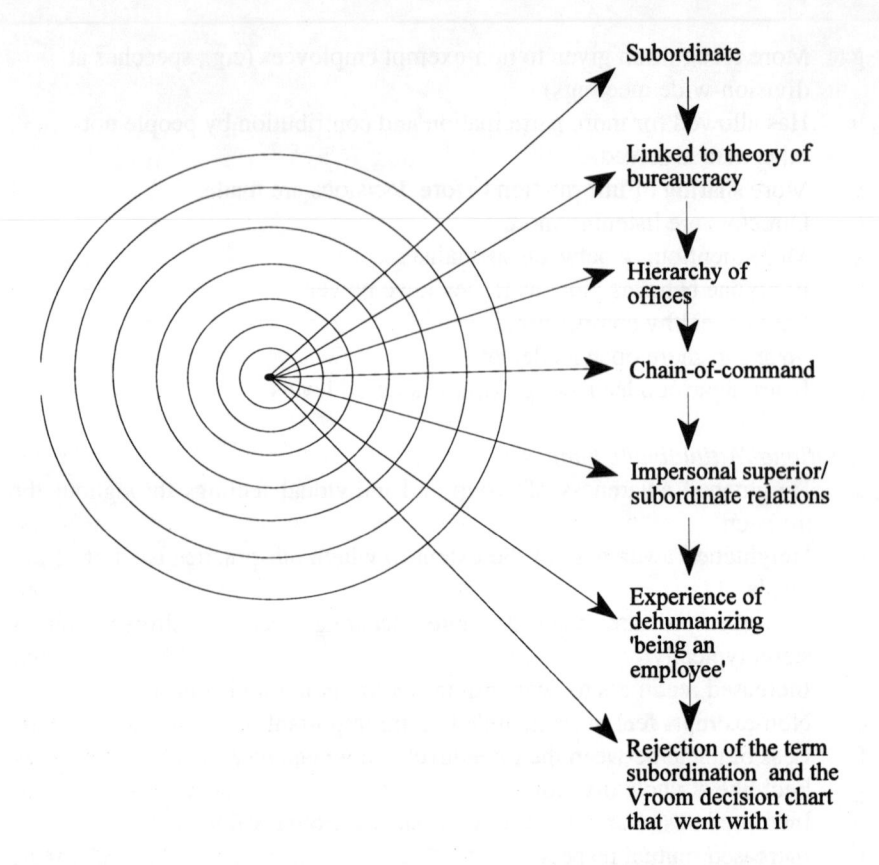

- Subordinate
- Linked to theory of bureaucracy
- Hierarchy of offices
- Chain-of-command
- Impersonal superior/subordinate relations
- Experience of dehumanizing 'being an employee'
- Rejection of the term subordination and the Vroom decision chart that went with it

Figure 9.1 The ripple effect of the power of theoretical language

References

Astley, W. (1985), 'Administrative science as socially constructed truth', *Administrative Science Quarterly*, 30, pp.497-513.

Austin, J. (1975), *How to Do Things With Words*, 2nd edition, Harvard University Press, Cambridge, MA.

Bakhtin, M.M. (1986), *Speech Genre's and Other Late Essays*, University of Texas Press, Austin.

Barrett, F.J. (1990) *The Development of the Cognitive Organization*, unpublished doctoral dissertation, University Microfilms International, Ann Arbor, MI.

Barrett, F.J. & Srivastva, S. (1991), 'History as a mode of inquiry in organizational life: a role for human cosmogony', *Human Relations*, 44, 12, pp.231-254.

Bernstein, R. (1983), *Beyond Objectivism and Relativism: Sciences, Hermeneutics And Praxis*, Basil Blackwell, Oxford.

Beyer, J. & Trice, H. (1982), 'Utilization process: conceptual framework and synthesis of findings', *Administrative Science Quarterly*, 22, pp.591-622.

Bloor, D. (1976), *Knowledge and Social Imagery*, Routledge Kegan Paul, London.

Booth, W. (1984), *A Rhetoric of Irony*, University of Chicago Press, Chicago.

Brown, R.H. (1978), 'Bureaucracy as proxies: toward a political phenomenology of formal Organizations', *Administrative Science Quarterly*, 23, 3, pp.365-382.

Castoriadis, C. (1987), *The Imaginary Institution of Society*, The MIT Press, Cambridge MA.

Cooperrider, D.L. (1990), 'Positive Image, Positive Action: The Affirmative Basis of Organizing' in Srivastva, S., Cooperrider, D.L. & Associates, *Appreciative Management and Leadership*, Jossey Bass, San Francisco.

Cooperrider, D.L. (1986), *Appreciative Inquiry: Toward a Methodology for Understanding and Enhancing Organizational Innovation*, unpublished doctoral dissertation, University Microfilms International, Ann Arbor, MI.

Cooperrider, D.L. & Pasmore, W.A. (1991), 'The organization dimension of global change', *Human Relations*, 44, 8, pp.763-785.

Cooperrider, D.L. & Srivastva, S. (1987), 'Appreciative Inquiry in Organizational Life' in Pasmore, W.A. & Woodman, R. (eds.), *Research in Organizational Change and Development*, 1, JAI Press, Greenwich, CT.

Dachler, H.P. & Wilpert, B. (1978), 'Conceptual dimensions and boundaries of participation in organizations: a critical evaluation', *Administrative Science Quarterly*, 23, pp.1-39.

Derrida, J. (1978), *Writing and Difference*, University of Chicago Press, Chicago.
Dubin, R. (1978), *Theory Building*, Free Press, New York.
Feyerabend, P. (1976), *Against Method*, Humanities Press, New York.
Fish, S. (1980), *Is There a Text in This Class? The Authority of Interpretive Communities*, Harvard University Press, Cambridge.
Foucault, M. (1972), *The Archaeology of Knowledge,* Tavistock, London.
Friedlander, F. (1984), 'Producing useful knowledge for organizations', *Administrative Science Quarterly*, 4, pp.646-648.
Gadamer, H.-G. (1975), *Truth And Method*, Seabury, NY.
George, J. (1988), 'International relations and the search for thinking space', *International Studies Quarterly*, 33, pp.269-179.
Gergen, K. (1990), 'Affect and Organization in Postmodern Society' in Srivastva, S., Cooperrider, D. & Associates, *Appreciative Management and Leadership*, Jossey-Bass, San Francisco.
Gergen, K. (1988), 'The social constructionist movement in modern psychology', *American Psychologist*, 40, pp.266-275.
Gergen, K. (1988), 'Toward a postmodern psychology', Invited Address, *International Congress of Psychology*, Sydney, Australia.
Gergen, K. (1982), *Toward a Transformation in Social Knowledge,* Springer, New York.
Gergen, K. (1978), 'Toward generative theory', *Journal of Personality and Social Psychology*, 36, pp.344-360.
Giddins, A. (1976), *New Rules of Sociological Method*, Basic Books, New York.
Glaser, B. & Strauss, A. (1967), *The Discovery of Grounded Theory,* Aldine Press, Chicago.
Gould, S. (1981), *The Mismeasure of Man*, Norton, New York.
Gouldner, A. (1970), *The Coming Crisis of Western Sociology*, Basic Books, New York.
Hartwell, S.W. Jr. (1985), *To Act as a Unit: The Story of the Cleveland Clinic*, W.B. Saunders Co., Philadelphia.
Hazelrigg, L. (1989), *Claims of Knowledge*, Vol.2, University of Florida Press, Tallahassee, FL.
Heidegger, M. (1927; 1967), *Being and Time.*, Harper & Row, New York.
Hopper, V.L. (1991), *An Appreciative Study of Highest Human Values in a Major Health Care Organization*, unpublished doctoral dissertation, Case Western Reserve University, Cleveland, Ohio.
Jensen, A. (1982), *Professional Approaches to Organizational Life*, unpublished doctoral dissertation, Case Western Reserve University, Cleveland, Ohio.
Kuhn, T.S. (1970), *The Structure of Scientific Revolution*, (2nd ed.) University of Chicago Press, Chicago, IL.

Morgan, G. (1986), *Images of Organization*, Sage, New York.
Pfeffer, J. (1982), *Organization and Organization Theory*, Pitman, Boston.
Ricoeur (1976), *Interpretation Theory: Discourse and the Surplus of Meaning*, Christian University Press, Ft. Worth, TX.
Rorty, R. (1989), *Contingency, Irony, and Solidarity*, Cambridge University Press, New York.
Rorty, R. (1979), *Philosophy and the Mirror of Nature*, Princeton University Press, Princeton.
Rosenthal, R. (1966), *Experimenter Effects in Behavioral Research*, Appleton-Century-Crofts, New York.
Sampson, E. (1989), 'The challenge of social change for psychology: globalization and psychology's theory of the person', *American Psychologist*, 44, pp.914-921.
Sampson, E. (1978), 'Scientific paradigms and social values: wanted: a scientific revolution', *Journal of Personal and Social Psychology*, 36, pp.1332-1343.
Saussure, F. de (1983), *Course in General Linguistics*, Duckworth, London.
Schein, E. (1985), *Organizational Culture and Leadership*, Jossey-Bass, San Francisco.
Skinner, Q. (1985), *The Return of the Grand Theory in the Human Sciences*, Cambridge University Press, Cambridge.
Srivastva, S., Cooperrider, D. & Associates (1990), *Appreciative Management and Leadership*, Jossey-Bass, San Francisco.
Srivastva, S. & Cooperrider, D. (1986), 'The emergence of the egalitarian organization', *Human Relations*, 39, pp.638-724.
Srivastva, S. & Associates (1983), *The Executive Mind*,. Jossey Bass, San Francisco.
Steier, F. (1991), *Research and Reflexivity*, Sage, London.
Sussman, G. & Evered, R. (1978), 'An assessment of the scientific merits of action research', *Administrative Science Quarterly*, 23, pp.582-603.
Thompson, J. (1966), *Organizations in Action*, McGraw-Hill, New York.
Unger, R. (1987), *Social Theory: Its Situation and Its Task*, Cambridge University Press, New York.
Warriner, C.K., Hall, R.H. & McKelvey (1981), 'The comparative description of organizations: a research note and invitation', *Organization Studies*, 2, pp.173-175.
Weber, M. (1947), *The Theory of Social and Economic Organization*, Free Press, New York.
Weick, K. (1983). 'Managerial Thought in the Context of Action' in Srivastva, S. & Associates, *The Executive Mind*, Jossey Bass, San Francisco.

White, H. (1978), 'Introduction: tropology, discourse and modes of human consciousness' in White, H. (ed.), *Topics of Discourse: Essays in Cultural Criticism Discourse*, John Hopkins University Press, Baltimore.

Whitehead, A.M. (1929), *Process and Reality*. Free Press, New York.

Winch, P. (1946), *The Ideal of Social Science*, Routledge Kegan Paul, London.

Whyte, W. (1982), 'Social inventions for solving human problems', *American Sociological Review*, 47, pp.1-8.

Wittgenstein, L. (1963), *Philosophical Investigations*, MacMillan, New York.

Wollheim, R. (1980), *Art and its Objects* (2nd ed.). Cambridge University Press, Cambridge.

Notes

1. We felt that this was especially important for a physician culture, grounded in positivist science. When the doctors received the statistical results of the survey, they spent little time arguing about the validity and reliability of the claims and instead discussed the relevance of the values and ideals as well as the transformations they were witnessing. Put simply, numbers and statistics constitute vital languages in this discourse community in that they make certain claims arguable and others not.

10 Relational knowledge in organizational theory: An exploration into some of its implications

Thomas S. Eberle

Cooperrider et al., in their chapter in this volume, aim to take the 'modern management insight' that organizations are 'made and imagined' 'to its logical conclusion'.[1] They say that if societies and organizations are made and imagined, i.e. are products of human interaction and social construction, they can be remade and reimagined. To take this argument 'to the hilt', the authors apply it to the organizational theorist and try to take systematically into account the constructed/constructing nature of the theorist's work: 'the postmodern implication that organizations are made and imagined can serve as an invitation to revitalize the practice of social science'. In other words, they want to explore 'what it means for organizational behaviour to take on its own constructive project - that is, to fashion for itself a practice of social theory that simultaneously includes an explanatory approach to organizations and a program for organizational reconstruction and development'. Their 'bedrock idea' is that 'the constructive co-enlightenment effect of all organizational theory is a brute fact'. In their conclusion, they recommend an 'appreciative approach' for organizational theory, one that appreciates the human cosmogony and focuses on social innovation. Thus 'new vistas of study and construction will continue to appear' and 'the theorist him - or her - self will soon come to experience what it is like to have their lives count, count affirmatively, as it relates to the creative and crucial questions of our time'.

While sympathetic with the thrust of this proposal, I sense a lack of elaboration in some epistemological and methodological aspects and in some fundamental concepts. In this chapter I intend to focus on the concept of relational knowledge and explore some of its implications. My basic thesis is that much can be gained if we draw on the insights of phenomenologically founded social constructionism. While basing my arguments primarily on the chapter of Cooperrider et al., I will develop them into a more fundamental critique of postmodern constructionism, where Cooperrider et al. locate their own approach, which in my view provides a problematic framework for clarifying the concept of relational knowledge. I shall proceed as follows. First, I examine what social construction means and, through this analysis, identify and eliminate some common misunderstandings associated with the phenomenologically founded social constructionism. Second, I discuss the problematic relation between postmodern constructionism and agency. Third, I examine the concept of socialty. Fourth, I go on to discuss some aspects of empirical reference. This allows me, fifth, to reconsider methodological individualism and, finally, to close with a brief statement on the 'appreciative approach' noted above.

Social construction

If, as Cooperrider et al. claim, organizations are 'products of human interaction and social construction' and the theorist's work has a constructed/constructing nature, then what do they mean by social construction? Is it a production or just an interpretation of a social phenomenon? If, as they say, organizations are 'made and imagined', then is there a difference between making and imagining or are they synonymous? The authors insist, following Hazelrigg (1989), that 'making/thinking/doing' and 'theory/practice/development' form a unity. I do not quite agree.

The talk about social construction originates from Berger and Luckmann (1967). Thus, it is worthwhile to remind ourselves of the basic constituents of their conception. Their sociological approach was deceptively simple: society must be grasped in its duality as both an 'objective' and a 'subjective' reality. The former, although produced by social action, appears to the individual as separate and independent from him or her, therefore the reference to objective. Subjective reality is the actor's consciousness of (social) phenomena, shaped in pervasive processes of socialization, and sustained and modified in daily interactions. In this dialectical duality the seeming dichotomy between Durkheim and Weber was reconciled, and the basic question for sociological theory could be put as follows: 'How is it possible that subjective meanings become objective facticities' (Berger & Luckmann, 1967, p. 30)? To avoid intricate philosophical reflections, they defined the key terms from the point of view of the natural attitude:

> It will be enough, for our purposes, to define 'reality' as a quality appertaining to phenomena that we recognize as having a being independent of our volition (we cannot 'wish them away'), and to define 'knowledge' as the certainty that phenomena are real and that they possess specific characteristics (Berger & Luckmann, 1967, p. 13).

The revolutionary idea was to declare common sense knowledge to be the central focus for the sociology of knowledge. Traditionally, the sociology of knowledge has been preoccupied with the history of ideas only; now we are told, it must concern itself 'with everything that passes for "knowledge" in society' (ibid., p. 26).

Berger and Luckmann's sociological theory was based upon a protosociological foundation, namely the phenomenological analysis of the life-world by Alfred Schutz. In a fine-grained descriptive analysis of the formal structures of the life-world (Schutz & Luckmann, 1973; 1989) Schutz tried to develop a philosophical foundation for Max Weber's interpretive (*verstehende*) sociology. After the idea of a 'phenomenological sociology' had spread among social scientists in the late sixties and early seventies, the phenomenological method soon fell prey to thorough misunderstandings. For example, it was denounced to be subjectivist or individualistic. However, the goal of phenomenology always has been the constitutive analysis of meaning structures, be it on a transcendental (Husserl) or on a mundane (Schutz) level. The phenomenological method chooses subjective consciousness as the locus of perception and cognition, but it does so to explicate the structures of phenomena not just in their noetic but also in their noematic aspects.[1] The phenomenologically explicated formal structures of the life-world are claimed to be the same for everybody, and thus neither subjective nor individualistic in any sense. In other words, phenomenological analysis attempts to describe those basic structures that all cultural life-worlds on this planet have in common. Consistent with this endeavour, Berger and Luckmann integrate Schutz' analyses with key aspects of modern anthropology (e.g. Arnold Gehlen, Helmuth Plessner).

In view of these widespread misunderstandings, it cannot be overemphasized that the phenomenological method is a philosophical, not a sociological method. This is the reason Berger and Luckmann draw a clear-cut distinction between 'constitution' and 'construction': constitution of meaning is a subjective process that takes place in consciousness and must thus be analyzed by phenomenology; construction is a social process and therefore should be analyzed by sociology.[2] However, what social construction means exactly also remains somewhat ambiguous. For instance, the term 'construction' has a static and a dynamic aspect. In its static aspect it denotes a reality-as-it-is (appears), while in its dynamic aspect it means the process of a reality-construction. Then again, it obviously makes a difference if we see a natural landscape with its mountains, rivers, meadows, cows, farmhouses and so on - a natural reality shaped by our cultural knowledge - or if we gaze at society produced, entirely, by human actions. To understand what is going on in society (e.g. in a social setting), the sociologist has - in Schutz' and in Berger and Luckmann's eyes - to grasp the meanings the actors themselves employ and in which they are embedded: the second-order constructs of social scientists have to relate to the first-order constructs people hold in their everyday life (Schutz, 1971a, 1971b; Berger & Kellner, 1981).

Although Husserl hoped to reach a kind of archimedic point of cognition, modern phenomenologists acknowledge that the phenomenological method, too, cannot escape the epistemic circle of reflexivity (e.g. Luckmann, 1980). Phenomenologists hope the same as Cooperrider et al. and Hazelrigg (1989, p. 8): that the 'threat' of an incessant reflexivity can be domesticated. Indeed, 'The Structures of the Life-World' (Schutz & Luckmann, 1973, 1989) offers such rich and detailed analyses of knowledge, its types, the relationship between subjective and social knowledge, its social derivation and the process of its construction, the transcendency's, and much more. These form, on an epistemological level, a frame within which the hermeneutical task of any sociological inquiry, quantitative or qualitative, inevitably has to be pursued.

In Berger and Luckmann's conception epistemological, methodological and theoretical aspects are intimately linked but analytically differentiated. In Cooperrider et al.'s paper their relations are less clear. On the one hand they proclaim 'the special charity of relativism', that societies as well as the relationship between social science and social practice are 'socially constructed'. At the same time, they talk of the 'truth' of human freedom, the 'fact' of collective existence or the 'truth' of human relatedness, and they call a 'brute fact' 'the contextual quality of all thought', 'the enlightenment effect of all inquiry', and the 'constructive co-enlightenment effect of all organizational theory'. While they treat different constructions at the level of organizational theory as an 'invitation to a relational understanding of knowledge', they do not seem inclined to do the same on an epistemological level. At this level there are 'truths' and 'facts', not meant as another equally relative world among many, but as a world that is superior to others including, for example, the epistemology of positivism. 'Changing virtually every assumption of a modernist science - including foundationalist verities', they obviously cannot do without 'foundationalist verities' themselves.

With respect to this new foundation, Cooperrider et al. imply an evolutionist view: That organizations are 'made and imagined' is called an 'essential modern management insight' which abandons the search for iron clad laws and the assumption that patterns of social-organizational action be 'fixed by nature in any direct environmental, technological, psychological or deep-structure sociological way'. However, to call this an 'essential modern management insight' is certainly misleading. First, it fails to say if this was an insight of managers or of management theorists; as experience shows they often do not cohabit the same world. Second, and in conspicuous contrast to phenomenologists like Husserl,

Schutz, and Berger & Luckmann, they do not explain what they mean by 'essential'. Third, the formulation conceals the fact that this 'insight', in its essence, goes back at least to Neo-Kantianism and Historicism: Heinrich Rickert and Max Weber developed the concept of ideal-type to come to grips with the ever-changing social phenomena whose constitutive difference to natural phenomena is that they do not follow any laws in a physicist's sense (cf. Burger, 1976; Eberle ,1984). Do Cooperrider et al. mean, that managers or management theorists are only now becoming aware of this?

Perhaps, instead, it is the radical implications drawn from that 'insight' that are new. Indeed, Cooperrider et al. claim that: 'no discipline has ever taken the idea of society as made and imagined to the hilt.' It is their goal to do this, and they are convinced that 'once done, ... there will be no return to the old'. Points of no return are always interesting places in a trajectory and worth a deeper study. In a somewhat secular statement the authors declare 'with confidence that the scoffers are uniformed'; uninformed of what? Are the ideas and arguments of the cited authors, such as Feyerabend, Rorty, Derrida, Wittgenstein, Kuhn, Habermas, Gadamer, Foucault and others, so compelling that all other epistemologies must be rejected? What about the 'special charity of relativism' in this context?

Let me emphasize that, since the turn of the century, Husserl's phenomenology has also rejected all those 'foundationalist verities' that Cooperrider at al. question - the Cartesian, dualistic epistemology and the picture theory of words. But phenomenology, as well as the philosophy of language, admit to a search for 'foundationalist verities', and both are capable of indicating a method of cognition that is able, in turn, to reflect its own premises. In comparison, the evidential grounds for Cooperrider et al.'s 'postmodern insights' remain somewhat obscure. They manage, as do some other postmodern thinkers, to bring together a broad spectrum of different approaches, including Heidegger and Gadamer, Wittgenstein, Habermas, Foucault, Feyerabend, and Rorty, all the way to Derrida. However, each of these thinkers has advanced their analyses to such depths that, in many ways, they are mutually incompatible. In my view, it is more fruitful to follow an epistemological reflection to its depths and draw the conclusions from there.

Postmodern constructionism and agency

I suggest that phenomenologically based social constructionism, in the tradition of Schutz, and Berger and Luckmann, can contribute a great deal toward clarifying several implications of the concept of relational knowledge. When Cooperrider et al. speak of a 'relational vocabulary of knowledge', or of a 'truly relational understanding of knowledge', they refer to Gergen (1988) who questions the concept of knowledge as a state of individual minds and places it within communities of discourse users. To confine knowledge to discourse is, in a phenomenological perspective, too narrow: Not all subjective knowledge is social or discursive knowledge.[3] Discourse certainly is an important and powerful sociological concept. It emphasizes the social aspect of knowledge, its collective character, its social origin and its interactional construction. However, the concept of discourse can be misleading, not only because of its linguistic implications, but especially when its relationship to agency is not specified. Are the 'users' of a discourse some kind of marginal attachment to the discourse or are they in any sense vital to it? Are we talking of a kind of auto-poietic, emergent discourse that takes on a life of its own, or is a discourse the result of the intricate coordination of two (or more) persons' practical actions? Do we dismiss concepts like consciousness, mind, experience, intentions and the like as subjectivist terms, as an inadequate discourse using traditionalist, obsolete or individualistic language, or do we integrate them with the concept of discourse?

Cooperrider et al., anyway, use such terms: they talk of experience, of minds, of actors - we,[4] students, physicians, researcher etc. - without saying what they mean and what epistemological status these concepts actually have. They even tie them together with the concept of an 'emerging organization'. Gergen, more radical, attempts to steer clear of avoidable ontological assumptions and considers agency a reified concept (Gergen, 1990). Luhmann (1984), who takes this argument to the hilt, so to speak, maintains that only communication can communicate and that any talk about an actor's action is a specific construction of the communication system. Gergen does not go that far, it seems, but has a special concept of agency in mind when reproaching it with reification, namely, knowledge as a state of mind, action as determined by an individual's intentions, and the like.

The constitution of phenomena, events, projects of action, and of acting in subjective consciousness and its intricate relations to pursuing an action and accomplishing social interaction, have been thoroughly analyzed by Alfred Schutz. His phenomenological description of the life-world furnishes a rich and detailed description of how phenomena in subjective consciousness are constituted, how experiences are formed, how actions are projected, how people make sense of their own and other's actions, how intricate the sequential organization of social interaction is, and much more. Phenomenology does not conceive of knowledge as a state of individual minds but as a process, as an ongoing constitution in subjective consciousness, based on past interactions and experiences. It does not assume that subjective intentions determine action (or worse: interaction) but analyzes the complex relation between projects of actions and actual acting in social or non social situations as an ongoing temporal process. I wonder why these process-oriented phenomenological investigations are overlooked when talking about 'individualistic' or 'subjectivist' conceptions, or when using terms like experience, mind or typifications of actors - terms whose meaning is neither epistemologically clarified nor explained by the context in which they are used in the text.

The phenomenological analysis of the life-world could, in my view, also elucidate the proclaimed 'unity of making/thinking/doing' (Hazelrigg, 1989, p. 113). The present task, according to Cooperrider et al., is 'to develop a new theory of theory with its own vocabulary that links knowledge with poiesis...'. Fortunately, they do not talk of 'auto-poiesis' - a concept in social science that, I contend, obscures more than it enlightens.[5] Thus their enterprise can be linked to agency more easily than other approaches of postmodern constructionism[6]. Their proposal, however, to bridge the seemingly contradicting quotations of Kurt Lewin ('There is nothing so practical as good theory') and Karl Marx ('The point is no longer to interpret the world, but to change it') by asserting a 'unity of making/thinking/doing' seems to me too simple. In a phenomenological perspective, thinking indeed can change the world: changing the interpretation changes the world-as-it-appears-to-me. In the 'natural attitude', however, it makes a difference if an actor just thinks and imagines something or if he or she expresses his or her thoughts and imaginations to other living persons. And it makes a difference if someone imagines the murder of someone or if he or she actually does it. Mundane phenomenology therefore considers thinking as acting but distinguishes between thinking and communicating, or between a discourse with oneself or with imagined others, and a social discourse with co-present others (physically present or 'appresented' by technical means, like telecommunication etc.). Baudrillard's assertion that the third world war has already happened because the simulation of it has taken place, his refusal to accept a difference between a 'simulation' and a 'real-life-event' (Baudrillard 1982), breaches the 'natural attitude' in a way that opens a nearly insurmountable gap between theoretical world and the world of people's practical concerns. Thinking hardly forms a unity with making and doing in the sense of real-world events, but doing and making in most cases - leaving aside unintentional consequences of actions - certainly include interpreting acts of an actor, in other words 'thinking' if we decide to treat interpreting and thinking as synonymous.

Mundane phenomenology also analyzes the formal properties of the perspective of someone observing an actor or interacting with him or her. This perspective is radically different to the subjective perspective of an actor. Understanding another actor means to make sense of his or her behaviour and to attribute him or her certain 'intentions' or 'motives' on the basis of specific cultural vocabularies and systems of relevancies. Obviously it is not possible to achieve direct access to another person's mind, experiences, thoughts or phantasies, but people interact with each other, interpret each other's actions, ascribe motives or intentions to each other, tell each other stories, engage in common discourses and common social constructions. On this, I think, all constructionists agree. Less clear is the concept of organization in this context. Gergen (1992, p. 207) is perfectly right to question why social theorists tend to speak of organizations as structures rather than as clouds, as systems rather than as songs, and as weak or strong rather than as tender and passionate. Organizations are abstract fabrics for which there is no direct empirical evidence. Concepts of organizations, lay or scientific, are therefore highly selective, anonymous and abstract; they are better viewed as 'images' or 'metaphors' (Morgan, 1986) or even as 'fictions' (Hitzler, 1991). The only way an organization is made accountable, however, is by human actions. Agency, defined as a theory of the human agent engaged in interaction and an account for the conditions and consequences of action (cf. Giddens, 1979, p. 49), runs less risk of being reified than organizations. Cooperrider et al.'s argumentation, with which I agree in many respects, could be strengthened by an explicit theory of action and less postmodernist talk.

The concept of socialty

The postmodern constructionism of Cooperrider et al. is a social constructionism based on a social as opposed to a dualist epistemology. But without having explicitly clarified agency, the concept of socialty remains somewhat obscure. While I concede that socialty always remains a kind of mystery, I would suggest examining the practices with which people construct their realities in concerted actions in far greater detail. Let us thus consider again how Berger and Luckmann proceeded. It is one of the main theses of 'The Social Construction of Reality' that cultural constructs are socially stabilized by processes of institutionalization. Constructions are thus not the subjective business of singular individuals. They are socially derived and intersubjectively enacted. The social constructionism of Berger and Luckmann therefore stands in strong opposition to the subjective constructivism that people such as Paul Watzlawick and others[7] sometimes defend. The subjective construction of reality is always based on internalized cultural knowledge and - leaving aside deep pathological aberrations - coordinated with other human actors in interactions or collaborations. As Goffman poignantly puts it: 'In some cases only a slight embarrassment flits across the scene in mild concern for those who tried to define the situation wrongly' (Goffman, 1974, p.1).

Subjective constructivism leaves out just what Berger and Luckmann's book is all about: reality construction in interaction and conversation, by means of internalized social objectivations, systems of relevancies and typifications, stabilized by routines, institutionalizations and legitimations, and so on. Viewed against this background, subjective constructivism is a-historical, asocial and blind to institutions. How about postmodern constructionism? How can the socialty of phenomena be conceptionalized without any ontological assumptions?

In Cooperrider et al.'s chapter one searches in vain for any reference to the plausibility structures of constructions. I agree that 'the world quite simply seems to change as we talk in it'. But we can sometimes observe rather obstinate resistance to new constructions. What are the conditions under which a reality 'shared' or constructed in common is altered? How can constructions be modified, developed, changed or replaced when they are firmly institutionalized and deeply entrenched in lore and legitimations? I would expect that in their reported medical clinic there exist several different cultural milieus, each with its own plausibility structure. I must admit I am quite puzzled that Cooperrider et al. do not report a multiplicity of perspectives when they explore and define the 'ideal membership situation' or when they envisage a 'vision of the good'. My own experience in management consulting suggests that what is good or ideal for members looks quite different depending on the actors' perspectives. I have met quite a number of persons who love to exert power and would emphatically resist any constructive change that could endanger their position. What seems good or ideal to them might be quite incongruous to what is good or ideal to other members of the organization.

Empirical reference in constructionism

Many of Cooperrider et al.'s theoretical considerations are indexical to the specific kind of research they are pursuing. Although the authors discard the difference between basic and applied research, it is important to acknowledge that there are different systems of relevance guiding concrete scientific endeavours. I certainly agree that an assembly line worker also theorizes, and that it is untenable to treat researcher and researched as isolated units if, I hasten to add, they interact during the research. Only then does it make sense to say, 'that the understanding of organizations and their/our practical transformation is a single, undifferentiated act' - our understanding of an organization affects that organization only if we interact with it (i.e. with its representatives). A constructionist view, however, does not require that the scientist help in inventing new constructions for people's everyday lives. Other constructionists, such as ethnomethodologists, conversation analysts or the German research groups around Thomas Luckmann, Hans-Georg Soeffner or Ulrich Oevermann, try to reconstruct concerted reality constructions as local, situational and interactional accomplishments. They have no practical concerns in the sense of changing people's lives. On the contrary, they attempt to avoid any influence on the people studied and favour data gathered by hidden camera microphone. Their research furnishes detailed accounts of the intricate workings of social milieus, without any direct ambition to change those milieus. In the realm of organizational theory the work of Deirde Boden (1994) offers a vivid illustration of such an approach, in the realm of clinical research there is also the earlier work of David Sudnow (1967). Of course, this is not to say that they do not affect society; they offer new discourses that affect other people, lay persons and scientists, but these discourses typically do not affect the people studied.

Against this background, the approach of Cooperrider et al. certainly represents a kind of applied research, not in the sense that it applies some extant theoretical results of basic research but in the sense that it pursues practical goals. A more appropriate designation may be to call it a (practically) committed research. If they combine 'an explanatory approach to organizations and a program for organizational reconstruction and development', they do not mean a descriptive reconstruction of people's past constructions in everyday-life-situations, as the other approaches mentioned do, but 'a constructive co-creation of the future in the here-and-now of inquiry'. Anyway, such a commitment calls for further meta-theoretical and methodological analysis. I suppose that Cooperrider et al.'s corpus of knowledge and their system of relevancies differs in many aspects from those of everyday theorists. For example, I would presume that they in some degree commit themselves to the specific scientific rationalities that Schutz (1971, a, b) and Garfinkel (1967) have identified: logical consistency, semantic clarity and distinctness (and this 'for its own sake'), the compatibility of ends-means relationships with principles of formal logic, and others. Thus I would expect that their work somehow differs from the work of management consultants who have no theoretical ambitions. It would be very interesting to analyse empirically the interactions, procedures and practices taking place in Cooperrider et al.'s research, as Knorr-Cetina (1991) did in a natural science lab.[8]

The unity of making/imagining and of theory, practice and development proclaimed by Cooperrider et al. is bound to their own approach. Ethnomethodological studies seldom affect the people studied; the latter do not even read the publications and accomplish their everyday lives quite well without them. Much of social research however does influence people, deliberately or not. If Cooperrider et al. strive with their inquiry for 'a constructive co-creation of the future', a puzzling question comes up: how can social change be conceived of in a constructionist perspective? How can humans, acting members of an organization or observing scientists, recognize social change? In everyday life, it seems to be relevant to people to discern if it is the 'things' which change or just peoples' 'interpretation' of those things. Avoiding the subject-object-dichotomy, Cooperrider et al. cannot distinguish the two. The same holds for phenomenology: as I suggested earlier, noesis and noema form an inseparable unity - there is no 'thing' stripped of its interpretation. The clue is not to be found in a different epistemology but in the institutionalization of social constructions: in everyday life we hold sufficient constructions constant over comparatively long periods; it is these stabilized constructions that furnish a firm basis for such decisions (if the things have changed or the interpretations).

Consider the case of that bed wetter who went to see a psychotherapist to get rid of his problem. After seven years of therapy he met a former friend who inquisitively asked him about the therapeutic success. 'I got rid of the problem', was the answer. 'I still wet the bed every night but now I like it.' To be sure, for our bed wetter the world has dramatically changed: he got rid of the normative interpretation that this is something to be ashamed of and therefore to be abolished. But if he spends a night as a guest in another bed, he will run into problems as his host may view the events in a different perspective. If we all agree that the 'fact' of bed wetting remained the same over the seven (and more) years, this agreement rests upon our practice of keeping constructions constant. A more radical therapy might have changed this basic construction itself: instead of a person wetting the bed we can picture the event as a mattress sucking the fluids out of an organic body, a scenario that could be dramatized by imagining some demons dwelling in there, planning new tricks to play upon their victim every night. Certainly, the plausibility structure might be confined to the therapist and his client and would, in a western culture, remain rather weak for a reality constructed like this.

The social actions relevant to social organizational theory and practice typically involve meanings that have little bearing on the physical aspects of bodily movements. How can people develop a sense for 'what has changed' and 'what remained the same'? In management development programs, members of an organization sometimes insist that it was only the rhetoric that changed while the actions remained business-as-usual. A vivid example is team work: the increased use of this term cannot conceal the fact that it is often employed to disguise old practices of hierarchical discrimination. This illustrates how important Schutz' postulate of adequacy of meaning is: the social scientist's constructs have to be compatible with those of people in their everyday lives. It is of utmost relevance to actors' orientations. Harvey Sacks' 'viewer's maxim', the 'if-can', although developed in a different context, may be helpful. Sacks' formulation of this relevance rule is deceptively simple: if one can see something in a certain way, see it that way! (Sacks, 1975, p. 224-225). This 'viewer's maxim', or better 'interpretation maxim', comes to terms with two epistemological insights: that there is no thing that is not interpreted, and that not every interpretation fits. Often there exist several interpretations that fit. In the context of our practical question, how can we recognize if social change has happened, we can use the 'if-can'-maxim in a modified way: If you can still see it in the old way, be alert - nothing may have changed besides the rhetoric.[9] Another relevant issue in this connection is the question of how certain agents manage to impose a specific reality on others - an issue that lies beyond the scope of this comment.[10]

Methodological individualism reconsidered

I have argued that central concepts in Cooperrider et al.'s contribution are somewhat ambiguous. My thesis was that the social constructionist approach as developed by Berger and Luckmann offers, based on the life-world analysis by Alfred Schutz, a rich resource for clarifying theoretical and meta-theoretical conceptions; for example, what social construction, relational knowledge or the relationship between social scientist and the members of an organization is all about. The present discussion does not allow more than to offer some hints regarding certain conceptual problems and their implications. As Cooperrider et al. refer to actors in their 'appreciative' approach and in their empirical illustrations, I contend that their arguments could be illuminated and strengthened more by a phenomenologically based social constructionism than by its postmodern version. The attempt of postmodern constructionism to steer clear of ontological assumptions inevitably backfires: the exclusion of agency, for example, keeps actors continually present backstage and lets them step forward as soon as an empirical reference is being established. In my view it is wiser to consider such implications at the metatheoretical level; they are readily overlooked within the practicalities of empirical research.

Moreover, it is difficult to clarify the concept of socialty without conceptualising the actors involved. Accordingly, the concept of relational knowledge remains inescapably diffuse. My thesis is that a relational theory that shies away from agency engages in exactly that which it tries to avoid: reification. There are no relations beyond actors enacting them, be it relations between humans or relations between symbols. The social does not posit itself. Apart from such ontological assertions, there arise methodological problems when the actors themselves are left untheorised. Structuralist theories of all kinds deliver vivid illustrations. And microsociological studies show well that any mechanistic metaphor, like Berger and Luckmann's (1967) 'conversational apparatus' or Sacks, Schegloff and Jefferson's (1974) turn-taking model as a 'conversational machinery', has inevitably to be considered in its context-free and its context-sensitive aspects, i.e. has to be related to the actual practices employed locally, situatedly and interactionally by competent actors.[11]

In the light of these arguments I wish to object to a blunt juxtaposition of methodological individualism and relation centred, constructionist approaches.[12] As the term suggests, it is a methodological, not an ontological individualism. What this means is that it is primarily dependent on the specific context of meta-theoretical and ontological assumptions in which it is embedded. In this sense, there exists a vast spectrum of different kinds of methodological individualism: economists treat their homunculus, *homo oeconomicus*, as if it were a completely autonomous actor and decision maker. Similarly, psychologists sometimes explain human action as caused by individuals due to their specific character traits and personality structure. The problem involved is not methodological individualism but the naive ontological assumptions being made. In the light of Schutz' arguments about structures of the life-world methodological individualism has a radically different meaning: a person is always born into the socio-historic apriori of a concrete, given society and culture. The stock of knowledge of a person is relational in a twofold manner: the concept of socialty says that it is socially derived; the concept of intersubjectivity describes it as constantly enacted, produced and reproduced in social interaction. Socialty captures the static or generic, and intersubjectivity the dynamic aspect of knowledge (the doing of knowledge). Schutz has delivered detailed accounts of the intricate interplay between actors and has shown, drawing on the premises of pragmatism (Mead, Dewey, Peirce), that actors interactionally produce their life-world as intersubjectively shared in the here and now.[13] I have stressed the fundamental difference between Berger and Luckmann's social constructionism as opposed to the so-called radical, subjectivist constructionism. Methodological individualism does not imply that actors 'cause' what happens in social settings, but rather that they enact it. It means to analyse social events at their very roots: at the practices producing and accounting them. In routine actions the subjective perspective of an actor has no special bearing, and there is often very little individualistic about it. But in others there is; neglecting this may lead to reifications from which there is no going back to reality-as-people-experience-it.

A phenomenologically-based sociology of knowledge presents a sophisticated version of methodological individualism that is highly consistent with a constructionist perspective. It differs a great deal from traditional versions that often operate with comparatively narrow and trivial assumptions (cf. the analysis of Lukes, 1977).[14] In addition, the sociology of knowledge does not adopt the narrow conception of explanation as many methodological individualists (e.g. rational choice theorists) do.[15] Instead, it is much more concerned with the practices of concerted social constructions, i.e. more with the how than with the why of social phenomena. It conceives of society as a complex fabric of interrelated social actions. Thus if a person externalizes and objectifies something it immediately falls prey to diverse, sometimes conflicting interpretations in a multiplicity of actors' and observers' perspectives - the so-called 'unintentional consequences'. In other words, a phenomenologically based sociology of knowledge heavily endorses - based on agency - a relational understanding of knowledge.

Towards an appreciation of the appreciative approach

Cooperrider et al. advance an 'appreciative approach to knowledge', one that should complement 'critical theory' which, for all its negativism, 'fails to tap into the inspiring potential of human cosmogony or social innovation and leads incessantly to a narrow conception of transformative possibility' (ibid., p. 23). Instead, 'appreciative ways of knowing are constructively powerful' (ibid.). They are convinced that:

> there will be no return to the old, not only because new vistas of study and construction will continue to appear, but because the theorist him or herself will come to experience what it is like to have their lives count, and count affirmatively, as it relates to the creative and crucial questions of the time (ibid., p. 15).

Cooperrider et al. do not care to describe for its own sake how members of an organization construct their life-world but want to help them to reinvent and reconstruct their world. Judged by this goal and commitment, their approach is inspiring indeed. In their empirical illustration they show that they succeeded in opening up the world for others and for themselves (in a co-enlightenment). They also show how they lived up to their epistemological considerations in their practical investigation e.g. in assessing the statistical numbers of their survey not as proof or disproof but as 'a concise rhetorical device', 'as yet one more form of theoretical language which again would enter the common culture of discourse'.

A constructionist myself, I found more in their chapter to agree with than to criticize. Thus my concern is more to expand and strengthen their approach than to dismantle it. In my view, epistemological reflections should be broader and more fundamental than just contextualizing a specific scientific approach. Closer ties to phenomenology and to a theory of action would probably be more helpful in clarifying basic concepts than the curtness of postmodern discourse. Cooperrider et al., on the other hand, may find my contribution not very helpful to them. Following Gergen (1978) they define good theory in terms of its 'generative capacity', that is, its capacity to challenge the guiding assumptions of a culture, to raise fundamental questions regarding contemporary social life, to bring about reconsideration of that which is 'taken for granted' and most important, to furnish new constructions (theories) and alternatives for social action. I doubt that my reflections increase the 'generative capacity' of their theory. For practical purposes it may be wiser to operate with rather vague concepts as most important is, as they say, 'not the content of the emerging theory per se, but the process of dialogue, debate, and organization/ theory/self-development' taking place. A too thorough concern for the basic concepts may in the end rather paralyse their endeavour, for the primary condition of successful organizational development will be their success in establishing fruitful social relationships with the members of the organization under study. My personal interest would be to study these very relations and social processes more closely, especially since they are major blind spots to the scientists-in-action. Such an investigation would not intend to change peoples' life-worlds but to teach us something about the subtleties of members' practical actions, about how they interactionally, situationally and locally construct and negotiate a common world, how they do discourse, how they do social change, and the like. Although all such findings inevitably are context-dependent, we may gain some insights that may reach beyond the context of their 'discovery'. It is these different systems of relevancies and interests of Cooperrider et al. and myself that account for some of the main arguments in our debate.

References

Baudrillard, J. (1982), *Der Symbolische Tausch und der Tod*, Matthes & Seitz, München.
Berger, P.L. & Kellner, H. (1981), *Sociology Reinterpreted. An Essay on Method and Vocation*, Anchor Press/Doubleday, New York.
Berger, P.L. & Luckmann, T. (1967), *The Social Construction of Reality; A Treatise in the Sociology of Knowledge*, Penguin, Harmondsworth, (Original: Doubleday, Garden City, N.Y. 1966).
Burger, T. (1976), *Max Weber's Theory of Concept Formation. History, Laws, and Idealtypes*, Duke University Press, Durham, North Carolina.
Boden, D. (1994), *The Business of Talk: Organizations in Action*, Polity Press, Cambridge.
Eberle, T.S. (1984), *Sinnkonstitution in Alltag und Wissenschaft. Der Beitrag der Phänomenologie an die Methodologie der Sozialwissenschaften*, Paul Haupt, Bern/Stuttgart.

Eberle, T.S. (1988), 'Die Deskriptive Analyse der Oekonomie Durch Alfred Schütz' in List, E. & Srubar, I., *Alfred Schütz. Neue Beiträge zur Rezeption seines Werkes*, in Haller, R (Ed.), *Studien zur Oesterreichischen Philosophie*, Band XII, Rodopi, Amsterdam, pp. 69-119.

Esser, H. (1991), *Alltagshandeln und Verstehen. Zum Verhältnis von erklärender und verstehender Soziologie am Beispiel von Alfred Schütz und 'Rational Choice'*, J.C.B. Mohr, Tübingen.

Esser, H. (1993), 'The rationality of everyday behavior: A rational choice's reconstruction of the theory of action by Alfred Schutz', in *Rationality and Society*, 5, 1, January, pp. 7-31.

Garfinkel, H. (1967), *Studies in Ethnomethodology*, Prentice-Hall, Englewood Cliffs, New Jersey.

Gergen, K.J. (1978), 'Toward generative theory', *Journal of Personality and Social Psychology*, no. 36, pp. 344-360.

Gergen, K.J. (1988), *Toward a post-modern psychology*. Invited Address', International Congress of Psychology, Sydney, Australia.

Gergen, K.J. (1990), 'Affect and Organization in Postmodern Society' in Srivastva, S. & Cooperrider, D. & Associates, *Appreciative Management and Leadership*, Jossey-Bass, San Francisco.

Gergen, K.J. (1992), 'Organization Theory in the Postmodern Era', in Reed, M. & Hughes, M. *Rethinking Organization. New Directions in Organization Theory and Analysis*, pp. 207-226.

Giddens, A. (1979), *Central Problems in Social Theory. Action, Structure and Contradiction in Social Analysis,* University of California Press, Berkeley and Los Angeles.

Giddens, A. (1984), *The Constitution of Society. Outline of the Theory of Structuration*, Cambridge, Polity Press.

Goffmann, E. (1974), *Frame Analysis. An Essay On the Organization of Experience*, Harper Colophon, New York.

Habermas, J. (1981), *Theorie des Kommunikativen Handelns*, Vol. 1+2, Suhrkamp, Frankfurt am Main.

Hazelrigg, L. (1989), *Claims of Knowledge* (vol. 2), University of Florida Press, Tallahassee, Fla.

Heritage, J. (1984), *Garfinkel and Ethnomethodology*, Polity Press, Cambridge.

Hitzler, R. (1991), *Organisation als subjektive erfahrung*, unpublished manuscript.

Knorr-Cetina, K. (1991), 'Die Fabrikation der Erkenntnis. Zur Anthropologie der Naturwissenschaft', Suhrkamp, Frankfurt am Main (elaborated version of: *The Manufacture of Knowledge. An Essay on the Constructivist and Contextual Nature of Science*, Pergamon Press, Oxford).

Latour, B. & Woolgar, S. (1979), *Laboratory Life. The Social Construction of Scientific Facts*, Sage, Beverly Hills.

Luckmann, T. (1973), 'Philosophy, Science, and Everyday Life', in Natanson, M. (Ed.), *Phenomenology and the Social Sciences*, Northwestern University Press, Evanston/Ill., pp. 143-185.

Luckmann, T. (1980), *Lebenswelt und Gesellschaft. Grundstrukturen und Geschichtliche Wandlungen*, Schöningh, Paderborn.

Luhmann, N. (1984), *Soziale Systeme. Grundriss einer Allgemeinen Theorie*, Suhrkamp, Frankfurt am Main.

Lukes, S. (1977), 'Methodological Individualism Reconsidered', in *Essays in Social Theory*, Macmillan, London.

Lynch, M. (1985), *Art and Artifact in Laboratory Science: A Study of Shop Work and Shop Talk in a Research Laboratory*, Routledge & Kegan Paul, London.

Maturana, H.R. & Varela, F.J. (1979), 'Autopoiesis and Cognition', *Boston studies in the philosophy of science*, Reidel, Boston.

Mehan, H. & Wood, H. (1975), *The Reality of Ethnomethodology*, John Wiley & Sons, New York.

Morgan, G. (1986), *Images of Organization*, Sage, Beverly Hills.

Prendergast, C. (1993), 'Rationality, optimality and choice: Esser's reconstruction of Alfred Schutz's theory of action', *Rationality and Society*, 5,1, pp.47-57.

Sacks, H. (1975), 'On the Analyzability of Stories by Children', in R. Turner (ed.), *Ethnomethodology,* Penguin, Harmondsworth, pp. 216-232.

Sacks, H. Schegloff, E.A. & Jefferson, G. (1974), 'A simplest systematics for the organization of turn-taking for conversation', in *Language*, 50, pp. 696-735.

Schutz, A. (1971), 'Common-sense and Scientific Interpretation of Human Action', in Schutz, A.,*Collected Papers I: The Problem of Social Reality*, Martinus Nijhoff, The Hague, pp. 3-47.

Schutz, A. (1971), 'Concept and Theory Formation in the Social Sciences', in Schutz, A., *Collected Papers I: The problem of social reality*, Martinus Nijhoff, The Hague, pp. 48-66.

Schutz, A. & Luckmann, T. (1973, 1989), *The Structures of the Life-World*, Vol. I+II, Northwestern University Press, Evanston, Illinois.

Srubar, I. (1988), *Kosmion. Die Genese der Pragmatischen Lebenswelttheorie von Alfred Schütz und ihr Anthropologischer Hintergrund*, Suhrkamp, Frankfurt am Main.

Srubar, I. (1989), 'Vom Milieu zur Autopoiesis. Zum Beitrag der phänomenologie zur Soziologischen Begriffsbildung', in Jamme, C. & Pöggeler, O. (Eds.) *Phänomenologie im Widerstreit*, Suhrkamp, Frankfurt am Main, pp. 307-331.

Srubar, I. (1993), 'On the limits of rational choice', *Rationality and Society*, 5, 1, pp.7-31.

Sudnow, D. (1967), *Passing on. The social Organization of Dying*, Englewood Cliffs, Prentice-Hall, New Jersey.

Watkins, J.W.N. (1959), 'Historical Explanation in the Social Sciences', in Gardiner, P., *Theories of History,* Free Press, Glencoe.

Watzlawick, P. (1976), *How Real Is Real? Confusion, Disinformation, Communication*, Vintage Books, New York.

Watzlawick, P., Ed. (1984), *The Invented Reality: How Do We Know What We Believe We Know? Contributions to Constructivism*, Norton, New York.

Weber, M. (1972), (1922), *Wirtschaft und Gesellschaft. Grundriss der Verstehenden Soziologie*, Mohr, Tübingen.

Notes

1. I thank Deirde Boden for very valuable comments to my first draft.

2. In contrast to other philosophers, Husserl affirms that noesis and noema form a unity: A (real life) phenomenon is always a phenomenon in consciousness, e.g. a phenomenon-as-it-is-perceived. We can change the phenomenon by noetic variations (e.g. by modifying our attention to something perceived), but the phenomenon can also alter its noema (e.g. a change of the something-perceived which is independent of our way of perceiving). Thus, Husserl delivers a highly interesting analysis of naive realism: we perceive properties of phenomena and attribute them to "things out there", concealing the fact that they are phenomena-as-they-appear-to-us (cf. Eberle 1984).

3. This distinction remained implicit in Berger and Luckmann's book but can clearly be seen in the context of Alfred Schutz' writings. I thank Thomas Luckmann for endorsing my interpretation in personal communication.

4. For a detailed account of this argument against the 'linguistic' conception of Habermas (1981) cf. Eberle (1984, pp. 172-187). Schütz/Luckmann (1973) provide a detailed analysis of the complex relationship between subjective and social knowledge. The subjective stock of knowledge is not completely contained in the social stock of knowledge, and - although in a different sense - vice versa.

5. Especially the 'we' is highly indexical in the text, sometimes meaning the authors, the researchers, the group of trainers and students, the group of reseachers and members of the medical clinic or the members of society at all.

6. Resurrected from ancient Greek philosophy for biological theory by Maturana and Varela (1979), the concept of auto-poiesis has been prominently launched within sociology by Niklas Luhmann (1984). There are even attempts to integrate Schutz' life-world analysis with Luhmann's autopoiesis (Srubar 1989).

7. Postmodernism is more about deconstruction than about constructionism. However, as Cooperrider et al. blend social constructionism with postmodernism, I label this and related approaches 'postmodern constructionism'.

8. Cf. Watzlawick 1976, 1984.

9. See also Latour & Woolgar (1979) and Lynch (1985).

10. For an ethnomethodological analysis of the intricate ways in which talking and acting are interrelated in social organizations, see Boden (1994).

11. On the imposition of reality in an ethnomethodological perspective cf. Mehan & Wood (1975, pp. 37-73).

12. While the terminology of 'context-free' and 'context-sensitive' was coined by Sacks et al. (1974), Heritage (1984) speaks of 'context-shaped' and 'context-renewing'.

13. This juxtaposition is constructed time and again by constructionist psychologists who refuse a specific individualistic ontology which has penetrated much of the psychological discourse; it has not been advanced by Cooperrider et al. As phenomenology mistakenly is often confused with an individualistic ontology, I try to clarify this misunderstanding.

14. Srubar (1988) calls this Schutz' "pragmatist turn".

15. Cf. also Watkins (1959). For further discussion see e.g. Giddens (1984).

16. For a lucid discussion of the relationship of a phenomenologically based social constructionism and rational choice theory cf. Esser (1991, 1993), Prendergast (1993) and Srubar (1993); cf. also Eberle (1988).

11 Reality is the basis of social construction which in turn creates reality

Mario von Cranach

Writing[1,2] in the context of this book, discussing in the context of this group is a new experience for me. Many years ago, with my first studies of goal-directed action, I began to deviate from the mainstream of social psychology, but I have never called myself a constructionist. The development of constructionism into 'relational theory'[3] suits my intentions well, but not completely. I feel tempted to define my own position as realistic systemic constructionism, but I do not want to attribute lack of realism and systemic thinking to others. I shall present my basic assumptions in the form of a few theses, and I shall illustrate these with examples from an empirical study.

I should like to point out that none of the ideas presented is original or new. All of them have been earlier and repeatedly stated and used by others in the same or another context. I have made them my own by introducing them into new combinations, by using them in practical research, teaching them and taking them seriously.

Social construction as self-organization

In this section, I want to outline my ontological and epistemological standpoint, so that the following psychological discussion is better understood; I do not intend to discuss the philosophy of relational constructionism. For my purpose it will be sufficient to reconstruct its basic principles (as I see them) in order to contrast them with my own convictions (but to have convictions may already be seen as unconstructionist).

Reconstruction of relational constructionism

As far as I have understood, relational constructionists maintain that

a   human reality is socially constructed in societal and cultural processes which are historically determined.
b   the medium of the construction process is some kind of language.
c   the results of these constructions are communicated in some kind of stories or narratives.
d   different views of the world, especially different and competing scientific descriptions, explanations and theories are in fact only different narratives, and as such neither true nor false or more true and more false.
e   the construction process is performed in the context of the relationships, in which individuals are embedded. It is in fact as much or even more a product of these relationships than of its individual participants.

Depending on how radically this position is maintained, it can have a deep impact on scientific work. One of its ontological conclusions could for example be: 'everything is socially constructed.' It would lead to the epistemological consequence: 'do not look for an explanation of phenomena but for the process of their construction.' And that could result in the heuristic maxim: 'whatever your topic and scientific aim, study relationships.'

My position

Now I want to describe my own position. As will be seen, I subscribe to the five constructionist principles as an essential part of the story, but not the whole story. Some important statements have to be added. I shall try to summarize my position in a few statements. Due to limited space, I must simplify the problems and restrict myself to what is most necessary, but the line of my arguments should become clear. Since mainstream social psychology models after physics, I shall discuss the situation of the natural sciences before turning to social science. In the following text, my theses are referred to by the letters a-r.

Reconstruction of the real physical world

a   In the following analysis, I distinguish between properties of the world in itself, properties of the human systems which construct representations of the former, properties of their discourse and language, and properties of their (constructed) representations.

b   The physical world is real and has real properties. This world in itself (paraphrasing Kant) is however not accessible to human knowledge.
c   Human social systems and individuals (in our case scientific disciplines, and their social subsystems as well as individual scientists; and also laypersons) aim to depict or represent the world in itself. This occurs in symbolic form in the context of communication. Languages based on code systems are used for this purpose.
d   The properties of these languages, and of the discourse in which they are used, depend on conventions which are related to the systems' circumstances: goals, self-representations and other knowledge, their histories, their supersystems, cultural and material environment etc. The represented contents are encoded in specific forms (narratives) according to social conventions.
e   The represented content, because it refers to the properties of the world in itself, is also functional for the representing systems' existence and determines their information elaboration and action.
f   These principles also refer to scientific disciplines, social systems which produce science. Their scientific representations are reconstructed from properties of the world in itself, from functions of the representing system, from properties of their discourse and language and according to social conventions. They are socially constructed narratives, but also world-in-itself representations. In this sense they are particular narratives.
g   Due to the aims and rules of the scientific systems, the world-in-itself representations should correspond as much as possible to the real but unknown properties of the world in itself. To the degree that this is the case, we can distinguish between better or worse scientific statements (provided we accept this aim). In this sense we can speak of scientific truth.
h   In some cases and to a limited extent, constructing representations of the world-in-itself can change the world-in-itself (e.g. Heisenberg's 'uncertainty relation'). Much bigger is the impact of activities which are based on these representations; in social practice these are normally not considered science, but technology.

Construction of the social world

i   Social affairs (social structures, processes and functions) are based on and incorporate the physical world (e.g. the self, however constructed, is based on and includes a physical body). This is a first source of reality in constructions.
j   Social affairs are constructed and reconstructed by social systems and individuals in the form of knowledge, which is to a large degree action-

related. They become real through the systems' actions which are derived from this information. This is a second source of reality in constructions.

k The construction process occurs in two ways. The first is practical societal activity. Here I refer to the coordinated acts of social systems and individuals, which are organized according to schedules of work division and coordinated through communication (e.g. all kinds of productive activity). The second is symbolic activity. Here the activity aims at symbolic effects, which create, re-create or change the meaning of social affairs (which in turn lead to acts with impact on physical reality, e.g. a changed definition of the embryonic state of human life leads to or accompanies a changed abortion policy and practice.Both these activities go hand in hand, as partial processes of human social self-organization.

l As a combined effect of both construction processes, the social world becomes real. (e.g. the army is real. Telling a recruit it is only a narrative will not comfort him. From his practical experience he knows better.)

m As all other human constructions, the statements of social science are related to its own systemic social organization.

n The construction of representations by social science is symbolic activity (in the sense of statement k): it partly creates the world which it investigates.

o To the extent these representations refer to social affairs that have become real, they can be more or less true. (Consider the hypothesis: the acceptance of abortion is related to value orientations.)

p To the extent these representations contribute to human social self-organization, they are more or less effective (e.g. the marxist view of social history has changed the world).

q Truth and effectiveness can both be considered as criteria for the constructions of social science.[2]

r Social construction occurs simultaneously on the various levels of the involved social systems and on the individual level: it is a multilevel process.

Let me summarize the essential points of these statements. The physical world is primarily real and secondarily reconstructed - by our cognitive activity in everyday life - and in a methodical way by natural science. Feedback effects from science to reality can be controlled or exported to technology. Therefore, natural science can make use of truth criteria referring to some kind of correspondence between reality and reconstruction. In addition, the social world is primarily constructed. It is primarily real insofar as its constructions incorporate physical reality; it is secondarily real insofar as its constructions create and change physical and social reality in productive and symbolic processes. These processes are always multilevel activities of human social systems and human individuals, as in our case the systems of social science and individual social scientists. I also hold that the social construction of reality is an aspect of human self-organization, and that constructions of social science can be subjected to criteria of truth and criteria of effectiveness.

Let me finally compare my standpoint with that of relational constructionists. I am sharing the general assumption of this position, that social reality is constructed in a social context. However, within this frame of general agreement, I am putting some of the weights differently, and I introduce additional ideas. In particular, I am stressing the idea that social constructions are based on and incorporate physical reality, and that they create and re-create physical and social reality in processes of self-organization. Therefore I propose the two criteria of truth and effectiveness. I believe that social productive activity is more or at least equally important as symbolic activity in the constructive process: to build a house is normally more effective than to speak about building a house. Both occur on many levels of the social system as well as on the individual level.

Action organization through social representations: an illustrative example

Aims and theory

Some illustration is certainly helpful. The study from which I shall draw my example has been published as a small book (Thommen, Ammann & v. Cranach, 1988) and in two articles (Ammann, 1987; Thommen, v. Cranach & Ammann, 1992). What follows is a summary: The study was performed to investigate how 'social representations' (Farr & Moscovici, 1984) are related to individual 'goal directed action' (v. Cranach et al., 1982, 1985). The concept of social representations refers to the dynamic part of the knowledge of social systems; we assumed that in order to have an effect on individual action, it must first be transformed (and thereby changed) into individual social representations. These are social representations that have become part of the individual knowledge system (it is important not to mix levels, in this case the individual and the social level). Individual knowledge, in turn, forms a basis for the cognitive and emotional processes that energize and steer the manifest, behavioral part of individual action (we could also say the action execution) - this is a core assumption of action theory. Thus, our theoretical model postulated the following chain of transformations:

Social representations → individual social representations → individual action-related cognitions and emotions → manifest behaviour in individual action.

Methods

In our empirical investigation, we compared psychotherapists who belonged to two different schools, namely client-centered therapists (CCT) such as Rogers and psychotherapists who worked according to the method of 'vertical behaviour analysis' (VBA) (Grawe & Caspar, 1984), a further development of cognitive behaviour therapy. We observed seven therapists of each kind during their real therapy sessions, took videotapes, and had extended interviews with them.

For an empirical representation of our model, we performed the following steps/operations.

Data collection, social representations   We reconstructed the social representations of the two psychotherapeutic schools from their basic literature and publications, from the statutes, regulations and from interviews with prominent representatives of the schools. The result was a comprehensive exposé of their social representations, which was approved by representatives of the two schools.

Individual action accompanying cognitions and emotions: immediately after the therapeutic session we confronted the therapists with videos of their own actions and asked them for their cognitions, perceptions, emotions etc. (Self-confrontation method, v. Cranach et. al., 1982).

Individual social representations: about two weeks after the therapy session, we questioned the therapists in a post-interview to give us further information in relation to those parts of the self-confrontation interview which seemed to relate to individual social representations. Thus we obtained additional information about the background of the action accompanying information processing.

Manifest behaviour in individual action   Here, we restricted ourselves to an analysis of the verbal client-therapist interaction from our videotapes.

Data evaluation   The central part of the evaluation was the content analysis of the self-confrontation data in order to classify the specific action-accompanying cognitions and emotions (environmental perceptions, attributions, goal-cognitions, various categories of planning activities, control cognitions etc.,). Similarly, the data from the post-interviews concerning the therapists' individual social representations were analysed, and their communications where evaluated as to their relationship to social representations and action organization. In accordance with many investigations of action-related cognitions (v. Cranach, in press; Tschan, under review) we assumed that these processes tend to run off in a sequence of three steps: situational orientation, action planning and execution control. We call this three-step sequence an information processing loop. (Fig. 11.1). The patterns of these loops where qualitatively and quantitatively analyzed to answer our research questions. The results generally sustain our model and give many insights into the connections of knowledge and action. However, it is not our aim here to report them in detail. Rather, we want only to provide a basis for the elaboration of an example to illustrate our arguments concerning the problems of constructionism. For this purpose, let us first look at the results in general and then choose a particular example, concerning the function of attributions in psychotherapy.

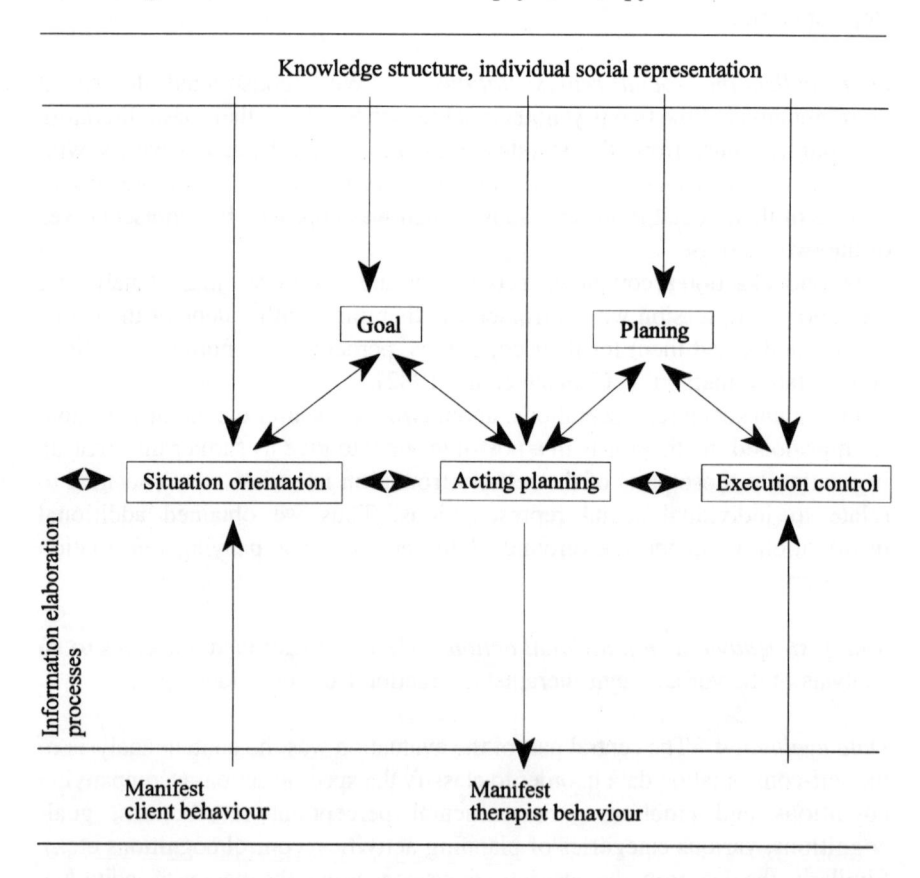

Figure 11.1 Model of information elaboration and action organization, information processes within a loop

Results

Of course I can hardly present this complex matter here in a short form. We found that the representations of both psychotherapeutic schools differ in a number of respects, which are significant for the organization of action in psychotherapy, and for attribution processes in particular. Let us here only compare these viewpoints.

Basic assumptions about persons   CC Therapy assumes that person is basically good, develops freely on the basis of a tendency to self-actualization and possesses a self which integrates experiences. Psychic impairments result from disintegration of important experiences. Psychic disturbances develop if a person is inhibited in his or her self-development. The person exists in the internal world of his or her experiences which is her reality.

VBA conceives of person as self-directed, autonomous and reflexive subjects which act on the basis of plans (a plan = a goal + operations). Plans are hierarchically organized. They are functional for behaviour. In psychotherapeutic interaction each participant tries to realize their plans. The interaction proceeds on two levels, that of content and that of relationship. Complementary behaviour of the therapist leads to a positive relationship, in which the client is more inclined to change. It is not promising to try to change behaviour which is related to several important plans.

Psychic health and illness, goals of the therapy   CCT aims at bringing the client near the ideal state of psychic functioning: reorganization of the self, congruence between real and ideal self, capability for intensive human relationships, conscious perception, acceptation and free communication of feeling, needs and wishes, independence from others' standards, autonomy and self-determination.

VBA assumes that problematic behaviour follows from unrealistic, incompatible plans. Events are unrealistically evaluated. Negative emotions result from interrupted and blocked plans. Therapy should lead the client to a state of greater autonomy and self-determination. Therefore, he or she should better understand their own behaviour and motives, develop insight into the relationship between plans and behaviour and change problematic plans.

Therapeutic means   CC therapists pursue the goals of not being directive, of concentrating on the experiences and not on the symptoms of the client, of avoiding diagnoses, hypotheses and explanations and of putting themselves into the clients internal frame of reference (empathy). In order to reach these goals, they must fulfill three general behavioral standards: empathic and non evaluating understanding, positive estimation of the client and authenticity. Other therapeutic means do not exist.

The VBA therapist should first establish a definition of the problem and reconstruct the clients' plans and their structure. For this purpose, he should use all indicators which the client delivers to him. He should establish a supporting relationship to cooperate with the client in the establishment of a new and better plan structure. For this latter purpose, some central heuristics and a number of detailed strategies are proposed. Let us now see how these social representations are related to the therapists' attributions during therapy sessions.

Attributions as dependent on individual social representations What is the function of attributions as mediators between social representations and actions? We departed from the assumption that attributions are based on knowledge, which consists mainly of individual social representations. We distinguished between different knowledge classes which might be important in our context. These were general (common sense) knowledge, knowledge about the social context of a specific behaviour or action, principles of professional ethics, general theoretical knowledge about personalities and specific knowledge about the personality of the client, action planning-related knowledge and situation-specific knowledge.

In our total sample, we found and evaluated 286 reported attributions. Contrary to our expectations, the frequency of attributions in the two groups was not different.

Action-related function of attributions As to the general function of attributions, we found that about 50% of attributions of both groups are used for planning future proceedings, especially choice of a specific intervention. About 45% of attributions of both groups serve the evaluation of the perceived client behaviour in regard of the attainment of therapeutic goals. About 25% also deliver information for the generation of new goals (these functions are not exclusive). Only for about 15% could we not find a function for action-organization.

As shown in Table 11.1, VBA therapists, in line with their social representations, attributed more often cognitive information elaboration, goals, and enduring dispositions to their clients. CC therapists attributed to a larger degree expectations and needs. There is a marked surplus on the VBA therapists' side in the interpretation of nonverbal behavior, probably caused by specific instruction during their training.

Furthermore, attributions in the organization of action, in connection with other cognitive processes, fulfill different functions for the members of the two schools. The VBA therapists use the attributions to construct a comprehensive client-specific knowledge. The CC therapists content themselves with situation-related attributions and do not use these for the further construction of client-specific knowledge.

Table 11.1
Frequencies of attribution by client-centered therapists and by vertical behaviour analysis therapists

Category of attributions	Client-centered therapists	Vertical behaviour therapists
Cognitive information elaboration	33%	67%
Goals	40%	60%
Enduring dispositions	33%	67%
Expectations, needs	64%	36%
Emotion, situation specific dispositions	48%	52%
Interpretations of verbal behavior	48%	52%
Interpretations of non-verbal behavior	39%	61%
Other categories	52%	48%

Total of coded attributions: 286

Let me finally summarize the greater part of the results, which are not related to attributions: they sustain the assumption that the action patterns of VBA and CC therapists follow a different type of action model. VBA therapists plan and act logically and are success-oriented, while CC therapists are norm-guided and value-oriented. Both groups form different relationships with their clients: VBA therapists structure the interaction according to their therapeutic goals and diagnostic assumptions, thus assuming a leading position; CC therapists follow the social representations of their school in controlling their behaviour for directive influences and leave the initiative to their clients. And finally, CC therapists reflect more about their own actions (evaluative meta-cognitions accompanied by self-related emotions) and mention considerably more empathic processes.

How this example illustrates my theses on social construction

Let us now relate this research to the theses which I have formulated above. In doing so, I shall proceed stepwise, from thesis to thesis; sometimes I shall have to refer to the same events repeatedly, but these repetitions are only apparent: the reference points of the statements will be different. The discussion refers to a single event of about 5 sec. duration: C (the client) turns his head and his eyes away from T (the therapist) and says: 'I cannot remember'. Let us begin with T's reconstruction of the real physical world.

To theses a and b   The attribution process is based on a perceptual process which (also) represents the world in itself. The movement of the head and C's utterance are physical events the images of which are transmitted to T by physical means, light and sound waves. They are real.

To theses c and d   T perceives C's eye movement because perceptual categories form a part of his cognitive system (e.g. Bruner, 1957; Erdelyi, 1974). These are kinds of schemata which may be based on both phylogenetic and cultural roots: turning towards or away from an interaction partner is highly significant both in animal and human communication (Argyle, 1969; Chance, 1976). In addition, its significance is especially emphasized in VBA, but de-emphasized in CCT, so that it is more likely to be perceived by the VBA than the CC Therapist. Thus, the sheer perception of the event is already dependent on social factors, although this is probably not social construction in its strict sense.

Similarly, hearing the utterance is based on innate human capacities combined with culturally acquired schemata. Here both therapeutic schools point to the importance of attentional listening.

To thesis e   The existence of a schema which emphasizes C's nonverbal behavior is important for the VBA therapist in the performance of his therapy.

To thesis f   Both the CC and the VBA therapist are not only perceiving as individuals: in noting or neglecting behavior of C they also transform the scientific convictions of their schools into reality. These schools exist and survive, because and as long as therapists apply their theories and dogmata.

To thesis g   Scientific systems, in contrast to other social systems, operate under a specific norm of rightness or truth. Thus, it is important for VBA that T does not overlook C's nonverbal behavior, just as it is important for CCT that he does neglect it; and both schools consider it indispensable that he or she properly understands C's verbal utterances.

As to thesis h this investigation does not provide good examples. But consider how the diagnosis of hysteria in 19th century psychopathology was part of the culture which produced this pattern of psychophysiological symptoms; or the wellknown 'Pygmalion effect' (Rosenthal & Jacobson, 1968).

But of course, psychotherapy is a communicative event and the processes of construction of the social world are far more interesting here.

To thesis i This thesis is more or less illustrated by the discussion of thesis a-h.

To thesis j Our research example has shown, how the therapeutic schools and their individual members have constructed their knowledge in the form of social and individual social representations. These representations become the basis of T's actions in therapy, and it is through these actions that they produce consequences (quite in line with W.I. Thomas' famous statement: 'If men define situations as real they are real in their consequences' (Volkart, 1951)). These consequences are different for the two therapists, because they interpret the behavior in a different way.

To thesis k Psychotherapy is a case of meaning oriented group action (v. Cranach, in press). There is no practical societal activity involved, as it where for example if T and C were building a house together.

There is however much symbolic activity involved, which defines and recurrently creates their social relationship. Thus, the VBA therapist may interpret the behavior (gaze avoidance and pretending not to remember) as resistance. Upon this interpretation, he builds his own next action, treating C as if he showed resistance, which in turn makes C defend himself or trying to understand his own, obviously inappropriate functioning. Thus C's behavior, whatever it was, may in fact become resistance through T's interpretation.

This becomes quite obvious if we compare it with the corresponding episode in CCT. Here, the therapists may interpret the behavior as an indication for incomplete integration of experiences into the self. He does not doubt C's message and tries to put himself into C's position, asking more questions about C's ideas and feelings. This makes C think why he forgot. Forgetting thus becomes an accepted fact.

To thesis l The interactive processes like those I have just described create and define the psychotherapeutic relationship, which is a real social system with all its components. Or, to put it in other words: the therapeutic dyads become real as social systems because (and to the degree) they are lived by T and C.

To theses m to q These are meta-statements in our context: they do not refer to the T and C dyads, but to our investigation itself as a scientific endeavour. As such, this study is unthinkable without the structure of the science system, of which psychotherapy forms a part too. This scientific system instigates the activities, among them also studies like ours, through which it exists. The investigation to which I referred itself is also an instance of constructed reality: so real, that it costs several hundred thousand Swiss Francs and two graduate students lived on it for more than two years. Furthermore, it is a more or less true description and interpretation of the investigated processes (more, I hope), and to the extent its results are used by therapists and their schools it will be more or less effective (less, I fear). I am well aware the ideas about self-organization which underlay these statements, are circular; moreover, I believe they must be circular. 'A pretzel-shaped world demands pretzel-shaped hypotheses' says a familiar and, so I believe, very wise joke. If the real world in itself contains feedback and feedforward loops, how could we investigate it by use of linear theories?

To thesis r   The information elaboration and action of social systems tends to proceed simultaneously on their various structural levels, and at the lowest levels there are always individuals involved (see v. Cranach et al., 1986; v. Cranach, in press). In a given case it is always necessary to make clear which levels we refer to. In the present study, the therapeutic schools construct reality through the actions of the therapists which are acting on the basis of their ideas.

By the term multilevel process I aim to replace the terms relational and relationship; their present use in social psychology and, I am afraid, also in relational constructionism is often unclear and vague. Sometimes they stand for social, sometimes for interactive, sometimes for a social system in general.[3]

Social practice, social research and the demand for truth

I have argued that social science theory should be subjected to two criteria, truth and effectiveness. Many social scientists do practical work such as instructing, consulting and influencing individuals, groups and organizations. In the course of these activities they gain important experiences and insights of the social world they are a part of. But to the extent they are as effective as we wish them to be, their insights are fleeting parts of the processes they induce, their constructive work, and we have no good judgment of how truly they represent realities of the social world. Truth of representation and effectiveness in change do not always go hand in hand.

Other scientists are more involved in pure research - the development of representations of social life which aims to meet the truth criterion. This is constructional work too, but its feedback on social reality is normally limited and slow. My own research has not changed the world. It has not even influenced the thinking of my colleagues very much, I am afraid. But its aim to develop a valid representation of social life is quite realistic, and the application of a truth criterion, if not understood in an absolute sense, is justified. The kind of methodological technique that should be used in such research depends on the question and the circumstances; what counts heavily is the spirit in which the results are evaluated.

Some social constructionists seem to have a certain contempt for what is called empirical research. Could it be they believe that with the development of constructionism empirical investigations are outmoded? Against such a view I would strongly object. Empirical research is justified and essential; it can give us insights we cannot achieve in any other way.

References

Argyle, M. (1969), *Social Interaction*, Methuen & Co, London.

Ammann, R. (1987), 'Attributionsprozesse und soziales Wissen', *Zeitschrift für Sozialpsychologie*, 18, pp.100-107.

Bruner, J.S. (1957), 'On perceptual readiness', *Psychological Review*, 64, pp.123-152.

Chance, M.R. (1976), 'The Organization of Attention in Groups', in M. v. Cranach (ed.), *Methods of Inference from Animal to Human Behavior*, pp.213-236. Aldine,Chicago. Mouton, The Hague.

Cranach, M. von, Kalbermatten, U., Indermühle, K. & Gugler, B. (1982), *Goal-directed Action*, Academic Press, London.

Cranach, M. von, Maechler, E. & Steiner, V. (1985), 'The Organization of Goal-directed Action' in G.P. Ginsburg, M. Brenner & M. von Cranach (eds.), *Discovery Strategies in the Psychology of Action*, European Monographs in Social Psychology, 35, Academic Press, London.

Cranach, M. von, Ochsenbein, G. & Valach, L. (1986), 'The group as a self-active system - outline of a theory of group action', *European Journal of Social Psychology*, 16, pp.193-229.

Cranach, M. von (in press), 'Towards a Theory of the Acting Group', in E. Witte & J. Davis (eds.), *Understanding Group Behavior*, vol. II, Small group processes and interpersonal relation, Erlbaum, Hillsdale, NJ.

Erdelyi, M.H. (1974), 'A new look at the new look: Perceptual defense and vigilance', *Psychological Review*, 81, pp.1-25.

Farr, R.M. & Moscovici, S. (eds.) (1984), *Social Representations*, Cambridge University Press, Cambridge. Editions de la Maison des Sciences de l'Homme, Paris.

Grawe, K. & Caspar, F.M. (1984), 'Die Plananalyse als Konzept und Instrument für die Psychotherapieforschung', in U. Baumann (ed.), *Psychotherapieforschung. Makro- und Mikroperspektiven*, Hogrefe, Göttingen.

Rosenthal, R. & Jacobson, L. (1968), *Pygmalion in the Classroom*, Holt, Rinehart & Winston, New York.

Thommen, B., Ammann, R. & Cranach, M. von (1988), *Handlungsorganisation durch Soziale Repräsentationen: Welchen Einfluss haben Therapeutische Schulen auf ihre Mitglieder?* Hans Huber, Bern.

Thommen, B., Cranach, M. von & Ammann, R. (1992), 'The Organization of Individual Action Through Social Representations: A Comparative Study of Two Therapeutic Schools', in M. von Cranach, W. Doise & G. Mugny (eds.), *Social Representations and the Social Bases of Knowledge*, Swiss Monographs in Psychology, vol. 1, pp.194-201, Huber, Bern.

Tschan, F. (under review), 'Communication enhances small group performance if it conforms to task requirements: The concept of ideal communication cycles'.

Volkart, E.H. (Ed.) (1951), *Social Behavior and Personality*, Social Science Research Council, New York.

Notes

1. Dedicated to Alfred Lang at the occasion of his 60th birthday.

2. I am grateful to Klaus Foppa, Ken Gergen and Adrian Bangerter for their comments on earlier versions of this paper.

3. I shall refer to this family of ideas as relational constructionism.

4. The irony of a purely truth oriented social science is that in order to avoid the fallacy of self-fulfilling prophecy, it should minimize its own effectiveness.

5. The reader can try to find out in what sense these terms are used throughout the chapters of this book.